HOW TO TASTE

HOW
TO
TASTE

A Guide to Discovering
Flavor and Savoring Life

MANDY NAGLICH

Advanced Cicerone® and Certified Taster

Kensington Publishing Corp.
www.kensingtonbooks.com

CITADEL PRESS BOOKS are published by

Kensington Publishing Corp.

119 West 40th Street

New York, NY 10018

All Kensington titles, imprints, and distributed lines are available at special quantity discounts for bulk purchases for sales promotions, premiums, fund-raising, educational, or institutional use. Special book excerpts or customized printings can also be created to fit specific needs. For details, write or phone the office of the Kensington sales manager: Kensington Publishing Corp., 119 West 40th Street, New York, NY 10018, attn: Sales Department; phone 1-800-221-2647.

ISBN: 978-0-8065-4229-4

First hardcover printing: July 2023

10 9 8 7 6 5 4 3 2 1

Printed in the United States of America

Library of Congress Control Number: 2022950828

First electronic edition: July 2023

ISBN: 978-0-8065-4231-7

To the readers who will stain these pages and leave them marked with the things they eat and taste and remember.

And to Wes, because having someone who believes in you makes a whole lot of difference.

CONTENTS

INTRODUCTION: TASTING IT ALL

"IT'S SUCH A TIGHT GAME, WE STILL DON'T KNOW THE WINNER. THIS is the fun bit for cup tasting." Suddenly, the announcer motions for the contestant to lift his cup and she shrieks, "It's a YES!" Beaming, she jolts up from her crouched position and addresses the crowd. "So France is leading right now. It's up to Daniel. If Daniel is a yes, he is the winner . . . but if it's a no, that means France is winning!!"

The crowd erupts with whistles and cheers at the mention of a French victory. After all, this competition is in Berlin, Germany. French spectators had a shorter trip to the World Cup Tasters Championship than the Irish fans there to support Daniel. It's hard to believe that less than ten minutes ago, this boisterous room had been nearly silent. The only sounds were the sputters of cup-tasting contestants slurping coffee from their specialty tasting spoons, then the *wooosh* as they spit it into their individual waste cups. Coffee cup tasting is an exercise in speed, skill, and decisiveness. In each round, the competitors start with eight sets of three cups of coffee. Within each set are two identical cups and one outlier cup. The tasters must select the outlier cup as quickly and accurately as possible. Daniel Horbat had slurped and sniffed and tasted for only two minutes and thirty-three seconds before locking in his selections. His competitor from France had taken more than five minutes to select his eight cups.

And now, the world championship has come down to the final cup. Currently, France has a score of seven out of eight correct cups. Daniel Horbat, representing Ireland, has notched six cups and if this last cup is correct, he wins because he had the faster time. There is only one way to know if Daniel is the champion: on the bottom of the correct cup there will be a mark.

"Are you ready, guys?" the announcer shouts into the mic as she kneels next to Daniel. She needs to be low enough to see the bottom of his cup when he raises it. Once she's in place she says, "Alright, I'm shaking," and gives Daniel the signal to lift the cup. There's a moment of anxious silence as she searches the cup's bottom and then, " . . . IT'S A YESSSSS!"

She draws out the final word as music blasts, the crowd leaps to its feet, and Daniel fist pumps. A flurry of camera shutters click from the front row. Over the clamor the announcer shouts, "Daniel from Ireland is the winner!" Daniel embraces the other three finalists representing France, the United Kingdom, and Guatemala. The United States representative, Jen Apodaca, isn't on this stage. She had been knocked out in the quarter final round.

"I did some things to prepare. I shied away from spicy food and things that were really salty. But it wasn't until I got to the world's competition that I realized there were these mega pros," Jen told me. "They had been on the world's stage the last three years in a row. And they were doing crazy things to maintain their sensitivity to taste. They were walking around the conference wearing masks to protect their noses from smells and only took them off to compete."

It was Jen who told me to check out the footage of the final round on YouTube so I could see what she meant by "mega pros." She was right; the feat was impressive. Daniel had taken less than three minutes to identify seven out of eight outlier cups. And remember, to find those eight cups he had to smell and taste twenty-four cups. He claimed the title of best cup taster in the world by spending less than seven seconds on each cup.

I wanted to find out what went into becoming a lightning-fast, super accurate taster. So, a few Sundays later, Daniel and I get on Zoom to talk tasting at the "mega pro" level. Right now, Sundays are Daniel's only free time because he's as dedicated to his newly launched roastery business, Sumo Coffee Roasters, as he once was to becoming the world champion cup taster.

I mentioned what Jen said about his extreme preparation for the worlds competition. "Yeah, that's true," he said with a chuckle, "I went crazy with the diet. I really ate only chicken and rice with no seasoning, and at first it was terrible, but then my body got used to it."

What we non-coffee tasters don't appreciate about the sets of three cups in a cup-tasting challenge is just how similar the coffees really are. At the world champion level, the difference in flavor between the outlier and the other two cups is almost imperceptible. The coffees could be roasted to the same color and grown in the same region on two different farms a few miles apart. They may be the same base coffee with one cup roasted just a hair darker than the other two. To an untrained palate, the three cups would taste virtually identical. But Daniel's palate was far from untrained. On top of sticking to his spartan diet for four months, "I was being very serious about it, practicing every day, and I realized I wanted to focus on bitterness. If I can tell just a slight difference in bitterness, if I can be really sensitive to it, that's how I can distinguish between the cups."

Daniel put everything into this strategy. To heighten his sensitivity, he eliminated all bitterness from his life. And all sweetness for that matter. Pretty much all flavor was off the menu, other than the taste of his practice cups of coffee. For four months, Daniel banished taste from his life in order to earn the title of world champion taster.

The good news for you is that to learn how to taste, you won't need to do any rigorous training or restrictive dieting. In fact, as you'll find in these pages, you'll do the exact opposite. Before Daniel endeavored to win the cup-tasting title, he started his tasting journey like so many: He learned to taste everything. And this appreciation of all flavors made him better (even the best!) at tasting the specific flavors of coffee.

But you're not looking to hoist a world champion taster trophy over your head anytime soon. So why should you care about tasting?

I could tell you that people who practice tasting experience more gratification from even mundane foods. (Every sommelier has their favorite boxed wine.) Or that those who maintain their sense of smell live healthier, longer lives. I could intrigue you with the fact that the memories we build around taste and smell are our most vivid and the ones we hold onto into the depths of our old age. Instead, I'll ask you a question: What is a habit you stick to every day no matter what obstacles get in your way?

During stressful weeks, our meditation practice slips by the wayside. When the weather is bad, we skip the exercise routine. After an especially late Netflix binge, you may go without brushing your teeth, just for one night. But at least once a day, you find the time to eat. It might be the activity you've practiced the most in your entire life. At thirty-two weeks, fetuses already display facial expressions as a response to tastes (carrots make them smile, kale makes them frown) in utero. By the time you reach adulthood, you'll spend roughly 15 percent of your income on food. For city dwellers, it is the second largest expense behind housing and for everyone else it comes in third behind transportation.

We spend our lives eating and drinking, without ever dedicating thought to what we actually taste. You have thousands of opportunities to cultivate your sensory skills. Let's start a journey into taste together, right now.

To be clear, the path to becoming a taster isn't expensive or snobby. It's not paved with Latin words or exclusive bottles of wine. I understand why you'd think that, though. Because I did, too. I used to believe people obsessively sniffing their wineglasses and trying to put words together to explain what they smelled were hindering their own enjoyment. As a hostess at a steakhouse, I'd overhear people debate whether the investment in a wagyu steak was worth it or whether a wine really had notes of leather in it and think, "Can't people just relax and enjoy things?" My resistance to this crowd I saw as exasperating and pretentious led me to start my journey as a taster with a different perspective from many others'.

I like to say I came into tasting through the side door, not through pricey snifters of whiskey or perfumers' school. I discovered the wonders of flavor inadvertently through one of the world's humblest drinks: beer. And a literal side door. In 2016, I snuck into a ballroom in Baltimore and my relationship to tasting changed forever. I only snuck in because I didn't know I had to buy a ticket, I promise. I was new to entering homebrew competitions and I figured the awards ceremony came with the cost of entry. Turns out, the awards ceremony of the National Homebrew Competition is also a banquet. When I found a side door into the event, I crept in and committed not to eat a bite or sip a beer; I just wanted to see if my French Saison won anything. I wasn't too hopeful considering there were more than 350 other brewers, all more experienced than me, entered in the category. I hung back in the corner while homebrewers feasted on dishes cooked with beer and paired with beer. When the award ceremony itself started, I slid into a seat. Immediately, my tablemates offered me an IPA. "Oh no I couldn't," I whispered. They took this to mean I'd rather have a Belgian Golden Ale; I politely declined but we chatted about my first homebrew competition in whispers as category announcements ticked by on stage. They told me they didn't have any of their own beers up for awards, but other members in their homebrew club did. Meanwhile, men from the crowd trotted up to the stage proudly accepting medals and photo-ops in the background.

"And now it's category nineteen, Belgian & French ale and it's a big one with 357 entries."

"Oh, this could be me," I told the rest of the table.

"In third place is James F. . . . " I shrugged; in my mind my chances were for a bronze medal or nothing.

"Don't worry about it. Getting a medal at Nationals is almost impossible," they reassured me.

I didn't even bother listening to hear who placed silver and gold. Instead, my tablemates and I discussed the nuances of club membership (I never joined a club).

"…Naglich from New York . . . "

Hearing my name, I paused. "Wait!" I said.

"Is that you?" asked someone in the group.

"…for her French Saison."

I'd won gold in one of the largest categories at the competition. After I went to the stage to accept my award, the evening took a turn. People approached me to recruit me to various New York City homebrew clubs. Others requested my Saison recipe. The representatives for the brewing equipment I used asked for pictures. And someone from the Cicerone program invited me to happy hour to learn about their certification.

The Cicerone program loosely mirrors the sommelier model: a series of tests to certify participants at increasing levels as we accumulate beer expertise. The first test, "Certified Beer Server," can be taken fully online. After that, each subsequent level—Certified, Advanced, and Master—include a tasting element in the exam.

Studying for my Certified Cicerone was the first time I considered individual flavors. I learned the scent of compounds like diacetyl (movie theater popcorn), acetaldehyde (unripe apple), and myrcene (green and herbaceous) well enough to recall and identify them in unmarked cups. To pass the Advanced exam, I had to become even more intimately familiar with tasting. I learned to parse aromas and assign each note to specific ingredients in the brew. (Yeast produced clove and white pepper aromas, but hops were responsible for minty or woody notes.)

At that point, I started noticing flavor far beyond beer. Flavor was everywhere: the way the office smelled different on Wednesday mornings after all the desks were cleaned. The drying tannins that roughed up my tongue after a sip of iced tea from the deli on the corner. That the bacon wrapped around the dates was smoked over applewood; would hickory smoke make the dish more interesting?

I expanded my vocabulary around beer flavor. I practiced identifying and describing the chemical compounds I smelled to audiences of both laypeople and brewery professionals—all while memorizing qualitative and quantitative characteristics for more than 100 beer styles, learning to build beer serving systems, and becoming intimately familiar with the chemistry of brewing. My dedication to my studies was enough to earn me a spot in the first one hundred Advanced Cicerones.

I knew the Master exam would be intense, so I took the advice of a current Master Cicerone and signed up for some classes. I got certified in cask beer, certified in draft line maintenance, took a cheese workshop, and an online malt workshop. By far the biggest investment of time, travel, and money was AROXA taster training where I met Dr. Bill Simpson (who you will meet, too, in chapter 5). This was also the most thought-provoking class in my studies.

My first attempt at the Master Cicerone exam I was completely blown away. I walked in ready for an exam that was measurably harder than the Advanced exam, but still recognizable. What I faced was akin to a marathon. Once I knew what I was up against, I resolved to prepare properly for the exam and take it again in 2020. Then the pandemic hit. It abruptly halted my plans to travel the world and learn from renowned beer experts and taste their creations. It also delayed the multiday Master Cicerone test that required extensive in-person evaluation. Early in the pandemic in New York City the only thing I had to look forward to each day was my walk to the grocery store. To entertain myself I started curating little tastings for myself and my husband. I'd come home with prosciutto that was aged two months, a twelve-month-aged prosciutto, and two-year-aged prosciutto to taste side by side. New cheeses. Manchegos soaked in wine or goudas made from goat milk. I took an online honey tasting class. I got my certified cider professional and WSET spirits certificates.

When I was finally allowed to sit the Master Cicerone exam again in 2021, I missed joining the ranks of the twenty other people in the world with that title by just one percentage point.

"You're so close; you'll get it next time," a Cicerone rep told me on the phone.

But I already knew there wouldn't be a next time. What I thought was a love affair with beer was really an obsession with capturing and understanding flavor by cultivating my tasting skills. My mission wasn't to elevate the world's most popular alcoholic beverage to some respectable pedestal, at least not anymore. Now, my mission was to share what I knew about our neglected senses of smell and taste. It wasn't tasting beer that I'd felt invigorated by but tasting it all. For all the books I'd read about tasting wine, appreciating cheese, assessing whiskey, shaping a palate for tea, and of course tasting beer, there was nothing that explained our capability for tasting, generally.

Looking back on the path to honing my tasting skills, I realized I had to be invited into private events, special educational programs, and conversations with hard-to-access professionals. Not to mention the huge investments of time and money that went into training. But learning how to taste doesn't need to be exclusive or expensive. I wrote this book to demystify the world of flavor, to take the conversations about tasting notes from exclusive back rooms to your living room. To kick the snobs to the curb and welcome in a full appreciation of coconut shrimp (a food pairing based on sweet complementing sweet), bottom shelf bourbon (the $16 bottle that whiskey experts love), as well as the extra special meals you want to remember forever.

After getting the results of that Master Cicerone exam, I spent the next year interviewing more than 100 perfumers, tasting specialists, scientists, and professional judges to compare what I thought about tasting to what they knew. Everything I've learned, as well as their collective wisdom, is captured in these pages. So here we are, the jumping off point to your adventures in the wide world of taste. This book is your guide to transform from a person who eats to a person who tastes. Inside you'll learn how your senses of taste and smell work, what influences them, and how to heighten them. You'll also learn how to better communicate what you taste and what it really means for a wine to "win" a gold medal. You'll get to know the lingo of professional tasters and the way smells impact your memory. Where the science exists, I'll include it as well as the context about where the studies of taste and smell may be headed. The study of our chemical senses (taste and smell) is ever-evolving and shifting while a book is not. As I worked on this manuscript, new science about olfactory sensitivity was released. I'm sure in the time since it went to press it has been updated once again. Luckily, this book is not meant to be a scientific tome presenting the totality of human sensory knowledge. Rather, it is a jumping off point to pique your curiosity about your senses and start your personal exploration of taste.

As with sharpening any skill, the gratification you get out of tasting increases as you improve. And since we taste several times a day, that's a lot of room for joy in our lives. To begin this journey toward grasping small opportunities for joy in the everyday we need to start at the most basic level: an understanding and appreciation for how our senses function. Then we'll explore how to hone and practice and improve our use of those senses. And finally, we'll discover how tasting impacts our life beyond what we consume. With this path laid out in front of us, let's get to tasting!

PART ONE

WHAT IS TASTE?

CHAPTER ONE

THIS IS YOUR BRAIN ON FLAVOR

TWO MEN SIT ACROSS FROM EACH OTHER IN AN UNASSUMING LEATHER booth. One is the student, one the master. The room is empty and generally unremarkable, with slate-colored walls and muted fluorescent lighting that makes the vivid descriptors being called out in a staccato rhythm pop all the brighter: "Lime candy, crushed apples, melon skin, green pineapple," the student declares to the approving nods of his grader.

A pen scratches on the score sheet in the momentary silence that accompanies his first sip of the white wine. So far, things are going well for Ian Cauble, the hopeful wine steward undergoing a mock examination for the blind-tasting portion of his Master Sommelier certification. He spits into a silver bucket and continues, accelerating his pace. "A crushed chalky note, crushed hillside, white flowers, fresh-cut white flowers, white lilies." Then he utters the now infamous "that freshly opened can of tennis balls and a fresh new rubber hose"—he begins to laugh—"is what I get."

Even the evaluator cracks a smile, stifling a laugh as he says, "That's a new one."

Of course, the wine in question didn't use any of these items as ingredients. And where does one source "crushed chalky hillside" anyway? But in the end, Ian triumphantly identifies the exact region and grape of the wine completely blind, making this one of the more memorable scenes from the documentary *Somm*. He goes on to achieve the most prestigious certification in wine: Master Sommelier. If a Master Sommelier smells it in a wineglass—rubber hoses, tennis balls, and all—does that make it a definitive tasting note?

If you ask Peggy Noe Stevens, a Master Bourbon Taster and Kentucky Bourbon Hall of Fame inductee, there are no wrong tasting notes. "In all sincerity, everybody has their own palate. One man's apple might be another man's pear," she says. "If I taste orange, someone else might taste apricot, so I never correct people on what they taste."

This is a fresh viewpoint and stands in direct contrast to those who insist on grading tasting notes as accurate or inaccurate. Many spirits makers and mixologists are working to demolish the gatekeeping tendencies of those at the top of the alcohol industry. Official tasting notes are one of the first snobbish fixtures they'd like to eliminate.

The truth about tasting, as with so much in life, lies between these extremes. Somewhere less whimsical than lists of flowers in a garden (or tennis balls!) but more scientific and provable than "if you taste it, you're right." To understand how both approaches are a little right and a little wrong, we start not on the tongue, nor up the nose, but squarely in the brain. The fact is that a flavor-active compound is definitively present or not present in a particular food or beverage. It is up to the miraculous work of our neural pathways and sensory cells to communicate their presence to the brain, where we make sense of them. There is no question that when there are more than three hundred parts per million ethyl butyrate in your glass of Australian Riesling or bourbon whiskey, there is some kind of tropical aroma. I may think it smells like a mango, you may say it's more like pineapple, but it is a fact that the aroma is there and humans can smell it. If a person takes a swig of white wine and tastes only the essence of black licorice, they should be sent to the doctor just as quickly as a person who sees a piece of black licorice and describes its color as green. Lived experiences influence our perception of flavor compounds (as we'll explore at length in the next chapter) but no matter how many rocks you've licked or Michelin-star restaurants you've dined at, your brain cannot change the chemistry of the food in your mouth. Anethole, the compound responsible for licorice flavor, is either there or it's not. Whether you describe that anethole as black licorice candy, fresh fennel, crushed anise seed, or absinthe depends on the encounters you've had with it in the past and how your brain has filed away and organized those memories. But you can't experience anethole if it isn't there.

These facts about flavor-active chemicals and the brain make sharpening tasting abilities far from an exercise in artistry. The practice and brain patterns required are akin to kindergarteners learning new vocabulary words rather than a craftsperson refining clay-sculpting skills. Just imagine a preschool class at circle time sprawled out on a rug being told by the teacher, "The furry animal you see in this picture has four legs, a tail, and floppy ears. We call this a dog. It is spelled D-O-G." Now imagine a class of tea experts sitting around a table at a certification training. "This aroma you're smelling right now, with herbal notes of spice and earth. We call this licorice." Instead of seeing a series of letters and assigning meaning to them, our gustatory and olfactory receptors sense a series of molecules and assign them an association or a name. This "assigning" isn't always conscious but rather a mechanism of the brain, a series of reactions as innate to the function of our body as any unconscious reflex. The doctor hits your knee with a mallet and your leg swings. You smell a whiff of smoke and think, *Fire!* It's automatic. And like other reflexes, tasting serves as an animal instinct, existing to answer one of the most primitive questions, an essential question: *Is this substance food?*

When you eye a slice of blood orange for the first time, your sense of sight identifies that it is similar but different from fruits you've seen before. The sense of touch affirms this similarity, and it is up to your chemical senses to determine if this new crimson color signals poison, sweetness, or something else. It takes only a small, exploratory nibble for your mind to start working simultaneously on two questions: *Should I eat this?* and *Wait, what is this?* The first answer is sought through your gustatory system, a network of receptors, neurons, and organs having to do with taste. When pungent blood orange fruit hits your tongue, it comes in contact with a series of mushroom-shaped bumps. You probably know these as taste buds, but today you learn their true identity: fungiform papillae (fungiform means having the shape of a mushroom, and papillae comes from Latin, literally meaning nipple; later it took on the connotation of small protuberance). Each of these mushroom-shaped bumps holds between three and five taste buds. And inside those buds, already too small to be seen by the naked eye, are between thirty and one hundred tinier taste receptors cells. These long, thin cells are where the tongue holds the tasting power, that those damned taste buds get all the credit for.

Taste-receptor cells are arranged in bundles similar to bunches of elongated bananas within the taste bud. Where the banana's stem would be, there are dozens of antenna-like structures called microvilli. These dainty antennas protrude through a hole on the taste bud called the taste pore and into the mouth. When that first miniscule bite of fruit enters the mouth, food compounds must dissolve into your saliva. Then they can float through the forest of microvilli waving in the saliva like seaweed on the ocean floor. One of the dozens of flavor compounds from the orange gets tangled in the microvilli and—boom!—tasting begins.

We'll focus on a singular compound from the orange, a sweet one, fructose. Fructose will only bind to microvilli connected to taste receptors that detect sweetness; these are type one or T1R–taste receptors. Once the fructose activates the receptor cell, it releases signals onto a gustatory nerve connected to the other end of the banana bunch–shaped cluster of receptor cells. These signals carry taste information to the brain. Finally, the brain can process this information and produce that beloved sensation we know as sweet taste. If you were a cartoon, this would be the moment a light bulb pops up above your head. The message from your primitive instincts is loud and clear: *Yes, yes, this is sweet! Eat it!* A secondary message follows: *Remember this place. There are calories and energy here, and we should come back for these orange spheres of nutrition.*

Bitter and umami taste signals also travel to the brain using T1R taste receptor cells. The receptors for umami, which send the message, "Keep eating! Big protein payoff!" won't be activated when tasting a blood orange. The microvilli tied to taste receptors for bitterness will see some action, though. There are some bitter flavor compounds in a blood orange, especially as we reach the white pith between the fruit and its rind. Bitter compounds that activate those receptor cells are the reason why we will stop eating the orange when we reach the bitter white pith.

To round out the full taste profile of a blood orange there is the tangy sourness. The pathway sour taste information takes to reach the brain is different than the one sweetness and bitterness use. To taste sourness, compounds must slip through the taste pore and react directly with ion channels on the taste receptor. This causes a chain reaction that tells the brain, *Sour! This doesn't taste good. Maybe we shouldn't eat this.*

The fifth basic taste, salty, is sensed when sodium ions open sodium channels in the taste-receptor cell beginning a chain of responses that ends in signaling the brain that we've got some minerals here and should eat more if the body is running low on them. This is why deer come to a salt lick only when they need salt. Humans have become pretty great at ignoring this instinct and reaching for the saltshaker even when we have abundant minerals.

However, anyone who has eaten a blood orange knows it is more than a sweet and sour and slightly bitter fruit. There's something faintly waxy, citrus essence, a fresh green note, a hint of floral almost like a whiff of the blossom that formed the orange itself. This complex lattice of nuanced flavors that makes a blood orange singular and unique is invisible to taste receptors because they are limited to our five basic tastes: sweet, bitter, umami, sour, and salty. In the future, metallic compounds, carbonation, starch, and fat may also emerge as basic tastes that send signals via their own receptors, but the science to confirm them isn't there, yet. For now, we will see these taste receptors are limited to the five tastes, and unable to decode anything else about what makes a blood orange different from a navel orange, or a tangerine, or any of the fashionable new citrus fruits like tangelos. Instead, it is up to your more than four hundred aroma receptors to identify these traits.

This collection of aroma receptors is where things get personal. Unlike the basic tastes that everyone perceives in generally the same way, variances widen from person to person when it comes to olfactory (the fancy word for *smell*) receptors. This stems from the fact that humans have around one thousand genes that help us decode aroma that travel through our olfactory pathway. To put this in context, the entire human genome is comprised of roughly twenty thousand genes; that means 5 percent of the genes that make humans uniquely human are tied to just one function of our sensory acuity: smell.

It may come as a surprise that odor detection could be important enough to the human experience to require such extensive, detailed genetic coding. And when scientists first discovered this fact, they were surprised, too. The groundbreaking finding earned the two researchers who identified these genes and the olfactory pathway, Richard Axel and Linda B. Buck, the Nobel Prize in Physiology or Medicine in 2004. But let's think about this for a second. When one considers all the questions our sense of smell can answer, one thousand genes starts to look like a more reasonable number. These genes are responsible for decoding all the aromatic clues that can give humans answers to things like: *Have I been here before? Is this food similar to something I've eaten? Does this drink remind me of things I like? Am I walking into a dangerous situation?*

Deciphering these olfactory clues starts with more hairlike structures. This time they are called cilia, and they sway in mucus lining the nose instead of saliva. Cilia are attached to the olfactory receptor cells housed in the olfactory epithelium, an oblong patch of tissue on the roof of the nasal cavity. Every time you smell something, you're actively sucking tiny pieces of that substance into your nasal cavity. Scent isn't a separate quality from the smelly entity, it is microscopic pieces of it. When you give old milk a cautionary sniff to see if it has spoiled, you just sucked some tiny rotten milk particles seven centimeters up your nasal passage, where they collide with the mucus that lines the olfactory epithelium. The tiny bit of rancid milk is trapped by the cilia, which stimulates the corresponding olfactory receptor that communicates with cells in the olfactory bulb. (Think of that the next time you notice the baby needs a diaper change!)

In order for any odor compound to be trapped by these cilia it needs to be the perfect size. The particles must be small enough to make the seven-centimeter trek to the olfactory epithelium without getting tangled in the forest of nose hairs that line the path. Yet they cannot be too miniscule to be caught by the cilia and brought into contact with the mucus layer. Without plenty of nasal mucus, our sense of smell is muted. Mucus has two important functions when it comes to aroma detection. First, mucus protects the olfactory epithelium (and its delicate aroma receptor cells) by keeping it moist and pliable. Second, it contains odorant binding proteins (OBPs) which are responsible for bringing the odor molecule and olfactory receptor together. Without the constant supply of OBPs in the mucus, odors aren't able to send information to the brain and are rendered undetectable. This is why competitive tasters swear by humidifiers ahead of big events or tasting exams. A taster who has a slightly drier nasal cavity than the competition may catch fewer flavor molecules simply because of the lack of mucus. Test it yourself. Next time you're on a plane, or perhaps in a very arid desert, sniff something you're familiar with, a favorite tea or packaged candy. Does it smell less vibrant and tempting than normal?

The pathway through the nose is what we commonly associate with taking in scents, but there is another road to that mucus drenched patch of tissue where odor synthesis begins. Let's dump out that spoiled milk and go back to our blood orange slice. During chewing, molars shred the orange, releasing aroma molecules. These molecules float up the back of the throat where they slam straight into the olfactory epithelium. This is called the retronasal passageway. When aroma travels this way, it plays a little trick on our brains. Because the aroma molecules are forced up the retronasal passageway via chewing, our brain misplaces the origin of the scent as the inside of the mouth. This sensory mismatch causes especially fragrant retronasal aromas to manifest as the sensation of flavor filling the mouth (see chapter 4 for strong examples of this). This illusion of the mind is why we often say a dessert "tastes good" when the blood orange pastry really only tastes sweet and slightly tart, but it *smells* good, specifically of rich custard, graham cracker, orange oil, and caramelized sugar.

Between these two scent passageways and the many genes humans have to decode aromas, at least 80 percent of what we consider flavor is attributed to what we sense through smell. That's a huge burden lifted by a small sliver of skin in the back of the nasal cavity. To intensify the load, this little patch of tissue has one of the most direct routes to the brain's processing power, much more direct than taste, and even quicker than touch sensations. Whether the odor-active compound took the route of the nose or the throat to become tangled in the cilia on the olfactory epithelium, once a signal is transmitted through the olfactory receptor to the olfactory bulb it is just a few fast neural snaps away from being processed in the olfactory (or piriform) cortex. It is part of the limbic system, which also contains the amygdala, where emotions are processed, and the hippocampus, where memories are formed and stored. Later in this book, in chapter 12, we'll explore the tie between strong emotions and scent and how this connection can be used for better tasting and better living. The hippocampus is also where much of our cognitive learning power lies. Another similarity between the act of identifying flavors and learning new vocabulary words.

This fast lane to the important areas of the brain isn't totally understood, but one definite function is protecting humans from danger. The aroma of smoke takes the most direct passage to send the signal, *Danger! Run!* to the brain before we ever see a flame or feel the heat of a fire. In less-dire situations, this superhighway to cognition is the reason memories of mimosas with friends or halftime on the elementary school soccer field are conjured when you smell the freshly cut oranges on your breakfast plate.

These millisecond-fast reactions and strong ties to memory go back to those primitive questions humans relied on their chemical senses to answer: *What am I eating? Is it a good thing? Have I had it before? Did it make me sick or give me energy?* The more modern questions might be: *Does this sample of wine smell like other chardonnays I like? Or should I send it back?* or *What perfume did Grandma wear so I can always remember her when I take a sniff?*

This is one way that flavor can make you feel—immediately back in your grandmother's embrace. But flavor can also make you feel much more literally. While the sour citric acid from that blood orange slips through your taste pore to signal your brain that something tart is afoot, it's also subjecting the tongue to tiny pricks of pain. This pain sends a separate message to your brain, via the somatosensory system (which is responsible for sensing touch, pressure, pain, temperature, and more). The message warns of dangerously low pH levels in the mouth and triggers a response to fix the imbalance.

To test how your brain reacts, let's do a quick experiment together. Imagine you're holding the sourest candy you've ever tasted inside your mouth. Maybe it is a Warhead or a Sour Patch Kid, or maybe you're not one for the candy aisle and instead you're envisioning the fruit of a fresh lemon in your mouth. What flavor notes are you noticing? How big is the bite in your mouth? What is the texture like? Now, turn your attention to the joints of your jaw. Are they clenched? Is your mouth pooling with extra saliva? I suspect that your answer to both questions is yes. And these things happen because you are experiencing an unconscious reaction to the perception of sour taste even without an actual piece of food or candy in your mouth. Sour items like vinegars, lemon juice, and fresh yogurt interact with touch receptors on the tongue and trigger the release of saliva to act as a buffer solution, which protects the delicate surfaces of your mouth from acid burns.

Flavor is sensational in other ways, too. Both the cooling of spearmint gum and the burn of dried chilies are responses from touch receptors in the mouth. Spicy isn't one of the basic tastes even though it is something undeniably sensed on the tongue. It's the touch receptors responding to the burn of capsaicin from chilies. These touch sensations are the information that help you detect if the salsa is mild, medium, or hot.

Everyone has these three types of receptors—olfactory, gustatory, and touch—and the good news for those on the path to becoming extraordinary tasters is they can be trained! As we'll learn in the next chapter, the legend of the supertaster, born with the ability to detect even the faintest trace of specific flavors, is a myth. However, it is true that we're all born into slightly different flavor worlds, and chapter 2 will show you how those worlds are shaped.

CHAPTER TWO

A MATTER OF INDIVIDUAL TASTE

THE MOMENT HAD COME: A TASTE TEST THAT NO TASTING EXPERIENCE could help me pass.

I'm in a stylish velvet-clad room with dim lighting that barely illuminates long and low couches that hover a few inches above the ground. A setting this chic calls for a chilled martini and conversation about the philharmonic's new season. Instead I'm preparing to stick out my tongue. It's the intended landing place for the tiny piece of paper hovering in front of me. World-renowned sensory researcher Charles Spence is offering me the white strip, about four centimeters long. A piece of paper that appears unremarkable in every way. And yet it will definitively reveal the level of my taster status.

I exhale, noticing my mouth has gone a bit dry with anticipation. I wonder if that will skew the test result. Or am I strategically producing imagined excuses in case I don't get the result I want? Too late for any more wondering, I take the piece of paper and drop it on my out-stretched tongue, waiting for what will come next.

IN THE PREVIOUS CHAPTER I ESTABLISHED HOW THE SENSES OF TASTE and smell function in humans. The same receptors connect the same neural pathways in every person's mouth, nose, and brain. The guy loudly slurping soup in the office cafeteria has the same wiring as the one quietly picking radishes out of his side salad. They might also have the same iPhones in their pockets. These phones make an apt metaphor for how taste systems develop and function in individuals. Each phone comes equipped with the same base capabilities and the same hardware. But no two people have their phones set up exactly the same way. Some differences are inherent to the phone. My father's ancient model has a camera incapable of capturing a picture in a restaurant with low lighting, while my newer version can not only capture a high quality photo, but also the GPS location of that photo, as well as the exact amount of light that hit the lens when it was snapped. Other differences stem from personal use. The Stocks app that came preloaded on my phone languishes, never once opened. While the various photo-editing apps I selected and downloaded get daily use.

Just like the settings, apps, and downloads on our phones, the factors affecting our personal tastescape can be inherent or added by choice. These factors include the sensitivities we're born with, the associations we learn, and those flavor responses our culture conditions us to possess. In this chapter I'll illuminate the idiosyncrasies that rise from our own genes, personal experiences, and cultural influences to shape the way we taste . . . everything.

It is this individual flavor world I am meeting with Charles to explore. He is showing me how different my experience of flavor is from every other person's. He sits politely across from me, watching as I place the filter paper laced with 6-n-propylthiouracil (more commonly called "PROP") on my outstretched tongue. It is only there a split second before I cringe, almost gagging, and grab for the paper. I can't get it out of my mouth fast enough. As I toss it into the trash can, I think to myself, *Victory!*

"Ah," says Charles, "it seems you had a reaction to that. What did you taste?"

I smile in a secret moment of triumph. "Intense bitterness, like taking medicine."

"Like uncoated aspirin?" he asks.

"Exactly," I agree.

This simple taste test was an analysis of one of the genetic traits that shapes our individual taste worlds. The gene being tested, TAS2R38, is the gene of "supertasters."

"It is not that gene that makes you a supertaster," clarified Dr. Linda Bartoshuk, professor at the University of Florida Center for Smell and Taste. And she would know, she's the one who coined the term in the early 1990s.

"We discovered supertasters when I was studying PROP tasting, when we were identifying the single gene for bitter tasting," she said.

Linda and her team were interested in PROP and TAS2R38 because the reaction to PROP is a simple test that could be used to categorize people by tasting sensitivity. There are "nontasters," who experience the PROP-laden sample as nothing more than paper in the mouth. There are "tasters," who sense some bitter flavor but don't find it particularly strong or unpleasant. Then there are "supertasters," who find PROP so bitter that the sensation borders on painful. Linda points out this status relates solely to tasting bitterness; when a subject is tested with PROP they are a bitter nontaster, bitter taster, or bitter supertaster.

"But you can be a supertaster without being a bitter taster," Linda emphasized. "There are other tests."

For the roughly 25 percent of the population who are supertasters, it's not only bitter tastes that packs a powerful punch. They experience a wholly more intense flavor world than the other 75 percent of the population. Sweet is sweeter, the burn of chili more acute, and the creamy texture of fat more apparent.

There are anatomical reasons for all of that intensity.

"A taste bud is surrounded by a basket of fibers that are pain-sensing fibers," Linda explained. "So the more taste buds you have, the more pain fibers you have, which is why you feel more burn."

And supertasters will have more of them. The number of fungiform papillae (those structures discussed in the previous chapter that house our microscopic taste buds) on the tongue vary with tasting status; a supertaster may have sixty or more in a square centimeter. An average taster will have around thirty per square centimeter, and a nontaster may have as few as fifteen; some counts have been as low as eleven.

The presence of extra taste buds lead supertasters to be flavor "superfeelers," too. One study set out to specifically prove these fibers surrounding the taste buds can feel shapes and textures just like our fingers. People were asked to determine which letter of the alphabet was embossed on a cube using only their tongue. Supertasters were two times more accurate at identifying the letters by feel than nontasters. A letter two and a half millimeters tall (that's about the size of a letter on this page) was large enough for supertasters to correctly name, while nontasters needed letters at least five millimeters tall.

In addition to PROP-tasting status and fungiform papillae, Linda uses one last test to characterize a supertaster: "On a scale where one hundred is the greatest pleasure of your life, the best thing you've ever experienced, and negative one hundred is the worst displeasure, and zero is exactly neutral, where would you put your favorite food?"

Linda doesn't mean just your favorite food like a hunk of cheese on a plate but your favorite food experience. My mind flickered to my first Trappist beer in Belgium, served alongside hunks of rich aged Gouda and sharply spicy mustard. I told her the high eighties, probably eighty-seven or eight-eight if I had to be exact.

"Good!" she exclaimed. "It's never one hundred. And don't worry, sex isn't usually one hundred for most people, either. For most people, one hundred is spending time with loved ones." Linda said people will generally slot their favorite food on the scale between sixty and eighty. And supertasters always rate food experiences higher on this pleasure scale than their taster and nontaster counterparts.

"We know tasters tend to have more taste buds. That's a peripheral anatomical feature. But this pleasure scale is handled in the brain." Defining exactly how a taster's brain relates food situations to the rest of their life experiences as compared to a nontaster is on the long list of phenomena Linda and her team are looking to study.

Bitter-tasting status, number of taste buds, and hedonic rating of food pleasures are the three criteria Linda turns to when declaring a supertasters. I was thrilled about my taster status, I mean, could a non-taster write this book?

Actually, yes. Despite a name that seems endowed with Wonder Woman–level superpowers, being a supertaster doesn't have any connection to descriptive tasting talent or the ability to pinpoint particular flavors. In fact, rather than comic-book-hero level courage, supertasters tend to have cowardice of the tongue.

"When supertasters are young, they'll avoid many foods because the experience is just too intense," Charles tells me back at my tasting assessment. "It's why my mother and I always hated our brussels sprouts but my father continued to insist we eat them." His father was a nontaster and likely didn't realize that the bitterness of a broccoli stem or a brussels sprout evokes more than a *yuck* in a young supertaster. It can be a truly day-ruining experience akin to the shock of staring into the sun. This leads to fewer novel food experiences and sensory memories, which, as we'll learn in chapter 12, are essential to thoughtfully tasting our way through life. In order to become adventurous eaters, supertasters have to actively fight their tendency toward bland foods and risk triggering their sensitive pain responses in order to enjoy the bitterness of an American IPA or radishes atop a salad.

"You know the 'super' doesn't carry a value judgment; it's just what I was calling them around the lab," Linda said. "Maybe I should have picked a different word."

I wondered if intense tasters was more accurate. Before I could suggest it, she added, "I'm not a supertaster, and frankly, I wouldn't want to be one."

Still, I felt excited to verify that I am one. Just as I'm beginning to lean back in my plush velvet chair to revel in the fact that I had bested the affliction of a supertaster by expanding beyond my bland childhood diet of cheese and crackers to bitter endive salads and gamey beef tongue soups, Charles begins the next step of the sensory evaluation. This will be a test of the nose. The supertaster badge of honor means being sensitive to the five basic tastes, but sensitivity to scent is the premiere ability when it comes to perceiving flavor. It's "supersmeller" status that the food-obsessed should really be seeking, and that's a genetic designation that scientists are exceedingly close to defining.

In the same way that bitter taster status breaks down into nontaster, taster, and supertaster, smeller status has its own categories. People who are highly sensitive to smell are hyperosmic, those with an average sensitivity are considered normosmic, people with a reduced sensitivity to smell are hyposmic, and finally, people with no sense of smell are considered anosmic. A series of studies shows that which category you end up in may be tied to the alleles on a single gene. Results consistently show that people with two A alleles on the odor binding protein gene (OBPIIa) are reliably normosmic. That's not quite as exciting as being hyperosmic or a "supersmeller," but these studies have shown that people with the two A polymorphism have an increased ability to sense single molecule odors as well as the ability to identify smells at a lower threshold. In the future there may be a proven designation for ultra-sensitive hypersomic smellers. Typically, in science fiction fantasies, when children can be genetically designed, the conversation steers toward augmenting height or choosing eye color and eliminating the genes that increase the likelihood of cancer. But maybe by the time we're selecting our future sons' or daughters' hair color in a lab we'll also specify two A alleles on the odor binding protein gene.

Back in the room with Charles, he waves a simple vial near my nose at just the right distance to waft a scent in my direction without blasting my nostrils with it.

"What color does this scent remind you of?"

I close my eyes and sniff the air.

"Any color coming to mind?" he prompts.

Here, I begin to spiral. My inclination is to blurt out "Magenta!" But no, it smells like a plant, definitely herbal, maybe a little powdery.

"Hmmmm," I murmur "maybe green?"

"Green?" repeats Charles, his eyes widening a bit in an expression of what I take as surprise.

Shoot. I overthought it, and in front of Charles Spence no less!

"Well, I was going to say purple, but it's too planty, sorry," I stutter. "*Planty* isn't a word. I mean it's too growing smelling, like a growing thing."

(Later, in chapter 9, we'll revisit the reason describing what I smelled reduced me to a bumbling mess.)

"It's beta ionone," he says, swiveling the lid to the vial closed. "As a full flower it's violets."

One in three people wouldn't be able to sense that green- or purple-smelling aroma wafting up from the vial, Charles tells me. Being able to enjoy the floral aroma of violet blooms on the street while you wait at a crosswalk all comes down to a single gene: olfactory receptor family 5 subfamily A member 1, more succinctly known as OR5A1. Those born with a pair of sensitive alleles for this gene may find the fragrant aroma of crème de violette (a liquor made by macerating violet flowers) in a classic aviation cocktail so pungent that it's akin to licking the flower itself. A carrier of the double insensitive alleles may not be able to detect the floral quality at all. In this case, people with a pair of insensitive alleles are considered to have a "specific anosmia" to beta ionone. The less clinical term for this condition is "scent blind" (or more casually, "nose blind") to a specific aroma.

Calling it blindness sounds devastating. Are these anosmics destined to wander the earth never experiencing the glorious natural scent hovering in the air around a field of vivid purple violets?

"There are more than two hundred compounds that make up the aroma of a strawberry," Professor Juyun Lim told me at the Department of Food Science and Technology on the University of Oregon campus.

"If you're blind to two of those two hundred compounds, and they aren't important compounds, then missing them won't matter," she said. "That is just what strawberry smells like to you." It's only when the compounds are the three or four that are essential to overall "strawberryness" that there starts to be variation in understanding what it means for a chewy candy to taste like strawberry.

A glass of wine emits as many as one thousand volatile aromas, with dozens of them being essential to the character of that distinct type of wine. "I can smell wine and say it smells like cherry to me,"

Juyun said, "but you say it smells like cherry jam, and maybe I don't think so. There is a huge range in the compounds we are sensitive to."

In this case, smelling cherry opposed to cherry jam could be related to a variation in sensitivity to the compound cis-3-hexenol, which has been tied to just two genes, and one study showed insensitive alleles for both genes "effectively abolished the response to the compound." Cis-3-hexenol contributes an aroma of freshness, sometimes described as grassy. A contribution that can take the aroma of cherry from dried fruit to plucked ripe from the tree. However, if you're blind to cis-3-hexenol, you won't be able to pick up on its contribution of freshness, leaving you less able to differentiate between baked cherry pie and fresh picked cherry fruit.

But specific anosmias can have their benefits, too. For example, people who are nose blind to the compound trichloroanisole (TCA) don't smell the musty-basement-like flavor in wine that professionals consider a flaw referred to as "corked." (TCA also rears its musty head in the world of beer and even balsamic vinegar.) The most expensive wines, those considered worth aging, are usually closed using the pricier natural cork material (as opposed to its synthetic TCA-free counterpart). There's always a risk opening a cork-sealed bottle more than ten years old. It might be worth every dollar, but it might also be tainted. However, those wine lovers who are blind to TCA don't run the risk of this specific flaw ruining their tipple: they'll enjoy a corked wine as if it were in pristine condition.

Another compound you may be happy to be blind to is indole. The 50 percent of people without receptors to sense it are saved from smelling the aroma of pigpen, or more specifically, pig poop. And there is the 6 percent of the population that's blind to isovaleric acid, a major component in the smell of sweaty socks and body odor.

As scientists continue to work through the more than four hundred individual genes tied to our perception of smells, it becomes clear how widely individual smellscapes can differ from person to person. Our genetic makeup decides the compounds we can and can't taste and how sensitive we are to them. Those sensitivities determine whether we'll find a specific scent pleasant or repulsive. The slightest variation in preferences can shape our flavor world. People with less sensitivity to bitterness may love hoppy IPAs and tannic red wines while the ultra-perceptive may veer toward sweet fruity cocktails and floral sakes.

Inherent preferences are not always baked into our DNA, though. They're also gained through experience. Sometimes they are instilled before our consciousness is fully developed, while we are in the womb and as days-old infants. Mothers who regularly eat pungent foods like carrots and garlic may be less likely to raise a child who picks all the healthy toppings off his or her pizza (we all know that kid, right?). Studies that analyzed mothers' diets during pregnancy showed that those who ate strong flavors had babies who made fewer negative facial expressions when confronted with pungent foods than the babies of mothers on a control diet. The absence of negative facial expression is correlated to food acceptance, meaning these babies are more likely to eat an adventurous diet if they are presented with one, and a more adventurous diet means more variety in pizza toppings!

These food preferences stay with us long after childhood. A simple taste test conducted in Germany is an illuminating example of this phenomenon. Adult participants were presented with two samples of ketchup and asked which one they liked more. The samples were exactly the same other than one ingredient: vanillin, which is the odor-active compound in, you guessed it, vanilla. Vanilla-spiked ketchup sounds pretty nasty, but there was a specific segment of subjects who consistently preferred the vanilla-ketchup abomination: people who had been bottle-fed. In Germany, baby formula contained low levels of vanillin. Adults who hadn't been bottle-fed in many decades unconsciously had a taste for vanillin.

Hundreds of variables confront babies in their first feedings. Any small shift in experience could be the explanation for the toddlers who want only the bizarre flavors at the ice cream shop (I never understood who was actually ordering the blue raspberry gummy bear blast with sour crunchies) compared to others who refuse to venture further than a chocolate chip away from their vanilla cone.

These hidden preferences are totally out of our control, yet they shape the way we experience the things we eat every day, and they only continue to pile up as we begin eating solid food. In fact, the way we chew solid food is another influence on the variation in taste perception from person to person. Each human "orally processes" food a little differently. You may think, how different could it be? A chew is a chew, it will get us the same end result, right?

Wrong. There are four particular ways people approach getting soft foods like crème brûlée or ice cream from mouth to stomach. "Simple" processors simply push the tongue to the roof of the mouth and swallow; the soft food is there, and then in one gulp, it's gone. "Manipulators" (sometimes referred to as "chewers") move the jaw vertically, letting the teeth do the work to move food from the mouth to the throat. "Tonguers" rely on the tongue to do the work, moving it from left to right across the palate to push food toward the throat. "Tasters" spend a little more time with the food either by sucking it against the roof of the mouth a few times, almost as if they are squeezing a little extra flavor out of it. Some taster-style processors also spread the food into the cheeks before moving to the throat so it covers more surface area of the mouth. According to a 2000 study, about 20 percent of us are natural "tasters" when it comes to getting a bite of custard from spoon to throat. Next time you dive into a bowl of chocolate mousse or creamy yogurt, pay attention to what you're doing with your teeth, tongue, and cheeks because whichever you depend on most influences exactly how that dessert tickles your taste buds.

Wageningen University scientists and the Unilever research and development department worked together on an experiment that forced participants to consume ice cream in two methods that weren't necessarily their natural chewing behavior: one group allowed the ice cream to fully melt in the mouth before swallowing it and the other group was required to chew the ice cream before swallowing. Participants found the ice cream to be firmer in texture and sweet while they waited for it to melt on their tongues. The group that chewed the ice cream found it to be noticeably fruitier and colder. From what we know about the importance of retronasal aroma, it seems that the agitation from purposeful chewing forced aromatics up the retronasal passageway, giving chewers a more intense flavor experience. A retronasal boost from chewing leads to a more flavorful experience for people who orally process with their teeth compared to tasters, who use their tongues to spread the food around their mouth.

At some point in our lives, perhaps on that very first bite of semi-solid baby food, we unknowingly decided how to approach getting nutritional goo from the spoon to our stomachs. That unconscious decision may lead to experiencing fruitier ice cream our whole lives because of it! Then again, the way we chew is just one tiny factor in how sweet or fruity a dessert seems to us. Before that ice cream was ever on the spoon, your cultural experience and familiarity with it modified how the bite would taste.

This influence of culture and expectation on our perception of flavor is an occurrence Charles is ready to trick me with next. Rather than a fragrant vial of oil, this time Charles holds a plastic squeeze bottle and poufs a few puffs of fragrance in my direction.

"What do you think here: sweet or savory?" he asks. He explains I might associate this scent more with meat dishes or more with things like cakes or desserts depending on my background.

"Hmm, maybe it's cloves? Not really," I think aloud.

"No, not really," agrees Charles.

"More woody, like maybe . . . allspice?" I look at him hopefully.

He doesn't respond and instead shoots a few more puffs of fragrance toward my nose.

"Or nutmeg?"

"There we go!" he says. "This one has been shown in studies, especially in North America, that it can be very sweet or savory, depending on the food culture you grow up in."

If you're familiar with nutmeg alongside a blast of sugar PSLs (pumpkin spice lattes, for the uninitiated) or as a small feature in the streusel that tops fruit cobblers, you'll lean sweet. Or you may be used to nutmeg in savory contexts, like creamed spinach and as part of sausage filling. Or you might not be familiar with it at all. A study of Vietnamese, French, and American subjects found that "spice" was the foremost descriptor of nutmeg used by Americans and French participants followed by "nature." Vietnamese subjects had a different impression and categorized the odor as "musty" or "plant." That same group of researchers conducted another study and found that both the French and American participants recognized nutmeg and named its scent "nutmeg" while Vietnamese participants were most likely to label the aroma as "plastic."

These vastly different reactions to the same scent remind me of the height of my beer taster training. During my most intense periods of studying for my Cicerone exams, I regularly met with other self-proclaimed beer nerds to taste classic examples of beer styles. We'd each bring a sample beer to pour for the rest of the group and dissect its flavor profile together. The idea was to learn to recognize classic styles by telltale aromas we all noticed, even when we weren't sure what exactly was in the glass. For example, notes of banana reliably point to German and Belgian styles. Big aromas of dried grapefruit peel indicate a classic American style. Beers that taste tart like vinegar are a Flanders Red, but beers that are tart like lemon are Goses or Berliner-style Weisses.

One night, I brought a California Common to one of these study group meetings. California common is a narrowly defined American beer style that is tied to its ingredients: Northern Brewer hops and toasty amber malt. Northern Brewer hop aroma is described as minty, evergreen, and woody. When we reached my California common sample in the flight, I leaned back and listed to my study group piece together a description of the hops.

"Tree bark in those hops for sure, hmm, maybe some sort of candied herb," said one.

"It's so, so medicinal," said the other. I raised an eyebrow and took another quick sniff of my sample. I didn't notice any medicine.

"Medicine? What about mint?" I suggested.

No, the aroma reminded my British counterpart of liniment, a term I'd never heard before. After some questioning, I realized liniment is another name for muscle rub, like Icy Hot.

That conversation stuck in my head long after study group. Should I be picking up medicinal flavors in some hop varieties? Was I missing something? After a quick consultation with the IcyHot in my first-aid kit (which definitely smelled artificial and medicinal), I hit Google. Turns out it's not just mint but specifically wintergreen (even more specifically the compound methyl salicylate, which gives wintergreen oil its aroma) that makes Brits think of liniment. Unlike Americans, who typically associate wintergreen with sugary contexts that include breath mints, chewing gums, or root beer, people from other cultures, especially in Europe, are first exposed to the aroma through liniment creams or other medical contexts. My online research sent me to You-Tube, where one very energetic British social media personality tasted

A&W Root Beer as part of a video recording his reactions to American sodas. After calling canned iced tea "really nice" and cherry-flavored soda way too sweet, he cracks open the root beer. He's not a fan. "It smells like when you cut yourself as a child and your mum and dad put like TCP or whatever it's called on you to kind of clean the wound. It tastes like cough medicine; I don't like it." Alas, this internet personality couldn't figure out what was triggering his association with first aid and ended up attributing it to the "aged vanilla" that is mentioned on the can. That video sent me down a mint-flavored rabbit hole. The internet provides no shortage of wild reactions to wintergreen-flavored or -scented things. A show-dog trainer was left distraught with the minty aroma of her nonaerosol coat conditioner for horses and dogs, leaving it a one-star review because "it smells like a locker room," noting that it made her entire room smell like liniment. She refused to use it on her dogs. It's worth pointing out here that the "scent" feature of this conditioner had a solid four-star rating from the other reviewers.

Your culture will not only shape how you interpret some flavors, but it also determines if you pick up on them at all. Yokan is a traditional Japanese confection made of gelled sweet bean paste. Japanese diners are familiar with the nuanced collection of flavors, including umami, that come together to produce the signature taste of the dessert. Researchers from the National Institute of Advanced Industrial Science and Technology in Japan studied both German and Japanese participants eating yokan. At first, they ate it under normal circumstances, and then the scientists increased the amount of retronasal aroma participants sensed from the dessert. The Japanese tasters had no problem noting an increase in umami flavor when there was more aroma present. Meanwhile, German tasters picked up on an increase in intensity of flavor but didn't notice a specific increase in umami. The German participants never really had a chance when it came to calling out that savory, brothy quality of umami. Especially when you consider that only 2 percent of participants hailing from Germany were able to identify umami when it was served to them in its purest form. While sipping on a monosodium glutamate solution, they struggled to come up with the right word to describe what they were tasting. A few of them came close with descriptions like "soy sauce," "soup," and "meaty" (all known to be umami-related) but the vast majority called the liquid "salzig" (salty) and the second-highest-used description was "eklig" (disgusting).

Their counterparts in Italy did just as poorly, with only 2 percent of that cohort coming up with the word for umami, while the Finnish participants came out with a surprising 15 percent correct identification. (Although 15 percent recognition is still dismal when you consider umami is one of just five basic tastes. We would think it was a problem if they couldn't come up with "sweet" to define a glass of sugar water . . . wouldn't we?) Having a word for the flavor in your native language helps you pick up on it when it's a part of a food or meal, but it's also being familiar with a flavor that leads you to recognize it.

Famed market researcher Howard W. Moskowitz conducted one of the earliest studies into how taste preferences are affected by both culture and class. He traveled to India, where he approached affluent students and found typical taste preferences: sugar was always good; salt was usually good but too much was bad; and bitter and sour were generally avoided. Rather than concluding his research with the typical sample of university students so many studies rely on, he went on to test the taste preferences of workers residing in India's lower economic class. These workers had less variety in their diet and also consumed less expensive foods. One ingredient in particular had an outsize impact on their eating habits: tamarind, which has a tart flavor that falls somewhere between an apricot and a lemon. They sucked on the fruit itself as a treat and used it to season meals like lentil soup, giving those dishes a distinct tang. When it came time for them to rate the intensity and pleasantness of increasing sourness levels (via increased concentrations of citric acid), their rating of pleasantness increased with intensity without leveling off. For this group, sour wasn't to be avoided, it was part of what made food delicious.

No matter the background we come from, humans will unanimously rate familiar tastes higher than a taste we don't recognize. Whether it's the tangy tamarind snacks of the Indian laborers or the minty notes in root beer in the United States, the snack we're familiar with is the one we'll reach for.

If you're an American reading this, your familiar diet is one of the most sugar dense on earth. Snacks like chips and sandwich breads are loaded with sugar, even though they're considered savory indulgences. Does this cultural proclivity for a high-fat, high-sugar, high-salt diet (especially when it comes to snack foods) tie back to taster status?

As many as 40 percent of people from European descent have nontaster status, while it may be as few as 5 percent of Asian people who are genetic nontasters. In the United States an estimated 30 percent of people are considered nontasters, with as few as 15 percent of men in America classified as supertasters. Now the fact that Germans had a hard time finding the word for umami when tasting yokan makes more sense. Since the tongues of nontasters indisputably feel fewer sensations than supertasters, it's not surprising that Europeans tend to like snacks that are crisp, crunchy textures and require some tooth work. On the other hand, people raised in Asian cultures prefer foods that require only "soft processing," textures of semisolid or malleable foods in the mouth. Things like tofu, custards, or the soft gel-like texture of yokan. The dessert, flecked with notes of umami and sweetness, offers a sensitive palate complexity in both texture and flavor.

For a less-sensitive taster, those subtleties aren't enough to pique interest or appetite.

This contrast between people who are culturally attuned to subtle flavors and those who are not was put on display during the 2019 holiday gift season when the Japanese government made an attempt to popularize yokan in the United States. A two-day event celebrating the traditional dessert was planned in collaboration with American media outlets and chefs. And for the first time, more than a dozen yokan makers came to New York City and brought with them thousands of years of experience crafting the jellied artisan sweets that were new to the American consumer. *Vogue* magazine got in on the yokan action, calling a collection of the Japanese sweets "a visual feast" as well as an edible one. The writer also emphasized to their fashion-conscious readership that they'll be "especially delighted to discover [yokan] is free of both gluten and dairy."

As if the emphasis on visual appearance and diet appropriateness wasn't a glaring indicator of the difference in cultural appreciation, there was the scene at the event itself. At one table an eighteenth-generation yokan maker showcased his delicate, earth-toned creations that he and his family had labored to perfect for centuries. Some of the uniformly sliced delicacies had carefully selected Japanese ingredients in addition to the standard trio of azuki beans, agar-agar, and sugar. A deep brown example had added kurozato (unrefined dark brown sugar) and a vivid green one was flavored with matcha. Directly next to this confectioner was a table occupied by American chefs presenting their own take on yokan. And how did they decide to introduce this nuanced, simple dessert with a thousand-year legacy to stateside consumers? They covered it in chocolate, rolled it in puffed crunchy quinoa, and stuck it on a stick. And if that wasn't enough, the customers had to answer one question when they came to the American chef's yokan lollipop table: "Which color would you like, pink or purple?"

They had to add crunch, color, and presentation to the yokan just so the average American could taste something.

⎯⎯⎯●

As Charles wrapped up his individual taster assessment he asked, "Now, doesn't it seem strange to just serve everyone the same thing without even asking a little bit about their taste world?" We had done several other mini sensory evaluations at this point.

When you look at all the evidence of our differences, it really does. A supertaster may want a little more vermouth than Campari in their negroni to keep the bitterness in check. Sprinkling nutmeg into a hot toddy might remind some drinkers of a meaty entrée, not usually what a bartender is going for with a sweet drink. And, of course, there's the beta-ionone blind diners who won't get any benefit from a violet-infused panna cotta. It's commonplace for servers and bartenders to ask, "Any allergies or dietary restrictions?" at the start of a meal. Maybe one day they'll start to ask us, "Any aroma blindness or favorite spices?"

Even if the waitstaff and chefs start working within or, at the very least, thinking about our individual flavor worlds, there are still other ways that the restaurant forces taste upon us that no questionnaire can account for. These factors are painted onto the restaurant walls, piped over the speaker system, and incorporated into the very plates dinner is served upon. In the next chapter we'll explore what the dining room itself tastes like, and how that changes our perception of the meal.

CHAPTER THREE

THE FLAVOR OF A DINING ROOM

M Y FOOT CATCHES ON UNEVEN COBBLESTONES AND NEARLY SENDS ME tumbling to the sidewalk, right in the path of an impeccably dressed couple walking their impeccably groomed dog down the impeccably clean (though uneven!) street.

"I know, these streets are crazy, right?" laughs the woman, maneuvering around me as I steady myself.

I am in Tribeca, a Manhattan neighborhood that is home to some of the most popular bars and restaurants in the city. Most of the establishments in this part of town are very impressive: pressed white tablecloths, sparkling wineglasses, and plenty of fresh flowers embellishing their dining rooms. In fact, flowers are the reason I am here. A conversation with floral designer Amy Eisenstadt earlier in the week sent me on a mission of curiosity. Amy knows her stuff. She designs floral arrangements for Michelin starred restaurants, star-studded events, and luxurious private residences. So, when she told me she was "shocked" by a certain Tribeca restaurant's choice of blooms, I wanted to see for myself what was so shocking.

"They have two massive arrangements of Casa Blanca lilies," Amy had said. "I always thought, '*Wow, those smell so strong!*'"

I was craning my neck to peer into the restaurant's window to see the flowers myself when I tripped. If the flower arrangements weren't big, like big enough that they look big from out on the street, I wasn't going to drop $20 (before tip!) on what was bound to be a mediocre cocktail. But they are big. Even through the window, the lilies look more like imposing alabaster statues than a flower arrangement. Soon, I am seated next to them and can see that each individual bloom is about the size of my fist, and carries more than a fistful of scent. The flowers tower over the bar seats, and even a few stools away the scent still invade my personal space. It is a heady sweetness mingling with a mild damp smell that edges on animal (so pungent I can't tell if my Bellini is made with the traditional peach or another stone fruit).

According to Amy, this sense that flowers are invading my personal space crosses one of her two cardinal rules of restaurant floral design. "Whatever the venue, there are only two things I really have to consider," she said. "How will the flowers look in a week? And will they smell too strong for a dining room? So no freesias or lilies. You don't want it to compete with the smell of the food." After pondering for a minute, Amy remembered one more consideration when it comes to restaurant arrangements, specifically arrangements for a midtown restaurant she designs for. "Oh, we also have a little battle going with some of the sommeliers. They'll say these flowers can't stick out so far because they have to get back to the cabinet to get glasses. But sorry, guys, they look good sticking out that far!"

Amy added that dining rooms don't always require huge glamourous arrangements; sometimes it's nice for the florals to blend in. She

THE FLAVOR OF A DINING ROOM

said they add a little something alive to a scene in a dining room, but they don't have to be a centerpiece and shouldn't be too distracting.

Here at the Tribeca restaurant, it seems to me that while Casa Blanca lilies are gorgeous, there has to be dozens of other choices of flower that would make the same visual impact without a perfume strong enough to obscure the flavor of my cocktail.

I set out to see if there was any reason a restaurateur may want to pummel customers with a floral scent while they dined. At first all I found were a handful of studies attempting to stop Casa Blanca lilies (also referred to as Oriental lilies) from producing their fragrance altogether. One paper states that eliminating the scent "would make Oriental lilies accessible to those who cannot tolerate their scent but want to enjoy their majesty." After digging into the chemical properties of the flower itself, I discovered it has four main aromatic compounds: benzyl alcohol, which smells slightly sweet and floral with under notes that smell damp; isoeugenol, the scent of cloves; cis-ocimene, which smells of sweet green basil; and linalool, a compound that smells of lily of the valley flowers and spiced bark. That last one, linalool, is also the dominant aroma in lavender flowers. Research has confirmed many times over that smelling lavender has a calming effect. In fact, its powers of relaxation are so potent that scientists are testing it as a medical treatment for anxiety. Reading through those piles of studies I also found evidence that lavender causes shoppers to browse longer at stores and feel more pleasant after nerve-racking dental procedures. Finally, I found what I was searching for: In an often-cited 2006 study researchers Nicolas Guéguen and Christine Petr noted that lavender aroma increased the amount spent in a restaurant as well as the length diners lingered. Bingo! If the team at the Tribeca restaurant weren't consciously placing lilies by my side to make me spend more, maybe they were doing it to soothe my unease as I opened the bill. (A single drink for $20, remember!)

The frustration of being unable to enjoy the juicy fragrance of my cocktail without interference obliterated any potential calming effect the flower aroma might have had. Interfering scents are obvious sensory triggers that alter how we experience food. For those seated close enough to the opulent arrangements, every bite of dinner would have a twinge of lily flavor to it. As discussed in chapter 1, smells don't affect what we taste; they are what we taste. An especially odoriferous trash can behind the bar is sure to obscure the delicate elderflower perfume of a St. Germain cocktail. And yes, your date's suffocating cologne will detract from the milky burrata on your flatbread (and possibly from the enjoyment of the night overall).

The things we hear, see, and feel around us shape the flavor of the meal as much as what's on the plate. And in turn, what we see, hear, and feel on the plate influences what we taste before we ever take a bite. Can wallpaper in the ice cream shop make your sample taste just slightly sweeter than the cone you end up eating out in the world? (Spoiler alert: yes, especially if the wallpaper is pink!) Will you notice the nuance in a glass of very expensive wine if you drink it in a loud bar? (Pro tip: save the good stuff for a quiet place if you can.)

In this chapter I will dig into the sensory inputs that surround us when we eat and drink and how they influence what we taste for the better and for the worse. To start, we'll look at the dining room as a whole and continue to zoom in until we the focus on the millisecond before the fork enters the mouth.

The scent of those lilies may have a wide circumference in the dining room, but there is one intangible that fills the entire room, from the steel rafter on the ceiling to the gleaming wood floor: music. Try to recall the last time you ate a meal in silence without any ambient noise. You might have to think all the way back to a sorry smushed sandwich eaten an hour before your final exam in the college library. (For me, it was always the sad but reliable snack of prepackaged hummus and pretzels, which were just stale enough that I could avoid my crunches echoing through the stacks.) When we're eating, we're listening, even if we aren't aware of it.

Some of the impact music has on our eating and tasting abilities is straightforward. Fast-paced music is proven to increase the number of bites diners take per minute. It also leads them to spend more. Low-pitched tones are associated with bitterness. Loud noise dulls our sensitivity to salty and sweet flavors, but we become more attuned to umami. We also notice the crunch of bar nuts or carrot sticks in a noisy setting. This connection between our ears and our palates is partially due to the literal wiring of our taste system. The chorda tympani nerve is one of the pathways that taste signals take from the taste bud to the brain. Enroute from mouth to cranium, this nerve passes through the middle ear. If the ear is vibrating from loud or tonal sounds, the chorda tympani gets jostled as well. Scientists aren't certain of all the effects these vibrations have on dulling or enhancing taste signals, but they know something is happening! Somehow, the specific vibrations of jazz music are responsible for diners' increased pleasure as the genre plays during dinner. In contrast, hip-hop diminishes the enjoyment of familiar foods—a fact that stuck out to me because there's a Michelin-starred restaurant in the Financial District that conspicuously bumps a mix of beat-driven music like nineties hip-hop and neo soul. However, every time I've been in Crown Shy, patrons seem to be far from experiencing diminished enjoyment. Then again, the team at Crown Shy isn't re-creating your grandmother's dishes tucked fondly into your memory. Perhaps the chef gets away with playing Janet Jackson and Biggie in the background because the menu features dishes like "Dorade, Mushroom Puree, Sunchoke XO Sauce" and "Treccione, Duck Ragu, Mushrooms" that use ingredients in original combinations that diners never considered, let alone considered enough to be familiar with.

"The music creates an energy and a mood," said general manager and partner at Crown Shy, Jeff Katz. "The idea behind this restaurant was that it's going to be fun and lively and boisterous, but with food and service that is tighter and sharper than you'd expect in a room like that." Jeff wanted everything to work together, from the pared-down aesthetic of the dining room to the carefully executed food coming from the kitchen and his partner at Crown Shy, chef James Kent.

"The food is always going to be beautiful and delicious."

But Jeff doesn't want Crown Shy to feel like a "food temple." He said some restaurants feel like guests are invited to come pray at the food altar. When it comes to sound and music in the dining room, Jeff doesn't think of it in relation to what's on the plate. "I'm not sure that it connects back to the way food tastes. I don't think that's the case. I think it's more about the way the room feels that impacts the diner." He added, "We want people to feel relaxed like they're having a good time and they don't have to act a certain way."

Which leads to the least surprising of all the research findings connecting our ears to our palate: we like what we eat more when we like the sound in the background. The conclusion of the paper from the Smell & Taste Clinic at the University of Dresden Medical School states, "The more the participants liked the preceding sound, the more pleasant the subsequent odor became." (If you've ever wondered whether that screaming baby is really ruining your dinner . . . Sorry, babies, wails of an infant's cry empirically stole away some of the pleasure people gleaned from the pleasing scents.)

Restaurateurs who place real significance on clientele finding each consecutive bite more pleasant than the last will hire someone like Joe Darling to curate a playlist for the space. Joe and the rest of the team at Uncanned Music have been creating sonic experiences for restaurants and bars for more than a decade. "The ultimate purpose is to disarm the guests of the restaurant," he said of the soundscapes designed for bars and restaurants around the United States. He believes patrons should feel comfortable, and the right music and sound levels subconsciously encourage them to relax and engage with one another.

"There's a golden ratio," Joe told me. "You play a familiar song and then a specific number of unfamiliar but really compelling songs." This balance allows clientele to notice they like the music, without it taking over their night. "Each restaurant seems to have a slightly different variation on that ratio."

Young Joni, Ann Kim's genre-defying restaurant in Minneapolis, serves pizza, meats, and other dishes fired on a series of woodburning ovens and grills to music curated by the Uncanned Music team. The goal is a soundscape that is playful, cozy, and classic without being immediately familiar. One playlist is a mix of seventies rock and folk that might be reminiscent of Chef Ann's parents' eight-track collection. While Sparrow, a Cuban-inspired cocktail lounge in Chicago modeled on the "great hotel lobby bars of the 1930s," shakes rum cocktails to a mix of jazz and African Caribbean music. The music mirrors the menu without being too explicit. It's a practice of creating a natural habitat for the food rather than playing music that sounds like fruity rum drinks personified.

Although there is music out there that *does* sound like fruity rum drinks.

Let's take whatever song is currently number one on the Billboard charts. If I had you rate it on a scale from soft to rough with a one being soft and a seven being rough, you could probably do that, right? The long drawn-out notes just glide by comfortably while rapid staccato beats feel bumpy and sharp. Okay, now rate that song on a scale from banana to lemon. Clearly more difficult, but still possible. In fact, that is exactly what researchers had sixty-six participants in a study do. Four songs were selected for their "sweet" (long note duration, low articulation, and low volume) and "sour" (high pitch, with high dissonance, i.e., when tones of different frequencies clash in a displeasing way) sounds. Consistently, the "sweet" songs scored high points as banana, chocolate, and meringue while participants rated "sour" songs as more lemon, crisp rye bread, and lingonberry. See if your ears can "taste" these songs yourself at howtotastebook.com/sweet-sour.

Without making a conscious thought, our senses come together to determine if "we're in a sweet place." Beyond this finding, the experimenters forged on to prove that we know exactly what a tune tastes like. Participants were then given sour and sweet fruit juices as well as honey and asked to mix a drink. Those listening to sour music made significantly more acidic drinks containing ingredients like grapefruit and lemon juice, while those with sweet tunes wafting through the room reached for the honey. When you order a zesty tropical tiki drink, are you really ordering it because you love rum, or is the playlist telling you it's time for something tangy in your day?

Across the lobby from Crown Shy is one of my favorite coffee shops, where the music is far from hip-hop. Black Fox has an atmosphere that is a little posh; it's sophisticated yet understated. Clean angular lines form a black-and-white-tile pattern on the floor. A large squared pillar on one wall is painted a dark gray blue; the opposing wall holding the wooden menu is the same hue. Countertops are a fashionable dark wood, and in the kitchen the setup is uncomplicated. A large, powerful-looking espresso machine dominates the counter. It's one of those shops that doesn't offer Wi-Fi in hopes of encouraging diners to have conversations and focus on the coffee. But little do they know, Wi-Fi is productivity's enemy, and that's why I wrote about half of this book inside Black Fox. I hesitate to call Black Fox my local coffee shop, even though it is merely four blocks from my apartment, because in New York City there are actually four coffee shops that are closer to me than Black Fox. What keeps me walking the extra block or two? According to science, it might be all that thought put into the interior design.

Our senses work together to construct a clear understanding of our surroundings. Unconsciously we'll take an auditory or visual cue and apply it to what we taste or smell. This is called crossmodal correspondence. It's the phenomenon that creates the association between sour ingredients and sharp, pitchy music. It's also what leads us to rate coffee served in red-hued coffee shops as sweeter. And coffee served in greenish ones as more bitter and sour. For most foods, this bitter and sour association is negative. But it turns out, these traits are what give coffee its characteristic flavor and depth. Participants in one study predicted coffee served in coffee shops with green interiors would be more bitter, more sour, and also tastier. Their positive affinity didn't end with the coffee in the cup, though; subjects also claimed they were most likely to visit coffee shops with dark color schemes and greenish tints. One has to wonder if a certain multinational coffee chain with a dark green logo made a similar discovery before this study was published. Generally, studies in crossmodal correspondence of taste and color show that shades of red are reliably matched with sweetness. White and blue with salty tastes. Yellow and green with lemon and lime, er, I mean sour. And the colors of coffee—black and brown, that is—with bitterness.

Before crossmodal correspondence was studied, there was another term used to describe the phenomenon of these colors jumping from the walls of a shop to our taste buds: *sensation transference.* Researcher and marketing innovator Louis Cheskin coined the term in the 1940s while he was working to improve the marketability of food products including 7UP Lemon Lime Soda and margarine. Cheskin used the same solution to improve the sales of both products: the color yellow. During World War II, butter was expensive because dairy was scarce. Margarine was intended to be a cheaper and widely available alternative. However, many homemakers refused to use it. Cheskin realized it wasn't the taste that was off-putting but its unappetizing grayish-white color. Once he dyed it yellow to look like butter, it was an easy sell. To

drive his point home, Cheskin served white butter and yellow margarine to guests at a luncheon. The guests reported that the white spread
(real butter) was "oily and greasy," but they enjoyed the yellow spread
(margarine). For the soft drink, yellow had a different but still sizeable
effect. This time, Cheskin only adjusted the packaging without changing the color of the liquid inside the can. He added 15 percent more
yellow color to the can and consumers reported tasting more lemon
citrus flavor in the drink.

The weight of the cup is another sensation that transfers to the
liquid inside. The same stands for a hefty fork and the food upon it.
Items served on heavier plateware are perceived as higher quality. This
is an opportune time to mention that my latte at Black Fox is served in
a weighty blue-gray mug with an equally substantial saucer to match
it. Even the to-go cups are made from sturdy but smooth cardboard,
which is a good move because several studies show that flimsy cups
lead to a decreased quality assessment.

The gray-blue walls of Black Fox may be giving me a calming, salty
vibe and the plateware makes me believe I'm getting high-quality coffee. All these sensations have transferred to my foamed vanilla date
latte with house-made nut milk before I even take a sip. Or it could
be the warm yellow-tinged light emitting from the industrial-chic fixtures that are having the real impact on my fancy latte. In experiments
testing the impact of ambient lighting on eating habits, multiple studies found that blue- and red-hued lighting extinguished the appetite
while white and most of all yellow lighting increased it. These findings
are consistent across a variety of foods including blueberry cake, apples, manufactured candy, bibimbap, bell peppers, and green salads.

Before you enjoy a midday snack, step away from the blue light
of your computer screen. You'll get a break for your eyes and a bonus
boost of flavor. Even better, step into a room with warm-colored bulbs
and your apple will be a little more delicious.

In addition to lighting, the temperature in your office may be a determining factor in what you're craving for a snack. If it's a little too warm that cool, crisp apple may be what you opt to eat. But if there is even a subtle chill, you are more likely to reach for a fresh-baked pastry or bacon, egg, and cheese sandwich from the coffee shop downstairs as a little treat. Our vices become harder to resist when we're cold. Researchers have found this effect applies to everything, from an extra glass of wine to a superfluous serving of dessert to an extended nap. While the frigid conditions might not impact what we actually taste, they do determine what we crave. Specifically, a few degrees' shift in ambient temperature affects our desire for umami-laden foods. Chilly temps at the grocery store might draw you to the butcher's counter. A warm cafeteria will steer you away from the ramen station. We perceive savory foods as being warmer than other categories like fruits, vegetables, and sweets, even if in reality that's not true.

Throw your next dinner party with the thermostat adjusted a few degrees lower than usual and serve steak or a tender rib roast. Your guests will find the meaty spread ultra-satisfying, but be prepared with extra servings for the guests who indulge a little more than they anticipated. And if you really don't want that extra glass of wine next time you go out to dinner, plan ahead and bring a scarf or sweater along to keep you warm.

The temperature inside the coffee shop influences your decision to order the excessively sugary latte you're craving or a healthy green tea, but the temperature inside your cup will also have an impact on how pleased you are with your choice. Han-Seok Seo, associate professor of sensory science at the University of Arkansas, has published a mountain of work on the role of sensory cues in food perception and acceptance. One study focused on coffee drinking temperature and found that people not only liked their coffee more but also associated more positive emotions with their drinking experience when the coffee was 149°F

(65°C) as opposed to 77°F (25°C) or 41°F (5°C). Participants reported the hot coffee made them feel "pleased," "peaceful," "satisfied," and, as expected, "warm" when compared to the other serving temperatures. Notably, the cold coffee left them "disgusted" and tasted "metallic."

This close-to-150-degree temperature falls in an interesting sweet spot. The pain threshold for liquids in the mouth is around 153°F (67°C). Participants reported this temperature as too hot and uncomfortable to drink. But 150°F is slightly below the threshold of actual pain.

Why do we like drinks at near tongue-scorching temperatures? One reason is that more volatile aromas are released by both solids and liquids at elevated temperatures. Heating a substance increases the energy of the molecules inside it. This makes the molecules move more rapidly and eventually break free from the food or beverage and become volatile. When it comes to tasting, those volatile molecules are buzzing around the surface of the coffee ready to be captured by the suction of a sniff and—boom!—smash into our mucusy olfactory epithelium.

Beyond there literally being more to smell when the coffee is warmer, there is the fact that our gustatory system recognizes the five basic tastes differently as temperature shifts. Our taste system becomes increasingly sensitive to sweet, bitter, and umami flavors as the temperature of the tasting increases from 59°F (15°C) to around 95°F (35°C), which is close to our natural body temperature. The receptors on the tongue are at the pinnacle of sensitivity when the coffee (or whatever we're tasting) enters the mouth close to the temperature of the tongue itself. As temperatures rise about body temperature (roughly 98.6°F/37°C), sensitivity to these flavors begins to decrease. One study of this temperature effect on bitter taste hypothesized that the reason sensitivity to bitterness decreases above 95°F is that the things we eat do not naturally exist at those temperatures. Therefore, humans don't need to use their taste sense to test for bitter flavors in foods that are hot. As we covered in chapter 1, the whole point of bitter sensitivity is to identify potential poisons in the food we eat. If we are consuming something hotter than 98°F we are cooking or warming it by choice. As researchers put it, "hot food was under voluntary control and therefore imposed no environmental threat." The only threat a hot coffee poses is burning our tongue, a risk we're willing to take because at this temperature it renders bitterness close to imperceptible and provides a fragrant nose full of volatile compounds. In the case of my 140-ish degree coffee at Black Fox, those volatile compounds smell like honey, apple, and lingering coffee according to the tasting notes posted by the register.

Upon discovering this relationship between bitterness and temperature, my thoughts turned to the people sipping on their iced coffee. How does temperature affect what they're tasting? Almost every flavor and aroma is harder to sense when the tastant is cold. At cool temperatures, volatile aroma compounds are slow to, well, volatilize, and therefore stay in place, a place that is far away from our sensory pathways. Have you ever had a bite of ice cream straight from the freezer that tastes like nothing other than . . . cold? Or melted ice cream that tastes so sweet it is nearly sickening? Just as we're less sensitive to some flavors when they're much warmer than our body temperature, it's also more difficult to perceive some basic tastes at temperatures far below it. In the case of frozen ice cream, our tongue physically warms the ice cream, causing it to melt. The small portion of frozen dessert that's now liquid provides all the sweetness and added flavors we taste. (Another thing to learn here: you get far more taste for your buck licking an ice cream cone than eating it with a spoon. Whether the potential mess is worth it is up to you!) When it comes to the iced coffee, only the coffee that has a chance to be warmed by the tongue as it flows over it will taste bitter. In fact, at about 33°F (1°C) the iced coffee won't taste like much. Hold that same iced coffee in your mouth until it warms and you're in for a bitter surprise.

This temperature/taste relationship is why Coors Light is served "as cold as the Rockies." At roughly 40°F (4°C), the light American lager won't taste like much of anything other than cold and refreshing. The natural bitterness of hops isn't noticeable until the beer reaches a temperature of around 59°F (15°C), by which time Coors is hoping you're on your next pint.

If the color of the walls and decor in the room can subtly shift the flavor of a meal, it's not surprising the pigment of the food itself alters flavor perception, too. Vanilla yogurt dyed pink with flavorless food coloring suddenly tastes of strawberry for more than 80 percent of participants in one study. Plain white rice dyed green conjures phantom spinach flavors. When rice is tinted orange, tomato aromas materialize in the mind. The flavor of strawberry in my homemade smoothies is always a bit lacking, but adding a drop or two of food coloring would do more to enhance the fruitiness I'm looking for than adding an extra handful of berries (as long as it was someone else doing the adding; once we're conscious of the color adjustment the effects are diminished). And before you balk at keeping food dyes on hand right alongside the oregano in your spice cabinet, know that professional chefs use this trick, too. While recounting his adventures in a French kitchen in his book *Dirt: Adventures in Lyon as a Chef in Training, Father, and Sleuth Looking for the Secret of French Cooking*, author Bill Buford found that the line cooks were adding a little extra "love" to many of the dishes on the menu, specifically noting food dyes used in wine sauce (a deep purple color), basil oil (a boost to the vibrant green), and ratatouille (to intensify the vivid red that should be imparted by expensive saffron). After making this discovery, Bill approached the head chef to ask him outright if he uses artificial coloring to enhance flavor. The chef considered whether he should disclose his techniques to a journalist residing in his kitchen and responded: "Never. Beet juice, of course. But not food coloring." Later, the intense yellow of the egg yolk pasta being prepared in the prep kitchen of a Daniel Boulud restaurant was also revealed to be augmented with a touch of artificial color.

Bill's discoveries surprised me, but I'm not disappointed in the chefs. (Although I think I now know why I can never get my homemade dill oil the striking emerald achieved at one of my cherished restaurants.) Our senses are so accustomed to the stimulation of bright, saturated videos flashing by on our cell phones that the colors of nature end up disappointing. I've never heard of a pastry chef admonished for a banana-flavored dessert that has a yellow color (which obviously doesn't come from the starchy white fruits), so why can't savory chefs enjoy the same luxury of increased flavor through increased color?

In his French-cooking adventures, Bill went on to learn to style dishes using the three principles of French plating: color (the visual contrast on the plate), volume (how the food fills the plate and towers above it), and texture (specifically, that there should be multiple textures). A concept we typically associate with visual beauty is conspicuously missing in those principles. Where's the balance? Balance, as a rule, is considered pleasurable by our feeble human brains. We're comfortable in rooms that feel balanced. Art that has balance puts us at ease. We'll stare at a symmetrical face longer than one that's uneven. A pair of back-to-back studies by Debra Zellner and her team at Montclair State University showed that our feelings about food presentation contradict these universal norms. She found that visual balance on the plate isn't important to how much we appreciate a dish or our desire to eat it. After all, an enduring trend at fine-dining restaurants is to plate a dish in a semi-circle shape that follows the curved edge of one side of the plate. This lopsided presentation wouldn't last if diners rejected the courses plated this way. In reality, these far from symmetrical dishes are the images we see posted to social media feeds as proof that a dinner was classy and modern.

What Zellner and her coauthors showed was that it's not balance on the plate that makes it tempting or tasty to a diner but instead neatness. So much so that she went on to title the paper "Neatness Counts." Intentional placement of ingredients is a visual cue that attracts us to a plate. Intricate dishes with thoughtfully placed, perfectly round dots of sauce and other ingredients lead us to anticipate delightful flavor, even though food isn't always practical to eat this way.

The roundness of those dots of sauce send their own hint about flavor. Have you ever noticed that most desserts are round? Doughnuts, cupcakes, cakes, cookies, pies, Bundts, lollipops—many of the goodies we crave are round, even though they don't really have to be. Square cake pans exist, as do angular cookie cutters, and pyramid-shaped Jell-O molds, but we don't see them used very often. That's because angular shapes are associated with sourness, saltiness, and bitterness, not the flavors we're looking for at the dessert table. A zigzag of yellow sauce invokes zesty and sour thoughts before we taste it. If that tangy expectation is met, the sauce will taste even more sour than it would if it were served in a round dollop. This association between sharp shapes and sharp taste goes for the shape of the plate as well.

Round, as you may guess by now, signals to our brain that we're about to enjoy something sweet. We assume chocolates with a rounded shape will be less bitter than chocolates with corners or angular shapes. And we expect round chocolates to be sweeter and creamier, too. Our desire for creamy, sweet wedding cakes might influence why most of them are round. Every now and then we'll see an angular wedding cake. Two memorable examples would be the octagonal six-foot stunner used to celebrate the nuptials of Kim Kardashian and Kris Humphries.

Another would be the angular 225-pound cake sliced by Princess Diana and Prince Charles at their 1981 wedding. Hmmm, maybe sharp-edge wedding cakes really will leave sour, bitter tastes in your mouth.

THE WALLS OF THE RESTAURANT, THE WARMTH OF THE ROOM, AND OF course the color and arrangement of the food itself are all sensory cues that come together to affect what you will taste before you lift a (hopefully heavy!) fork to your mouth. I took note as all of these environmental elements came together to affect my dinner on a winter evening at Blue Hill at Stone Barns. There were many things I was looking forward to tasting at Dan Barber's two-Michelin-star restaurant thirty miles north of midtown Manhattan. The chef had a reputation for growing flavor into the vegetables and animals he served at the restaurant, starting with how they were treated out on the farm. The idea is that flavor starts in the field, and food grown with the final taste in mind won't need much seasoning in the kitchen because it would already be close to perfect. I had heard of the new type of squash developed for the restaurant and the specially cultured butter from individual cows. I was curious to taste so many things that would come out of the Blue Hill kitchen. But more than anything, I wanted to taste *the carrot*. A dish consisting of a single carrot perched alone on a plate was highlighted during an episode of the streaming series *Chef's Table*. The orange beacon flashes across the screen as former *New York Times* restaurant critic Ruth Reichl breathlessly gushes about the chef and his vegetables: "You taste things that just taste better than any pea you've ever had before, any radish you've ever had before." Then the line that motivated my trip upstate: "A carrot that is, like, the carrotness of carrot." She goes on to explain how the vegetables served at Dan Barber's restaurant Blue Hill at Stone Barns taste like the very essence of what they are, like an ethereal, perfect specimen capturing and intensifying the ideal of that vegetable.

One could choose to believe that this carrot is truly imbued with heavenly qualities, that the soil used, and the care given make it wholly different from the carrots at the grocery store. But when we bring all the qualities of the setting at Blue Hill at Stone Barns into focus, maybe we have another explanation for this carrot's deft command of its own carrotness.

To be clear, I didn't just go to Blue Hill at Stone Barns because I wanted to taste some carrot. This was the celebration of both my birthday and my anniversary, and the fact that I stayed up until midnight for the exact moment the reservations would open so I could get an ideal 7:00 p.m. slot. All of this coordination meant I came to the sprawling farm the restaurant sits on when it was fully lit by the sun on a clear day. Before heading to the large wooden doors of the restaurant, I walked the grounds to see the pigs in a hay-filled barn adjacent to a greenhouse brimming with row after row of microgreens. By the time I settled into a cozy leather chair in the restaurant's bar I was thoroughly charmed, and it was still twenty minutes before my dinner was scheduled to begin.

As soon as I set down an empty predinner glass, I was swept into a long dining room with vaulted ceilings supported by steel beams. The room would have felt large and cavernous except the long central table was adorned with foliage I'd seen earlier on the farm, effectively bringing the outdoors into the room with us. The branches, dried grasses, and flowers twisted up toward the beams filling the space, making it feel at once refined and homespun. We walked past white-linen-enshrouded tables to our corner booth. I remember thinking, *Ah, this is a good table.* (Surely this made the food taste better!)

Then our twelve-course meal began with a flurry of fresh-picked vegetables, cured meats from animals raised on the farm, and tiny morsels crafted from a combination of the two. Each of these small bites were intriguing, made even more significant by the fact that I could see the ground they were plucked from right outside the window. The active farm was now illuminated in shades of ruby and coral under the setting sun.

Finally, *it* was placed in front of me. It was a bright orange, nearing a neon hue. The greens were still attached. Draped across the plate in a deliberate curve, I thought it looked like one of those children's matching cards, the visual definition of a carrot. It was clear that it was unadulterated; it took only a glance to see there was no seasoning, no sauce, it's simply a carrot on the plate. The plate was a stark off-white color with a matte finish. This finish ensures that no light bounces off the plate. There's no gleam of overhead bulbs. No faint orange reflection of the carrot itself. It is as if the carrot is sucking up all the light around it, shining as the sole beacon of food in front of you. It is all-encompassing; it is a plated message that says, *I am carrot.*

It was a good carrot. I closed my eyes, hoping to absorb its carrotness to know that I was tasting the most carrotful carrot flavor I would likely ever savor. Sitting under the soaring ceilings of the dining room in my cushy gray booth with my eyes shut, a thought crossed my mind: *If this carrot were served in a stack next to a bowl of hummus at an office cafeteria, would I think differently?* I opened my eyes hoping to find the carrotness. For my second taste of the dainty two-bite vegetable I kept my eyes open, taking in the dining room, the idyllic farm surrounding me, the special occasion I was there to celebrate. Ah, I did like this carrot.

PART TWO

HOW TO TASTE

CHAPTER FOUR

THE TASTING METHOD

Ben Wald slides across the table from me in a whirlwind. "I know I'm late. I'm sorry. Work is so crazy; we're redoing the cocktail menu." At the time, he was in charge of beverages at YUCO, a restaurant in New York City that melded French techniques with ingredients from Yucatán. But Ben called it an "agave bar." Every day he worked around tequilas and mezcals, mixing drinks, taking inventories, making recommendations, and recommending pairings. The night of our meeting, after he shoots off a few final texts, he's leaving work behind because we're not here to talk about anything agave-based.

"You know women are more likely to be supertasters; that's scientifically proven," he says while we try to catch our server's eye. "More and more women are becoming master blenders, and guess what, whiskey is getting better and better."

Ben is a finalist in the World's Top Whiskey Taster competition, which takes place in Bardstown Bourbon Company in Kentucky in three days, or as he keeps saying, "[in] seventy-two hours." When I ask what special steps he's taking to prepare, he quips, "For this? Nothing. Nothing!"

However, I soon found out that fellow whiskey-heads are blind tasting him on a collection of pours as soon as he leaves this bar. And he's done at least a half dozen practice blending runs, mixing and tasting what he creates. He also has a bar owner lined up to take him through the ropes when he arrives in Kentucky on Friday.

"As far as diet, obviously no spicy food and nothing too hot, but nothing other than that," he reveals. "No, I'm not going to skip coffee if that's what you're thinking."

I wonder if Ben has had coffee just now, or if tasting always gives him this energy.

The World's Top Whiskey competition requires participants to identify different whiskeys in a blind taste test. Although there is no certification awarded in this event, it may remind you of the rigorous testing used to fain Master Sommelier status. To achieve the height of wine expertise and enter the small, revered circle of Master Sommeliers you must pass an onerous multiday exam encompassing both theory of wine and the serving of it, and of course, the widely known and glamorized blind-tasting portion of the exam—or as one Master Sommelier candidate referred to it, "the six glasses that stand between me and never taking a wine test again." The Master Sommelier test has been the subject of several documentaries and has inspired dozens of similar certifications: honey sommeliers, olive oil sommeliers, mustard sommeliers, and the most clever take on the title—cider tasters are "pommeliers," though the requirements to hold these title are not as well defined as those set forth for the wine stewards. And not every specialty food community chose a twist on "sommelier" for their certified experts. Cheesemongers can become Certified Cheese Professionals, bourbon experts seek the title of Bourbon Steward, coffee specialists pursue the Q Grader certification, brewers aspire to be Master Cicerones, while chocolatiers and cocoa makers can become Certified Chocolate Tasters.

You might expect each type of taster to approach their specialty with their own method, something secretive known only to those initiated into the club or trying to get into it. But this is not the case. The fact is that whether it be cheese, olive oil, chocolate, or sherry, tasters approach their task in much the same way. In fact, other than the container the tastant itself sits in, most tasting professionals appear almost identical as they put their sensory abilities to work.

"Listen, once you can taste, you can taste anything," Ben tells me while eyeing the selection behind the bar. This evening we're going to run through a whiskey tasting together. It's the ritual that got him through qualifiers and regionals for this whiskey competition, and it comes to him as second nature now. The routine doesn't require flourish or grandeur; Ben and I could as easily run through this tasting at a crowded burger joint as we could in this hotel lobby bar. The person next to you at a café may do it, without interrupting your conversation in the slightest. In fact, it's possible to conduct a quick yet thorough tasting mid-conversation, although that does defeat the point a bit. Wouldn't we rather stop talking and taste together, if only for a minute?

It's a good time to note that this is the premise of this chapter. And really this entire book. A few seconds of our lives, the briefest meditation on our sensory world, is all it takes to build tasting skills and also tasting appreciation. Here I'm going to share the seven-step tasting method I use. This method has come together after years of sensory training, both in formal classrooms and more casually tasting with specialists like Ben. At last count, I've conducted 114 interviews for this book. Before that, I spent almost a decade taking tasting classes of various caliber and expense, and then there are the countless times I've practiced, been tested on, and taught some iteration of this method.

It's been shaped by guided tastings in Freising, Germany; West Village, New York City; and Reims, France; and virtual interviews from Japan, Australia, and Canada. In cheese caves, island vineyards, hop yards, and urban distilleries we marched through the same basic beats.

I've named the steps set(ting), see, sniff, swirl/snap, sip/sample, spit/swallow, and finally sit and synthesize, and I'll take you through each of the seven steps with some of the tasters and scientists who inspired and confirmed them. Then, at the end, we'll run through it together. You can start daydreaming of the first thing you want to taste with it, but no rush quite yet; there's still learning to do before we get to putting anything in our mouths.

SET(TING)

You don't have to be at a preplanned event to get to tasting; hopefully you'll do it in many different settings. The hotel bar Ben and I find ourselves tasting whiskey in, a friend's house, or out on the street in front of the taco truck are examples of settings that you don't have control over. In that case, this step is all about taking note of your surroundings. A quick way to assess your setting is to run through your four other senses: sight, touch, sound, and smell. What do you see around you? Remember the influence of color: red walls or large red artwork may add a dash of sweetness to your tasting, while a mahogany wood interior could literally taste a bit bitter as molecules of the wood float toward your nose and mouth. Lights may be too bright or too dim. Find some natural light if you can; it's the easiest lighting condition to replicate so that you can attempt to keep your lighting consistent at every tasting.

At the bar, Ben and I are sitting in front of a set of large windows, although the sunlight is quickly disappearing. The walls are a neutral off-white and there are warm-toned wooden accents around the room. It's a generally attractive but not very memorable space, the kind that exists with tiny variations all over the city. It's as close to a perfect visual setting for a focused tasting as you can find. There is nothing to distract you or influence the tasting.

How are you feeling? Are you warm? Overheated? Do you have a chill and wish you'd brought a sweater? It is cold in this bar, cold enough for me to want to put my coat back on. Cold enough that I have an inkling the whiskey will taste better, more warming, than it might if I were more comfortable.

Now, take a deep breath. If the air is cold and dry you may have more trouble picking up the aromas of what you're about to taste. There's nothing to be done about this; it's just a factor worth noting. (I suppose you could bust out your travel humidifier, but then your senses may be dulled by the overwhelming embarrassment you'd feel for the rest of the meal.)

There are other things to feel: Unfinished wood on tables or benches is a little scratchy. Hard wooden benches are also uncomfortable. And uncomfortable is no way to taste. It's distracting, like a little bug buzzing around your head pulling attention away from the task at hand.

Do you hear anything distracting? As we covered in the previous chapter, boisterous noise will dull your taste and music can affect it. The same glass of whiskey will taste different with loud salsa music pumping through the sound system than it will sipped in front of the television in your living room. Inside this bar, someone has thought about acoustics; even though there are a reasonable number of people milling around, the noise doesn't rise above a murmur. The music is quiet enough that I can't exactly pick out what is playing on the system. Sounds are perceptible but not distracting.

The most important aspect of your setting to note, the element that will really interfere with the taste memories you're creating, is smell.

What do you smell around you? Most cuisines have a signature scent. In Elisabeth Rozin's book *Ethnic Cuisine*, which sits somewhere between cookbook and researched manifesto, she outlines combinations of three ingredients called "flavor principles" that generally define global cuisines. For example, if you're sitting in a Greek restaurant, you're liable to smell olive oil, lemon, and oregano. A Hungarian spot will have an ambiance replete with the fragrances of onion, lard, and paprika. If you're out in front of that taco truck, especially if that truck is on a busy street in midtown Manhattan, you're probably getting a whiff of gasoline or maybe garbage with your side of salsa. And, of course, there's your smelly dining partners. It's hard to imagine that diners at Nobu can taste the nuanced flavors of sushi amid air saturated with whatever Le Labo perfume is considered "in" at the moment.

Now if you're the one in control of the environment, even if it's just tasting a cup of drip coffee at home in the morning, you have some options to improve your experience. There are three factors you'll want to consciously set up for a tasting: the plateware or glassware; the ideal temperature for what you're tasting; and eliminating distractions where possible.

A glass has influence over what you taste but probably not as much as you think. Usually, a restaurant with an extensive wine collection will also have an extensive glass collection. Burgundy glasses have wide bowls (the part of the glass just above the stem) with sides that curve almost as much as the sides of a globe, while flutes tend to be straight up and down to show off the leisurely ascent of the bubbles within champagne. Then there are the whiskey snifters with belled edges where ethanol vapor is said to collect. Better to hold the sharp fumes there than inside your nose.

If it was up to Maximilian Riedel, the collection would be more expansive. He's the eleventh-generation CEO of glassmaker Riedel, known for their line of varietal-specific wineglasses. Maximilian takes it a step further: he believes every winery should have their own specific glasses that highlight the winemaker's philosophy. He's the president of a glass manufacturing company that's been around for more than 250 years, but he still attends design meetings with winemakers and winery owners. "I like to be there because I like to see the emotions come forward," he says. "It's so interesting when they call the entire team together to experience the wine that they're so familiar with, maybe too familiar with. I open the spectrum of flavors just by serving it in different glasses."

It starts with twenty glasses that Maximilian and the winery team can narrow down to three to five. He says glasses can emphasize any aspect of the wine, from specific flavors to smooth texture, "any aspect except alcohol; we never emphasize the alcohol." In this case, both Maximilian and the winemakers he designs for are in luck. Japanese researchers used a "sniffer camera" to create visual models of ethanol vapor emitting from wine in various glasses. A martini glass and a straight-sided rocks glass (like the ones Ben and I sampled whiskey from) showed alcohol vapors rolling across random areas of the glass like steam rising from a hot spring in the morning air. The wineglass showed a completely different pattern of vapors. The ethanol was most intense around the edges of the wineglass, forming a distinct circle with an open center where ethanol concentrations were low. Watching the vapors rise from the glass in a ring around the rim is mesmerizing; you can see the sniffer-camera footage at howtotastebook.com/glasses. This open center circle is exactly where your nose is meant to hover as you take in the aroma of the wine. Of course, no one on the winery team is looking to accentuate the sharp burn of alcohol, either. But everyone might have differing opinions on what they do want to highlight. Maximilian says this is when it gets tough. The winery owner might like the glass that seems to bring out bold tannins, while the winemaker wants the glass that underscores the subtle fruitiness. "And then we'll make them a custom prototype to bring those two aspects together," he says, beaming. A new wineglass is born.

What factors shift in a glass to change the perception of what we drink? There are a few ways glasses really do influence what we taste.

- A lip of a glass that curves inward toward the top of the glass has the effect of trapping the scent right at the rim of the glass, so a nose gingerly placed below the lip has a plethora of fragrance waiting to be inhaled. This holding effect is the same for all scents including the sharpness of ethanol, so very high alcohol beverages shouldn't be served with a lip that arches inward. "The traditional cognac snifter is the dumbest glass in the world. Alcohol can't escape," Maximilian scoffs. "It's like Mike Tyson gives you a punch, that's how concentrated it is."

- A lip that flares outward, on the other hand, causes a waterfall effect on the liquid. It creates a sort of cascade as it falls into the mouth. All that froth of a waterfall knocks aromatic compounds out of the liquid right when you want them flying about: when they're directly under the nose. This shape is seen on the classic Teku beer-tasting glass or tulip glass for whiskey.

- A narrow mouth will direct a potent stream of liquid down the center of the tongue, concentrating mouthfeel sensations like zippy carbonation or drying tannin. A wider mouth encourages each sip to spread over the entire palate, emphasizing sweet and fruity flavors across the front of the tongue.

- A stem of any kind keeps warm hands off the glass's bowl and allows the liquid inside to maintain its temperature. An especially long stem keeps hands far away from the rim, and therefore out of sniffing distance, where hints of fragrant lotion or hand sanitizer can interfere with tasting.

- A wide bulb is said to give more contact with oxygen, which allows the flavors to "open up." To this I say fie! Anyone capable of flicking their wrist is capable of swirling liquid, therefore introducing as much oxygen as they'd like. It's not their fault, but people drinking from the massive bowls of cognac snifters or bulbous burgundy glasses are making a statement more about the types of drinks they indulge in than any sort of necessary aeration.

Which leads me to my long-held philosophy on glassware. The only thing a glass is there to do is to make the drink you're sipping feel special and by association give you the special feelings, too. As long as you're using one that's easy to drink out of, the type of glass doesn't matter at all. Any advantage an outward-sloping lip or a long, elegant stem gives a taster can be outdone by contributing an additional modicum of focus. Yes, I'll concede it's easier to swirl liquids in taller glasses with rounded sides. It's very easy to get some centrifugal force moving in a Scotch Whisky Association–endorsed Glencairn glass. But if you want something to swirl, it will swirl. Ben and I are drinking our straight pours of Knob Creek Rye out of square-sided rocks glasses, which make swirling difficult but not impossible.

Don't stress over choosing a glass. The dozens of judges that work the Great American Beer Festival, the largest beer competition in the world, each year in Denver all use the same kind of glass. Guess what they are tasting out of? Plastic! Plastic is cleaner, less likely to carry contaminating odors, and in the end may be easier on the environment. Cleaning thousands of sample glasses would use extensive water and heat for drying. Furthermore, in order to keep up with the demand of a competition that evaluates close to ten thousand entries in the span of three days, thousands of glasses would need to be manufactured for this competition. If there is nowhere to store such a large number of glasses, they, too, would end up going to waste. Consider this your permission to use whatever glass you'd like. If you want to drink every beverage from a Gatsby-esque carved crystal coupe, go for it! It's the conventionally "wrong" glass for rosé, but your fondness for it and the vast opening for aroma release will combine to make the box of wine in the fridge taste even better.

It works in the other direction, too. At a Radio City Music Hall show you may be forced to drink your tipple out of a plastic cup screen-printed with the words *THE ROCKETTES*. Don't let that stop you from ordering the nicer wine you really want. Your focus and appreciation will bring forward more flavor notes than a carefully curved wall of glass ever will. (By the way, cocktails at the seminal holiday show used to be served out of martini glasses that had a pair of women's legs where a stem would be. And yes, I do think that would change the way you tasted your cocktail, though I haven't tested my theory. If anyone wants to, the plastic "Rockettini" glasses are available for $15 a pop on eBay.)

The most important thing about the glasses you're sampling out of is that you have a glass. Please don't drink ciders, beers, canned wines, or anything else you're looking to truly enjoy from the container it comes in. Narrow bottle and can openings offer almost no path for aroma compounds to make it to your nose. Plus, the feeling of the can or bottle on your mouth is not going to send your brain the message that what you're drinking is worth tasting. Any old glass will do, including a plastic one.

Still, there are specialized vessels designed to draw the best flavor out of specific mediums. Professional olive oil tasters use thick blue glass bowls to obscure the color of the oil. A "snake eye" sake cup, about the size of a shot glass with a more rounded bowl-like shape, is white with a bright royal blue bull's-eye printed on the bottom of the interior, and helps tasters assess quality because even the finest sediment suspended in the sake will be more obvious when observed over the blue bull's-eye. For plating things like cheeses, chocolate, or fully composed hors d'oeuvres, sticking to white is best. Additionally, a rounded edge is worth seeking out simply because it's what we're used to seeing food served upon. However, approach your plates with the same mentality as the glassware. If all you can get your hands on is white paper plates, you will still have a worthwhile tasting!

———•———

OKAY, YOU'VE PICKED YOUR GLASSES AND PLATES (AND HOPEFULLY didn't spend too much time on the picking!) and now it's time to get to the actual food or drink you'll be tasting. As we discussed in the previous chapter, the temperature your food is served at has an effect on how it tastes for a variety of reasons. First, our taste buds are physically able to taste more sweet, umami, and bitter compounds at temperatures that approach our body temperature. Second, the warmer a food or drink is, the more volatile aromatic compounds will be. A warm slice of pizza has aromatic molecules buzzing around it like a swarm of microscopic fruit flies, ready to be carried up to the olfactory epithelium as opposed to a cold slice. (Sorry, you "pizza tastes just as good cold" folks. It's science!) Finally, we have expectations for the temperature certain items should be served at and messing with our expectations can make us unconsciously dislike what we're tasting without attributing that dislike to the temperature. For instance, even well-made vodkas taste harsh at room temperature and the very best cheeses will taste bland at cold temperatures.

The chart on page 67 has the ideal serving temperature for foods and drinks that are commonly the focus of planned tastings. Notice there is also a column for the *ideal* consumption temperature. Temperature is a constantly moving target. Rather than remaining static the temperature of your tastant is always assimilating to the temperature of the air around it, whether that be the air in an oven, a refrigerator, or the room. This means a perfectly chilled glass of wine will only stay that way for a few moments. You'll be consuming whatever you taste over a range of temperatures. For cold- and room-temperature items, nature works in our favor. We'll naturally perceive the flavors as opening up as more aromatic compounds volatilize as we're enjoying it. Warm foods or drinks are not as lucky. As they cool it feels like the flavor is deadening. For this reason, it makes sense to pour something like coffee samples one at a time, or make sure your guests are ready to eat as soon as food comes off the stove.

Chilled beverages can maintain temperature in ice buckets filled with chilled water. Twenty to thirty minutes outside of the fridge allows beer, wine, and sake to come to the ideal temperature. Items like cheese and chocolate, which are best tasted at room temperature, should be set out about an hour ahead of time. Certified Cheese Professional (CCP) and award-winning cheese monger Brian Gilbert says cheese should be served warmer than people think. "I always say ambient temperature but not sweating." He emphasizes that this serving temperature is the way cheese is made to be tasted. "Sometimes people get nervous about letting something like cheese sit out, but they shouldn't. It would be fine for five hours or more depending on the cheese." By the way, a cheese plate appetizer is an excellent shortcut for judging whether you should stick around the wine bar for dinner. Cheeses shouldn't be cold, they should readily spread, crumble, or slice. Serving cold cheese is a subtle sign of a lack of preparation and attention that likely isn't limited to the appetizer course.

As your tasting supplies come to temperature, keep them covered with something breathable like a tea towel to help keep their aromas contained. Brian adds that this covering method also goes for stinky pairing items like fermented pickles. If the aroma is allowed to waft through the room each taste of cheese will be somewhat reminiscent of pickle. It's best to keep the aroma at bay until you want to taste the pickles and cheese together.

TASTANT IDEAL SERVING	TEMPERATURE (F) IDEAL SERVING	TEMPERATURE (C)	SERVING TIPS
Olive Oil	82F	28C	Olive oil can be warmed in a small container in the hand or by using external heating before tasting.
Cheese	65-72F	18-21C	Cheese should be removed from the refrigerator at least 30 minutes before tasting. For large servings, cheese can sit at room temperature for up to an hour.
Chocolate	65-72F	18-21C	Chocolate should be served at a cool room temperature; it's up to your mouth to add the extra few degrees of heat to bring it to its melting point.
Caviar	46-48F	8-9C	Allow the caviar to warm as you eat it; this will expose a wider range of flavors. For very small portions, try one bite chilled and one bite after it has warmed.
White Wine	48-55F	9-13C	White wines with higher alcohol content should be served at the higher end of this range, as should very sweet dessert wines.

Then there are items like olive oil that are ideally tasted at above room temperature. Once you've tasted olive oil gently warmed, you will never find the cold oil served next to bread at Italian restaurants appetizing again. The slightly greasy texture becomes silky, and peppery aromas from natural phenolics will remind you why olive oil—"good olive oil," if you ask Ina Garten—is so often denoted as a seasoning in itself. Professional olive oil tasters use heating pads or specially designed warmers to warm their small blue glass bowls before lifting the oil to their lips. A dip of the bottle into a warm water bath works well and will save you somewhere between $22 and $868, depending on the warming gadget. One way to pour and maintain a warm water bath at home is using an electric kettle. Kettles with digital temperature displays are the easiest way to ensure that the water is heated to the correct temperature down to the degree. And with this method there's no need to worry about scorching your oil, or yourself in the process. At the risk of being too obvious, this device is also the best tool in your kit when it comes to tasting teas that require specific brewing temperatures.

Once the plating and serving of the samples is under control, the last thing to do is a sweep of your room to tame potential distractions. Follow the same questions about your five senses we ran through at the beginning of this step, but this time ask what you can control in each realm. For tastings that act as exam preparation or other professional pursuit, be as stringent as possible with eliminating the distractions. Sit in a comfortable chair (or stand if you'll be standing at your assessment) and face a white wall. Ideally, it will feel like it's just you and your sample alone in the world without even a stray scrap of paper in sight. If you're just tasting casually or with some friends, there's no reason to be so diligent about avoiding visual distractions. But it's still a good idea to pick up those scraps of paper and to keep your area from being cluttered. It's amazing what our minds will choose to pay attention to in order to avoid singular focus. Music should be unobtrusive. Scented candles should be banished from the room, as should fragrant flowers.

By the end of this step, you'll have taken note of your setting if you can't control it, or you'll have set up your desired tableware, decided how to serve your samples at the proper temperature, and made the room as comfortable and distraction-free as possible.

SEE

"THERE ARE TWO REASONS TO DO THE WHOLE THING WHERE YOU TILT the glass and hold it up to the light," Ben says as he does the tilt, holding the glass six inches above his forehead. "It's because you feel like you should or"—here he squints his eyes into an expression of exaggerated concentration—"you're trying to signal to everyone around you that you are very serious. That your opinions on whiskey should not be messed with."

I laugh and imitate his stance, screwing up my face in a look of sheer effort. "So the color, what is it telling me, then?"

"You literally cannot tell anything by the color."

Surprised, I snap my eyes away from my whiskey glass. "Nothing?"

"Nothing."

And you can't tell much about a drink by its "legs," either, although it is fun to swirl liquid up the glass and watch it trickle back down, clinging to the sides in thin, well-defined streams or slow-moving sheets. Some people say the speed these legs or "tears" flow to rejoin the liquid at the bottom of the glass indicates age and alcohol level. But the oils from barrels that wine, spirits, and vinegars are aged in also affect this speed. So do additives like coloring or sugar. Like Ben said, most of the gawking into tilted glasses is done out of a sense of obligation to some unknown tasting standard rather than any useful knowledge.

Across any medium, from wine and sake to honey and chocolate,

experts confirmed to me that you can't infer all the much about flavor from appearance. As I've noted, olive oil judges intentionally obscure the appearance of their oils with thick blue glass bowls because
visual characteristics reveal nothing about the quality of the oil. So why,
then, all this focus on appearance? I call it the fondant effect. Many
cakes made to mark special occasions are covered in elaborate swirls
and shapes made of fondant. You've seen them; rather than looking like
fresh-baked things that have come from an oven, they're reminiscent of
a museum display of model race cars or hand-shaped butterflies. Fondant is made of gelatin, vegetable fat, sugar, and glycerol. It tastes about
as terrible as that ingredient list sounds. And the texture is no better;
it's powdery yet gooey with the malleability of a stick of unchewed Juicy
Fruit gum. Huge swaths of this edible gum are molded around a cake,
completely enclosing the pastry inside. The fondant can be brightly
colored, a deep saturated blue molded into ocean waves complete with
flying seagulls, or it can be pale pastel shades twisted into floral arrangements. All of this ornate decor around the outside has no impact on the
flavor of the pastry within. Baby shower cakes plastered in pink fondant
may have lemon cake and vanilla buttercream hiding underneath. A
jubilant red lunar New Year cake can be a basic chocolate on the inside.
Depending on how elaborate the fondant on the outside is sculpted, the
cake inside can be a welcome relief (I was worried I'd be biting into
something ocean-flavored when I saw the blue seagull cake aforemen-
tioned, but it was red velvet!) or a disappointment. Judging your tastant
too closely at this step has the same ramifications.

The fondant effect is why the see step is the briefest of the seven.
Brief, but still necessary, this is the observation of our tastant in its
perfect form. The composed dessert. The freshly poured coffee. The
whole unsullied wedge of cheese. Whatever you're tasting, it will never
be more beautiful than it is right now. And that's worth a moment
of appreciation. That perfection is fleeting, as nearly everything we're

served begins to change in appearance moments after we receive it. The fluffy crown of head on a beer starts to dissipate, a soft cheese spreads towards the edges of the plate, or the froth of a foamed sauce languidly exhales its volume.

The reason this step exists in every professional tasting method is to check for flaws and imperfections. Chocolate may have a waxy white sheen, an indication that it has come out of temper and "bloomed." Sake, wine, and some beers may cast a slight haze that doesn't affect flavor but will affect a quality score. Ice cream may have clusters of ice crystals that show a fault in production and must be observed and noted before evidence of the flaw melts away.

Don't scrutinize your sample too closely; in chapter 6 we'll discover just how far astray visual cues can lead us, and every second spent analyzing appearance is another chance to follow those cues in the direction of a wrong conclusion. Simply note what appeared before you, what has shifted, and whether anything looks a little off. This, the see step, is the first time in the process to make notes either on paper or casually in thought. There are three more "notes" pauses throughout the seven steps. These pauses help you identify a few keywords to remember the sample as a whole at the end of the process.

Speaking of process, it's time to get to the most in-depth step, smelling.

SNIFF

"Whenever I'm guiding a tasting, I always remind them of this"—Ben lifts his glass—"start far away from your nose." He extends his arm so the whiskey tumbler hovers about eight inches from his face. "I know how far I personally need to go just by what's in the glass, but you have to remind people or else they'll just shove it in their face right away."

Shoving your face in the glass is only a big deal because our schnozzes are such extraordinarily sensitive tools. As few as four molecules of an odorous substance can activate an olfactory receptor. (Though activation doesn't guarantee we'll be consciously aware of what we're smelling.) This sensitivity shapes how you'll approach the entirety of the sniff step. In order to get the most joy and detail out of the sensual aromas and effectively deliver aromatic compounds to the receptor cells on the olfactory epithelium, there are several different smelling techniques to employ. It's like attempting to pummel an opponent in a game of dodgeball. Your ball strikes are more effective if you can throw from different angles at varied speeds. Using a medley of sniffs ensures our dodgeballs, in this case aromatic molecules, are guaranteed to make contact with our target, the olfactory epithelium. Consequently, this step is the longest and most intricate part of the tasting method, and yet, it's still not complicated enough to tip off your dinner mates that you're doing it (although, c'mon, bring them along to sniff with us!).

As we progress through five specific olfactory assessment techniques, the goal is to steadily increase the volume and concentration of each puff of fragrance we take into the nose. In the first one we're aiming to take in the least intense dose of aroma. As Ben demonstrated, this is the "distant sniff." Hold your fork, glass, or plate about six inches from your face. I usually think of it as a Sharpie marker's length between me and what I am sniffing. Then take three to four short explosive sniffs or about one half second each. That's all there is to the distant sniff!

Frankly, this sniff is often useless, and it feels easy to skip. At six inches away you might smell nothing, and you can immediately move on. If at this range strong aromas are apparent, it's time to pause and take note, because they might soon disappear. This sniff is akin to releasing an olfactory canary into a coal mine in search of danger. The distant sniff is a line of protection from a two-pronged threat to the entire tasting process: temporary blindness and adaptation.

Diving your nose deep in a glass is tempting. How will all those scent-packed molecular dodgeballs hit their target without a close-range strike? But like a pool without a lifeguard, dive at your own risk. When a sample has a high concentration of one aroma and you dive in there . . . poof! In the span of a single sniff, you may go completely nose blind to the most important scents. You'll be no more able to detect those components than the people born naturally anosmic to them. And this blindness could last for thirty minutes or more.

"There are compounds that you can smell for a second, and then you can't smell them again for several minutes," says Pamela Dalton, a chemosensory scientist at the Monell Chemical Senses Center. "We're not totally sure why these bouts of temporary blindness occur." Pamela tells me it could be that some molecules bond to our olfactory receptors and are very resistant to breaking that bond. They stick around, blocking the receptor for that scent, rendering us incapable of noticing its presence. Or it could be that they don't clear out of the nasal passageway as fast as other odors; if there is already a high concentration of the odor in the nose, adding a little more won't make much of an impact and we won't register that odor as present.

Musk aromas immediately came to mind for Pamela. "Perfumers will say when they're evaluating something with a musk component, they have to wait a pretty long time, like several minutes before they can go back and smell it again because it just disappears after one sniff."

The distant sniff is a cautious approach that allows a small amount of a potentially blinding compound into the nasal passageway. In taking a scant sample, the hope is that there will be fewer molecules of that blinding compound than available receptors. This way, you'll get at least one more sniff before the receptors are temporarily blocked.

You've successfully circumvented temporary nose blindness. Now onto thwarting the nose's natural tendency to adapt.

"Our sense of smell was probably a danger detector," Pamela says. "So if we smell something and then we stick around, there's little valuable information left to be gained from that [scent] for the most part."

In order to remain sensitive to potential new threats, we quickly adapt to whatever scent environment we remain in. The nose is really savvy at detecting differences. That's why quality-assurance panels are given a perfect "control" sample to test all other samples against. A panelist will essentially adapt themselves to the smell of that control, so much so that the control has no scent anymore. Then, if any of the other samples have an aroma, they'll know that sample is different than the control.

"It's like lowering background noise," Pamela says. "It could have been a very weak signal initially. But if you can reduce the background, then the signal becomes much more apparent." Upon the first whiff of a freshly poured cocktail, the predominant scent is herbal, vibrant thyme. However, within seconds of close-up study your brain will start to write off the potent odors in search of hidden ingredients. During that focused search for other scents, it's easy to forget that initial nose full of thyme ever existed. Keep in mind what you notice during the distant sniff. With each progressive sniff we'll increase our exposure to the scent, making sure to focus on what we sense and what changes along the way to piece the aroma puzzle together.

The next piece of the puzzle comes from the "moving sniff." So, which is moving—you or your tastant? This time it's the tastant; we'll get you moving that snout soon enough. In the distant sniff we crept up on the aroma from afar. Now, with the moving sniff we can get a little closer, but still inhale cautiously because potential blindness and rapid adaptation are at stake. Back to the fork, glass, or plate you have hovering a Sharpie's length away from your face. We're going to move it in a pattern that traces a perfect right triangle. First, move it toward your nose in a constant motion until it reaches a spot about one to two inches below the nostrils. You just drew the base of the triangle. Then, trace the hypotenuse of the triangle a straight line moving up and away from your nose at a forty-five-degree angle. Now it's time to draw the third side of the triangle, which is a roughly six-inch drop back to the starting position. The final resting place is that same Sharpie's distance from your nose. While you trace this invisible triangle, continuously take short, half-second sniffs. To give you an idea of how large the triangle is and how fast to move, it takes me roughly seven short sniffs (about four seconds) to trace the whole triangle.

The reason for this triangular movement is twofold. It goes back to our goal of pelting the olfactory receptors with aromatic dodgeballs at all angles: the way aroma falls down toward the nose is different from the way it is sucked up into it. A few tasters I interviewed for this book mentioned heavier aromatic compounds falling differently than light ones that more readily float up the nasal passageway. I haven't found much science to back this claim, but I think it sounds like a good theory. I did notice the aroma of a brown mustard shift as I sniffed the aroma falling back to me from the high point of the triangle. The bright sharpness dulled, and a subtle nutty fragrance emerged, similar to the skin of a peanut.

The second reason for the triangular movement is that there are fewer volatile aromatic compounds available below an object than there are above it. This goes back to our slow progression of aromatic intensity; only two or three of the sniffs made while tracing the triangle should be at close range and carry substantial quantities of scent. During this step we're still being introduced to the scent profile, taking in its most overt characteristics.

The distant sniff is comparable to seeing someone from across the room. The moving sniff is learning their name and title. This next one, the "short sniff," is the first handshake. The short sniff is as straight-forward as smelling techniques come. Hold the tastant just below your nose, an inch is about perfect, and take three or four half-second sniffs in quick succession. Then move the tastant away from the vicinity of your face, at least six inches away but more is preferable. Now we're bathing in the full picture of the aroma and can take in all of its complexities. Take a moment to meditate on it—does it match what you were picking up on in the distant sniff and the moving sniff? Is it what you expected or not?

No matter how glorious the fragrance was, how tempted you are to smell it again, wait a few seconds to give the software in your brain and the hardware in your beak time to reset. Speaking of resetting, there is a reason we've been taking these quick sniffs rather than the deep inhales depicted in just about every image that is intended to portray someone smelling something. Every picture you see of a suited-up somm or even an overall-clad lavender farmer, they're striking the same pose: their snoot right up next to the glass or their handful of just-picked flowers, taking a deep inhale implied by the faint smile on their face and their tightly closed eyes. When I see this romanticized version of smell, I think of one thing: mucus.

As covered in chapter 1, a dry olfactory passageway is an ineffective, dull olfactory passageway, so when professionals get to sniffing, they make every effort to keep moisture—and therefore mucus—intact. Like a spiderweb and a fly, mucus (and the odor binding proteins within it) traps aromatic compounds as they float by the olfactory bulb. While captured, the aromatic compounds connect with odor binding proteins and come in contact with olfactory receptors. This contact creates a scent signal that goes off to be interpreted by the brain. The first half of the mucus's job is done, but if all is functioning properly it has another important role to complete: waste disposal. After capturing the compounds, the mucus will continue to flow down the back of the throat, carrying the trapped compounds with it. And with a swallow mucus enters the digestive system. Meanwhile, a new sheet of mucus is coating the olfactory bulb to capture new aromas, flow away, and the loop continues endlessly. That's one reason the short explosive sniffs are the ideal method to bring aromas to the olfactory receptors. They don't bring in much excess air that will dry the nasal passageway and potentially eradicate precious mucus supplies. Furthermore, Pamela says that these rapid explosive sniffs also work in favor of the way air moves in our nasal passage. She worked with a bioengineer in her lab who created a model to show how odors travel once inside the nose. He showed that turbulent airflow inside the nasal cavity causes compounds to bounce off structures inside the nose, eventually reaching the olfactory bulb.

"The dogma was that only about ten percent of what we actually inhaled, in terms of the concentration of an aroma, would make it to the olfactory area," Pamela explains, "but now I would say that's wrong. It might be right for some people, but for some it's more and others it's less. There is more variation than we ever realized." In the same way all noses look different on the outside, the interior structures of our noses are also diverse. Each half-second sniff brings new airflow and movement into the nose, which starts the process of compounds ping-ponging off the landscape features. Hopefully, more than 10 percent of them end in contact with the olfactory area. One big, long, grand, Hollywood-style inhalation creates a single constant stream of airflow with all the bouncing around of molecules happening in the same pattern.

"Basically, the best way to do it is explosive, short sniffs," Pamela says. "A short, very discreet kind of sniffing rather than one long inhalation."

And so, we have the reason for our short sniff. A first handshake with the scent that sends all those odoriferous compounds bouncing off the walls or the nose toward our moist, mucusy receptors. Clearly you can see why quick, explosive sniffs are the best technique.

Now, let's throw it out the window and risk it all on the "long sniff." First, take a beat and make sure you've wrapped your head around what you've smelled thus far. Every scent, even the most basic like the smell of a fresh-cut lemon, has more than one thing going on. As expected, with lemon the core of the smell will be, well, lemon or citrus. This is the primary aroma; it's your answer to the question "describe that scent in one word." Boom, *lemon*!

By definition, the primary aroma can't be two things. It's tempting to think that a peanut butter and jelly sandwich has primary aromas of peanut butter and jelly. But it doesn't. Depending on the work of your sandwich artist, the primary aroma will either be peanut butter, or, more likely, bread. Jelly holds tightly on to its aromas unless it's quite warm; go ahead and sniff some for yourself. Although it's not the primary aroma, jelly won't be left out of the sensory description for the sandwich, unless it has no scent to speak of. This is where secondary aromas come in. There can be a small handful of secondary aromas; this could be berry notes or oat-like characteristics from bread. A lemon might have a secondary aroma that's waxy and rose-like , or maybe a woody green quality from the white pith that comes between the fruit and the rind. This bouquet of secondary aromas consists of all the other descriptors you notice consistently during the distant, moving, and short sniffs.

The final category of notes within the aroma is, unsurprisingly, tertiary aromas. Did you pick up a note of rose only on the moving sniff of the lemon? Maybe it wasn't until the short sniff that you noticed a sharper fruitiness that is similar to a mashed raspberry. For now, all of these belong in the tertiary aromas: scents you noticed but don't seem to be intrinsic to the character of whatever you're smelling. This is a first attempt at categorizing every scent we picked up on. There will be chances to move things around as you continue through the sniffing process. Which, as of this moment, we are more than halfway through.

And so, the "long sniff." To perform this sniff, bring your tastant into the same position as it was during the short sniff. Then take a gentle inhale for two to four seconds. As you inhale, move your head so your nose crosses back and forth over the center of your tastant. If you happen to be smelling something in a wineglass, the goal would be to cross over that open space in the center of the ring of ethanol aromas. Once the four seconds are up, move your tastant at least six inches away from your nose. Long sniff complete.

This is the most time you'll have to sit with the scent. It's like the conversation that follows after shaking someone's hand. You learn more details about their life and get a clue about their personality. But nothing too intimate. During the long sniff you might notice some tertiary aromas come forward; maybe you should think of them as part of the secondary-aroma category. Or maybe you came upon a new tertiary aroma. Take note.

Moving on to the last sniff in this step: the "retronasal sniff." If we've now seen our new acquaintance across the room (distant sniff), been introduced to them (moving sniff), shook their hand (short sniff), exchanged small talk (long sniff), then now we're about to get to know them over dinner. The retronasal sniff reveals a whole new side to the aroma we've been getting to know, literally. This step forces the aroma up the retronasal passageway toward the olfactory epithelium. When the aroma arrives there, the air it's carried by is flowing in the opposite direction compared to the four previous sniffs.

Sometimes what you pick up during the retronasal sniff is notably distinct from what you've perceived in the aroma so far. Other times it will be almost identical. "We aren't sure if it is different because the odors are sweeping over the epithelium in a different direction and lighting up different receptors in a reverse order," explains Pamela. "It tends to be a weaker sensation because we have less control over it than orthonasal sniffing."

In order to encourage the most intense possible sensation retronasally, there is some choreography. It's a routine that takes some practice. I suggest trying it a few times without a tastant to avoid any choking or sputtering. This is a common occurrence when overeager students jump into this step during my tasting classes. Although the tastant will hit your palate for the first time in this step, you shouldn't focus on what you taste. This choreography is also specifically designed to block orthonasal smelling. When performed flawlessly, this sniff will create the sensation of a third type of flavor. Noticeably different from the previous five sniffs.

First take a deep breath. Skipping this step regularly results in sputtering and coughing. All together now, a big chest-raising breath. Next use your nondominant hand to pinch your nose shut. The nostrils will remain pinched until I tell you to release them. From this point forward you are a one-handed, nostril-less beast in pursuit of retronasal perception.

Now, take a medium-size sip or bite of your tastant into your mouth. Medium-size is enough that the sample feels substantial, but you have no problem chewing, swishing, or swallowing it. Close your lips. They will remain closed throughout the next steps. See why we needed that big breath now? Do some minor chewing and swishing to get your sample moving in your mouth, but there is no reason to do anything uncomfortable. You only have a split second for this, as we're ticking away seconds on our remaining oxygen level. And now, muster your coordination. Several things need to happen in synchronous motion. All in the same moment swallow, let go of your nostrils, and make a gusty exhale out your nose. Your lips are still closed; you left them closed, right? The instant you began to exhale, a sensation of flavor filling your mouth is unleashed. That is aroma masquerading as taste.

SWIRL/SNAP

NOW THAT YOU'RE ACQUAINTED WITH THE AROMA OF YOUR TASTANT, it's time to examine its appearance again. The goal in the see step was to take in appearance without making assumptions about what flavors would come from it. This time, after so many sniffs, you have an idea of the flavor and are less likely to be misled.

It's time to snap, smear, or cut into solid tastants. The snappiness of a food is an important indicator of freshness. In fact, the loud crunch of a crisp apple or snap of a baby carrot is the best indication of its freshness. Crunch is a gauge of freshness because of tight cell walls stretched around plump, well-hydrated cells. Think of the cells in a carrot as thousands of tiny basketballs. Fully inflated or even overinflated basketballs will be taut and push back against your hand if you try to crush them. In the case of a carrot, the air in the basketball is water, but in the case of snack food like chips or the crispy skin on fried chicken, the cells are inflated with air. As you compress the carrot with your fingers (or teeth!) to break it, the well-inflated basketballs fight back until the pressure is too much and they finally burst, loudly blowing a hole through the rubber wall. The crunches of fresh celery or bell peppers are made from the sounds of hundreds of cell walls exploding at once. As vegetables sit around losing their freshness, water seeps out and leaves behind cells similar to mostly deflated basketballs. This time when you push the ball flat it might eventually pop, releasing the remaining air with a dull *pffffffft*, if it makes any sound at all. A carrot in this state has more of a mush than a snap to it.

The biological reason we like crunchy foods is tied to nutrition. It takes just three days for a fruit or vegetable to lose 30 percent of its nutritional value, sometimes more. And after a week, anywhere from 15 to 55 percent of a vegetable's vitamin C content is gone. That rubbery broccoli in the back of the fridge isn't the healthy snack you were hoping for anymore.

Not all snaps are related to vitamin content or freshness, though. In relation to chocolate, a lively snap can indicate whether the bar is "in temper." Temper is a state when the crystalline structure of the chocolate is still intact. Chocolate that has melted and resolidified is considered "out of temper." An in-temper dark chocolate bar will have a clean, clear snap while one that is out of temper might have a soft bend to it. The "snap" of a sourdough bread is more like a chorus of crunches rather than a single sound. This crunching of a fresh crust gives way to the soft, fluffy center.

Not every tastant will be snappable, but there's still a lot to learn from cutting and spreading. The way a cheese smears under the pressure of a knife gives clues about the density of its "paste." Smearing cheese this way also releases a trail of aroma molecules as cell walls are crushed and pulled. It's a good idea to get your nose in there while you smear. For that matter, any manipulation of the tastant, whether stabbing it with a fork, breaking it with your hands, scooping it with a spoon, or swirling it in a glass will release volatile aromas.

Beyond being another approach to observing your sample, swirling, snapping, or smearing is another chance to pelt the olfactory receptors with the maximum possible aroma molecules. In order to do this pelting, we'll employ a technique I call the swirl and sniff. If you're tasting something unswirlable it's called the snap and sniff. And if you're tasting something unsnappable it will be the cup and sniff, which is maybe not as catchy but still effective. To begin, make sure your hands are clean and scent-free. If that's not possible, try rubbing them together or on your shirtsleeves to neutralize as much scent as possible. Now, take one (hopefully mostly clean) hand and press it into the top of a glass or bowl until it forms a seal. The seal should be tight enough that you'll see a small ring on your palm once you lift your hand, but you don't need too much pressure, especially when dealing with fragile glasses. Keep the seal intact, while swirling the sample under it for about five seconds. If you've had a hard time pinning down the aroma of your sample swirl for eight or ten seconds. During this time, it's imperative that you do not lift your hand or allow the seal to soften. Now, move the rim of the glass or bowl until it is aligned with a point an inch below your nostrils. Simultaneously lift your hand from the glass and take three to five short half-second sniffs through your nose with your mouth slightly open. You may feel a bit like a panting dog (you may look a bit like one, too), but having your mouth open means some of the aroma may waft up the back of your throat as you sniff. We never turn down an additional chance for retronasal olfaction!

While you were swirling, aroma molecules were breaking out of the solution, and instead of drifting up and out of the glass, your properly placed hand forced them to collect in the space below it. And by removing that hand you've ushered the aroma out of the glass and into the jet stream that is your sucking nostrils. In the same way, covering and swirling a liquid builds a concentration of aroma molecules, snapping, cutting, or breaking your tastant also releases an intense puff of aroma ready to be inhaled. The snap and sniff requires less coordination. All you need to do is hold whatever you're tasting about two inches below your nose and break it a few times, taking a short sniff each time you make a break.

And for everything unswirlable and unbreakable, cup your nondominant hand around your tastant as if you are trying to capture the aroma like a net. After a few seconds use your dominant hand to lift the plate to your nose with your other hand still cupped around the tastant. Once the plate is in place, remove your hand by sweeping it toward your nose, ushering all that scent in the right direction, which is toward the olfactory epithelium.

"So how much swirling are you going to be doing to the whiskeys during the contest in Kentucky?" I ask Ben.

"None of the aggressive kind of wine swirling you're thinking about," he says. "With high-proof spirits that aren't diluted, that's just going to kick out a ton of alcohol."

"I feel like everyone swirls."

"It's a gentle swirl; it's more just to get things moving. There can be a layer of oils from the barrel on the top, so you get it moving to get that out of the way and release other flavors."

"Okay, gentle swirling, that's a new one for me."

"All swirling looks fancy, so it has that benefit."

I swirl slowly, thinking about how if rye was poured into a wine-glass I would have the clear spot over the middle where I could sniff with less ethanol.

"I can tell the alcohol, or get a close idea just by the nose; I would say this is ninety-five-proof. Do you get that burn when you get in close?"

I did get a little burn, but I'd gotten it when taking my first sniffs, too. Before I was gently swirling. Maybe I wasn't noticing the burn now because it has been there for a while. I needed to give my nose a break.

Stop! Palate cleanser time.

At this point in the tasting method, food or drink has only barely touched your palate, but it's time to talk about palate cleansers. These should really be called sensory cleansers, or maybe flavor cleansers, but like so many things involved in tasting the name ties back to the idea that flavor happens in the mouth. It's a funny conundrum because the palate cleanser most people have likely come in contact with is one for the nose. Even if you've never used them, you have probably walked by the petite jars of coffee beans on the perfume counters at the front of department stores. Even airport shops and some drugstores have coffee beans on the fragrance displays. Sometimes you'll see them at a whiskey tasting or other introductory tasting course. However, practiced professionals steer away from them. The smell of coffee may mask any other scent lingering in your nose, but it will also obscure the aromas of the next thing you smell. Coffee shares more than one hundred aromatic compounds with chocolate, wine, beer, and even cheese. Sniffing coffee beans while tasting has the opposite effect of cleansing your senses; instead it introduces additional aromas.

The goal of palate cleansing is to get your senses back to neutral. The most neutral scent available, the ideal thing to sniff to give your senses a reset, is yourself. No, you don't need to lift an arm to whiff some of your more potent musk. A dose from the crook of your elbow or even the shirt on your shoulder will work. After a particularly intense flavor, tasters might rub their hands together, then cup them and cover the whole bottom half of their face while taking a few breaths. The only scent we can't escape, the smell of ourselves, is exactly the ticket to getting our senses back to zero.

Tasting yourself, unfortunately, does not work as well. To cleanse the physical palate, we'll need something else. The most common palate cleanser is room-temperature water. This water should never have ice in it because cooling the tongue dulls the sensitivity of taste receptors, which is the opposite of the purpose of a palate cleanser. I use sparkling water when critically tasting because I think there is some mechanical cleaning action at work. It could be those Scrubbing Bubbles commercials at work, but I am fully convinced that the tingling of carbonation on my tongue is lifting away some of the flavor compounds.

"Warm water is the best palate cleanser when tasting anything that contains fat," international chocolate judge and the cofounder of the Specialty Cocoa Association Brian Cisneros tells me. "It needs to be at or a little warmer than your body temperature to melt away the fat."

I'm surprised by his warm-water assertion because the palate cleansers in chocolate tasting get pretty wild. Standard palate cleansers consist of bland foods like unsalted crackers or rice cakes. But on a chocolate taster's table in additon to crackers you might see sliced green apples and torn bread. A favorite among some chocolate judges, and the most bizarre in my opinion, is unseasoned polenta made to a loose soupy consistency.

"The problem with using food [as a palate cleanser] is you're not brushing your teeth between samples," Brian says, "so the next chocolate you taste, maybe it has a little corn grit in there because you used raw polenta as a palate cleanser."

This is true; those dry, unsalted crackers are nearly impossible to remove from your molars. I do find them as a nice occasional nose cleanser, though. On a day when I might have to taste forty or more beer samples, smelling myself over and over gets old.

Cocoa beans are up to 51 percent fat, and much of the complexity of chocolate is carried in this fat. As it carries flavor, it also coats the mouth. "The best way to get any fat off your palate is by melting it; that's the only way to get rid of it," he says. "That's why I use the warm water." This is good advice for palate cleansing while tasting other high-fat items like cheeses or ice creams.

Brian clarifies that this applies to a professional setting where scores count and judges are trying to stay as neutral as possible in between settings. "If you're tasting chocolate for fun, eat whatever you want as a palate cleanser, the sky is the limit!"

SIP/SAMPLE

FIVE STEPS INTO THE TASTING METHOD AND IT IS FINALLY TIME TO AC-tually, legitimately. genuinely taste something. Our olfactory receptors get credit for as much as 80 percent of what we perceive as flavor, but there is still a lot to be learned through our taste receptors. In fact, simply having something in our mouths actively improves our sense of smell. Pamela Dalton, along with other sensory scientists at the Monell Chemical Sense Center, devised a set of experiments to investigate the impact of sub-flavor threshold tastes on olfactory sensitivity. Volunteers held a solution that tasted like pure water in their mouths while they sniffed vials. In truth, the volunteers were holding one of three solutions: water; a subthreshold umami solution (MSG and water); or a subthreshold sweet solution (saccharine and water). The volunteers were asked to identify which of the vials contained benzaldehyde, which has a cherry almond aroma. We learned in chapter 3 that everyone has differing sensitivities to individual compounds, but in this experiment the volunteers could reliably identify benzaldehyde at lower thresholds when they held the sweet solution in their mouths. Even at levels below the flavor threshold, the presence of sweet tastes made participants more aware of a scent that is associated with sweetness.

Sniffing and tasting—they're better together!

So, let's get to sipping and sampling. We're going to go through three different tastes, each one building in complexity the match taste, the mouthfeel taste, and the aftertaste taste.

The match taste is straightforward. It's your opportunity to relax and finally taste what you have been sniffing for the last minute or so. The only thing you need to do here is notice if the taste you experience matches the aroma you've sensed. Simply take a medium-size sip or bite of the item you're tasting. You want enough to fill your mouth but not so much that it is hard to orally process, or as the pros refer to it, *masticate*—two fancy ways of saying to chew it. For drinks, a medium sip fills your mouth but leaves room for swishing the liquid around.

(Here is where you will spit or swallow, but I'll cover that decision in the next step.)

For the most part, the match taste will result in a match. This is due to learned "flavor congruences"; we assume something that smells of vanilla will taste sweet and something with an aroma of lemon will be sour (even though citric acid itself has virtually no aroma). However, this taste will not always result in a match. For example, if you had never tasted coffee, you would note that it smells like chocolate, toasted nuts, and a hint of red fruit, and you would note that it tastes bitter. There's a mismatch between aroma and taste because nuts and red fruits are not bitter, and neither is most of the chocolate you've tasted. Yet, after that first mismatched taste, every consecutive taste of coffee would also smell chocolatey and nutty while tasting bitter. Soon you would note, yes, the tastes and aroma match when you smell coffee and taste bitterness.

Because compounds like salt (salty), caffeine (bitter), saccharine (sweet), MSG (umami), and citric acid (sour) all have strong flavors but no aroma, occasionally you'll be surprised during the match taste. I find this usually happens with lurking sourness. A dessert or cocktail can smell like cherries and vanilla but have a dose of tangy acid hiding in the taste, not always unpleasant but definitely not a match.

And that's all for the first taste; it boils down to a true or false question. Aroma and taste match: true or false?

Let's move on to the mouthfeel taste. *Mouthfeel* tends to be a polarizing term; people consider it to be jargony or pretentious, but there's a reason I use it here rather than using *texture*. Texture is something we see (remember, it's one of the three French principles of plating!): it looks crunchy; it looks creamy. It might feel crunchy or creamy when we snap it with our hands. But until it's in our mouth, we can't know the mouthfeel. Human teeth can sense grit that is just 10 microns in diameter. For context on just how teeny tiny that really is, a human hair has a diameter of 70 microns. Our mouth feels a grit we assume is the size of a grain of sand, but even very fine sand is about 60 microns in size. A pudding that appears to have a creamy texture might have a gritty mouthfeel because the naked eye has a visibility threshold of roughly 40 microns. Thus, we may be incapable of seeing particles we can feel very clearly in the mouth. And that is why the mouthfeel taste keeps its name.

So, what exactly is mouthfeel? It is the somatosensory (or feeling) component of tasting, meaning how bodily sensations like pressure, pain, or warmth contribute to flavor.

A good introductory exercise in analyzing mouthfeel is tasting various milks side by side. Assess the difference between a nonfat milk and a full-fat one; if you're daring, compare it to cream. For the dairy avoidant, try the base version of your nondairy milk, maybe almond milk and then the "coffee creamer" version. Both may be described as slick or creamy, but the full-fat version is more dense and feels heavier. It coats your tongue and your cheeks. And even a few moments after you swallow you can still feel it. The glaring difference between the two milks isn't taste or aroma, but rather the *feel* of the milk in your mouth.

That same syrupy-coating sensation gives the luxe mouthfeel to a T-bone steak as the fat melts on your warm tongue. It's also the difference between a satisfying ice cream and the ones that seem to disappear the moment you close your mouth, usually made of more air than any other ingredient.

While milk is a good way to compare light to heavy sensations in the mouth, a sparkling-water tasting is a way to assess touch sensations. Do a side-by-side comparison of two different brands of sparkling water. If you can find them, San Pellegrino and LaCroix work well for this exercise. The former has a fine carbonation that feels like a tingle on the tongue. In contrast, LaCroix has big rough-and-tumble soda pop bubbles that feel more like Pop Rocks bursting than the fizz of champagne. Noticing these tactile differences on the tongue prepares you to pay attention to more nuanced variances like the difference between sticky and syrupy honey.

To examine the mouthfeel of the tastant, take a slightly smaller bite or sip than you did in the match taste so there is room to move it around your mouth. For the first several seconds hold that taste on your tongue and notice how it settles there. Is it melting at all? Changing shape? Are carbonated bubbles bouncing off your tongue? Or is it holding its shape? Now, move the tastant around your mouth. Note if it is sharp like the shattering crust of baguette or smooth and creamy. Finally masticate, orally process, or chew (whatever you like to call it!). How does the sample break or mash? Are there any new qualities emerging you didn't expect? This can be as pronounced as a creamy filling inside a waxy chocolate or as subtle as a mushy spot in an apple.

Swallow (or spit) and inhale air over your tongue and cheeks. This airflow will enhance any potential cooling or warming on the palate. A tingling warming may indicate alcohol or capsaicin (the spicy compound in peppers). A master bourbon taster told me "breathe in and the higher the tingle, the higher the proof!" Cooling sensations are usually tied to menthol, but there are other compounds that activate the TRPM8 ion channel, which is responsible for the cooling sensation, like eucalyptol and some compounds found in nutmeg.

HERE ARE SOME MOUTHFEEL TERMS YOU MAY HEAR THROWN AROUND:

Astringency, also called "tannic," is the drying sensation of drinking an overbrewed black tea or a very dry red wine. It feels like saliva is being sucked out of your mouth, leaving it very dry, because that is exactly what is happening!

Tannic polyphenols cause your saliva to coagulate and pull it away from your tongue and cheeks, leaving your palate feeling dry.

Viscosity literally refers to the measure of a fluid's resistance to flow. You'll hear it come up often in wine tasting with references to "medium viscosity" or "high viscosity." Behind the fancy lingo this term refers to how a liquid moves. Low viscosity liquids have a consistency similar to water; high viscosity liquids flow and spread slowly like syrup.

It can be hard to find the words to describe mouthfeel, especially when you're new to evaluating it. These are some less technical terms you may come across or use yourself:

- thin, watery, syrupy, creamy, viscous, heavy, light;
- coating, waxy, pasty, gummy;
- fuzzy, leather, tough, chewy;
- harsh, drying, rough, tannic;
- tingling, prickly, bubbly;
- hot, cooling, warm, cool, burning, icy, numbing;
- soft, silk, suede, supple;
- crispy, crunchy, hard, stale, chalky, powdery, crumbly;
- sticky, thick, slick, gooey.

The final taste in the sip/sample step is the aftertaste taste. To assess aftertaste, take a final medium-size taste, chew or swish it to coat your mouth, swallow it, and breathe out gently. Wait for five to ten seconds without taking a sip of water or another bite. Observe which flavors linger and for how long. You may also notice mouthfeel shift or new sensations arise, especially numbing sensations or spicy heat.

Aftertaste can tell you a lot about the quality of what you're tasting. There are general aftertaste rules for different specialties. When it comes to sake, both long aftertastes and quickly vanishing aftertastes are acceptable, but the latter is much harder to achieve and signifies a very skilled producer. In wine, a finish that quickly disappears from the palate is an indicator of a manufactured wine. The word "short" is a negative term to describe this affliction. A wine described as "too short" has no aftertaste and is judged to be poor quality. If an oyster has a long, bitter aftertaste it may have been harvested during breeding season; it won't hurt you, but it's not the briny sea delicacy you ordered. Acacia honey should finish sweet and clean, while late-season honey always has a subtle bitter aftertaste. Overall, the most important thing to notice about aftertaste is how much you enjoy it.

A sample may seem delightful until a five- to ten-second pause has you reaching for the water glass to wash away a bitter, mineral flavor. Aha! This is why we can't forget aftertaste when evaluating flavor! It can change how we feel about what we're tasting as a whole.

In summation, during the sip/sample step you will take a note of whether the taste matched the aroma of your sample, how it felt in your mouth, and the length and overall pleasantness of the aftertaste.

SPIT/SWALLOW

TASTING IS NOT EATING. THE TWO ARE OBVIOUSLY RELATED, BUT EATing means swallowing. Tasting—sometimes—does not. Especially in settings when many of the same item will be tasted in succession, or the item has high calorie density or intoxicating effects, a tasting could be cut short by fullness, drunkenness, or caffeine buzz. So we spit. Or as the cheese tasters over at Tillamook outside Portland, Oregon, put it, "expectorate." The floor of the quality-assurance lab has spit buckets that the lab techs can maneuver with their feet. "Oh, yes, with a little experience, anyone can expectorate in a way that is, well, classy. We don't even notice each other doing it."

Ben prepares me for our first sip of whiskey. "The first taste of whiskey is a wash; you're just going to be blown away with alcohol," he says. "You can basically just take a drink and not think about it because all you're doing is acclimating to that alcohol." Now, this is an ideal time to spit if you have a spittoon (or the less classy spit bucket) around. Since there is no flavor to be gained from this first taste, spitting out the wine or spirit saves you from drinking unnecessary alcohol. We're tasting here, not taking shots!

If you're going to be spitting in front of others, you should practice. A bowl in the sink makes a good target to get comfortable with the aim and velocity of your stream. Remember you only need to practice with a medium-size sip. I recently heard of someone practicing by spitting water in the shower, which is both hilarious and honestly not a bad idea. You can pick a target like a shampoo bottle or the drain and pretend it's the spittoon.

With enough practice, you'll develop your own technique, but here's how I do it: I purse my lips to make the shape of a zero lying on its side rather than an O. I find an O-shaped stream travels with too much force. And by that I mean too much splashing. And by that I mean making a mess.

Before you spit, imagine a nice constant stream traveling from mouth to bowl. Now use a little force and spit the liquid. Do not even think about letting your lips go slack before the stream is completely ended. I find myself holding my lips pursed for a half second after I'm finished spitting just to avoid the dreaded dribble—the last few drops that run off your chin and, if you're especially unlucky, onto your shirt. And this is why we practice: to avoid the dribble and avoid getting totally sloshed at a tasting event. Using a spit bucket at an event can be intimidating, but don't let that keep you from spitting; there is no shame in using a spit cup.

It's valuable to know how to spit, but there are also good reasons to swallow. Perhaps the most important is the fact that there are taste receptors on the back of the throat, lining the esophagus, and present in the gut. After a food or drink has left the mouth, we continue to taste it. Second, the act of swallowing is one of the best ways to push aroma compounds up the retronasal passageway to the olfactory epithelium. However, if you don't want to swallow, there's still hope for retronasal action. Pamela says, "The act of swallowing is what gives us a lot of that retronasal aroma, but if somebody's unwilling to swallow, what they should do as a replacement for that action is agitate what is in their mouth to try to get some of those molecules . . . retronasally."

Each taster will have to decide their own course of action, depending on what and where they're tasting. Ideally, you'll give each item you taste at least one small swallow. At a tequila tasting, a bartender told me he spits out three-quarters of the spirit and swallows the last quarter to understand how smooth it feels "going down." And with the final spit or swallow ends the tasting portion of the method.

SIT AND SYNTHESIZE

YOU JUST WENT THROUGH SIX DISTINCT STEPS TO COLLECT DATA ON something you're tasting. Without this seventh step the previous six don't matter. The synthesize step is the moment to reflect on what we've perceived, how it fits in with the rest of our lives, and how we'll remember it. This step is simple: pause to consider what you've tasted, file it away in your flavor memory (we'll learn more about this in the next chapter), and simply revel in the experience of taste. This tasting method is really a way to force you to take a few seconds to examine the world from a different perspective.

We can sit next to each other while we conduct a six-step method and determine what we are each personally tasting. This seventh step is the conversation that comes after—the discussion of what we sensed and how our personal flavor world relates to your companions. Sometimes these conversations feel like fortune-telling. We agree the coffee tastes like chocolate because it makes sense that it would taste like chocolate. Sometimes, though, there are these moments when you hear the right word for what you're tasting, and it's like a shock goes through your system. You can viscerally feel that it rings true. In my classes, people are just learning to think about what they taste. They sniff and swirl and sip and sniff again, hesitant to say anything at all. Words like *caramel* and *toasted bread* are met with polite murmurs of support but not true agreement. Eventually someone says in a volume just above a whisper, "Um, soy sauce?" The rest of the class erupts, "Yes! Yes! Soy sauce." It's like a collective exhale. It's as if for a moment we spoke with one another telepathically. We feel absolute certainty that there is less that separates us than we originally thought. A moment of collective revelation from a simple sip (and sniff!) of beer.

These moments aren't guaranteed at every tasting, but it is guaranteed that they won't happen without a pause to sit and synthesize. Tasting companions aren't required for a revelatory synthesize step. Sitting alone after a great cup of tea and considering how it relates to all your past tastes of tea can border on meditative. Reading about the grove the olives you're eating were grown in and using flavor to connect that geographic location to your snack elevates the experience. This pause to sit and synthesize gives meaning to what you experienced during the first six steps of this tasting method. To recap those steps, this is what you've done to fully appreciate what is in front of you: You checked the setting for things that might interfere with the tasting, or selected the plateware, serving temperature, and distraction level if you could (set). You saw how beautiful the creation in front of you was and checked it for potential flaws (see). You sniffed it from a distance, sniffed it while you moved it, sniffed it short, sniffed it long, and sniffed it with the back of your nose (sniff). As you took your first forkful, swirled it, or snapped it, you observed it again (swirl/snap). Finally, you tasted its flavor. You chewed or sloshed it, observed its mouthfeel, and noticed its aftertaste (sip/sample). You took the final swallow or spit (spit/swallow), and now it's time to think about all you've done.

"Sometimes I smell something, and the thumbprint of the distiller is right there," says Ben. He compares the whiskey he's tasting to what he knows about all the whiskeys and other spirits he's tasted in the past. For Ben, flavors of grape jelly and the dry skin of a peanut signal it's a whiskey by Wild Turkey. Whiskeys like Woodford Reserve will always be more clean and precise. "But then there are times you have to sit and put things together and say, 'Okay, what's not here?'"

Young whiskey tastes like mothballs and malty corn to Ben, so no mothballs in the aroma means it can't be young. Chocolatey or heavily floral notes indicate a high percentage of malted barley. Whiskey that "tastes as crunchy as almost burnt sugar crystals" is aged more than twenty years. Ben has a mental list of these differences, and eventually you'll build one, too. As you're starting out, it's helpful to take notes during your tasting so you can run through them without needing to hold all the flavors in your memory.

Ben stays away from hedonic descriptors; he avoids calling whiskeys or agaves good or bad for the most part. Instead of saying a spirit is good he'll say, "This is something that would be on my bar." It's a personal decision rather than an absolute statement of quality. "At the end of all of it, tasting is subjective, and it's always going to be. How I remember this [whiskey] is going to be completely different from how you do."

Remembering it is what sitting and synthesizing is all about. This step doesn't need to revolve around picking apart the elements in what you taste or assigning a rating. It's a few moments to focus on the flavors in front of you, what they meant to you in the moment, and what parts of them you'd like to capture to bring with you for the rest of your life.

———————

A LITTLE OVER SEVENTY-TWO HOURS LATER I STAND AT A TABLE IN A dive bar outside of Louisville, Kentucky, with Ben and a group of his whiskey-obsessed friends. They are talking about making barrel picks, a holy grail of the whiskey-nerd experience, where a group works with a distiller or blender to select an entire whiskey barrel that will be specially bottled for them.

The World's Top Whiskey Taster competition is over. Ben didn't win, but he didn't get last, either.

As we stand with the other competitors, whiskey blenders, and their colleagues, I noticed we are all nosing our drinks. I am drinking what must be at least my five hundredth Yuengling (I did grow up outside of Philadelphia), but I asked for a cup to pour it in. I swirl it and raise it to my nose between sips. I see some people pursing their lips to pull oxygen in over the whiskey or wine they're drinking. Ben exhales gently over his palate after he swallows, just like me. I consider how I like the mouthfeel of Yuengling more out of a bottle than on draft. It's more prickly, the bubbles pop with little zaps rather than the soft tingle that flows off the tap.

A recap of recent barrel picks is exhausted and the discussion turns to evaporation rates and how they affect mature whiskey.

"Affect the flavor? Fermentation is the flavor. The angels' share leaving doesn't change the fermentation profile!"

"But barrel character will cover it up. Smell this, smell this." One of Ben's support group extends his arm across the table. "Would it smell like that through a bunch of vanilla?"

We each take a sniff of the whiskey to determine if vanilla character from oak would be beneficial or offensive. The group just behind us is sipping beer from their bottles and cans. I sort of wished I could show them how much better it would taste poured into a plastic cup, so they could get a nose full of hops or clean crackery malt character with every sip. But I also realize not every beverage is for thoughtful tasting; some of them are for unthoughtful drinking.

Just then, one of the event organizers from Bardstown Bourbon Company, invites all the competitors to get together for a drink to toast their efforts.

"No! No, here we do not shoot bourbon," he says. "Bourbon is not for shooting. We are shooting chardonnay."

And with that, the bartender pours a round of half glasses of dive bar white wine. The competitors raise a toast to whiskey tasting and toss back the chardonnay. There is no sniffing, swirling, sipping, or synthesizing happening on this one.

CHAPTER FIVE

COLLECTING FLAVORS, REFERENCES, AND REFLEXES

"NOT A SINGLE PERSON WAS SPITTING. I COULDN'T BELIEVE IT!" Logan marvels.

"I know," I laugh, "the buckets were right next to the glasses, too. They were practically begging to be used."

I met Logan Hanes at the World's Top Whiskey Taster competition at Bardstown Bourbon Company and we immediately got to talking about tasting. We both recognized that the judges' speeches ahead of the tasting competition were a little too flowery, a little too precious. We agree that tasting isn't about philosophy.

"You get too many thoughts going, and you're trying to remember too many things," Logan says, "and you're not going to be able to taste at all."

Logan was a member of the in-house tasting panel at a Kentucky distillery well known for its highly collectible whiskeys and bourbons.

"I had no idea what to expect. I just thought, if I fail, hopefully I get to taste some cool whiskey first," remembers Logan about his decision to try out for the panel.

For years, his nose and palate had a say in which barrels were considered truly exceptional, with contents good enough to be packaged under the distillery's ultra-collectible brand, and which were mediocre; these barrels of whiskey would be blended away in the still delicious, but not so rare bourbons. Logan and his fellow panelists had to be sensitive to even the faintest out-of-place flavor note, or a nearly imperceptible change in mouthfeel. After all, people would spend anywhere from a few hundred to many thousands of dollars for a bottle to display on the bar. Perfection wasn't a goal; it was a requirement. With the stakes so high, tasters like Logan had to go through a many-month audition process before being accepted onto the panel.

For the first test potential panelists face forty to sixty cups of water filled with different concentrations of the five basic flavors. Cups with liquid so sweet they hold a candle to Southern sweet tea. Cups filled with water augmented with just a whisper of bitterness. This is considered the "beginner" test, a straightforward way to whittle down the group to candidates who already have sensitive palates. The surviving group moves on to tasks that require identifying specific flavors like lavender or leather; perhaps this is a sneaky way of testing for individual blindnesses (discussed in chapter 3) to important compounds. The finalists who pass these tests then begin a six-month training program.

Logan and I have so many similar ideas about tasting and flavor, I suspect he must have been trained in the same way as I had, but while he was learning on the job in Kentucky, I started out in a San Diego conference room at a five-day intensive taught by Dr. Bill Simpson, founder of Cara Technology, a company that establishes professional taster planners for food and beverage brands. From our experience and training, both Logan and I know that if you want to be a good taster you can't be trained like an artist—you need to be trained like a dog.

In the international terminal at JFK airport, passengers are always met with a troop of sweet-faced beagles. On my last pass through baggage claim, one of them gave my suitcase a sniff right as I slid it off the carousel. His vest denoted that he was a working dog, which kept me from giving him a couple of encouraging pats and "good boys." My luggage might have smelled of wine bottles or the wooden holder for the champagne saber I brought back with me. Luckily, this gainfully employed canine was not screening for decorative weapons. This was a member of the "Beagle Brigade," a team of dogs employed by the US Department of Agriculture to detect prohibited products and stop them from coming into the country. The expertly trained beagles are our last line of defense against highly contagious diseases like African swine fever, which could devastate the American pork industry. In fact, this dog may be coworkers with the beagle that made headlines for sniffing out a roasted pork head illegally brought through the Atlanta airport.

Pork or not, whatever the dog was searching for appeared to be in a silver duffel bag a few feet behind me. The duffel was resting under a firmly placed paw. The paw remained adamantly in place for a few seconds until the dog's excitement took over and he had to rise briefly to wag his tail before gaining enough composure to sit and once again place a paw on the bag.

I didn't want to stare, so I'm not exactly sure what happened next between the dog and his handler, but I have a good idea. Excitement like that comes from the anticipation of a reward. Detection dogs don't track down target aromas because they're interested in discriminating scents. The dogs set out expertly searching for the specified odor of narcotics, agricultural products, or victims lost in a snowdrift because if they find them, they'll get a reward. Sometimes it's a standard treat or praise from their beloved handler, but other times it's the really good stuff like the opportunity to play catch or tug of war.

At the beginning of their journey to become a professional sniffer, the dogs start with simple foundational exercises. The trainer grasps a treat in one hand and a container holding the scent in another. Once the dog leaves the hand with the treat alone and ventures to sniff the scent stimulus, he is rewarded with the treat and a word of encouragement. This exercise is repeated over and over again until the dog realizes it's not the aroma of treat that earns it a reward but the aroma of the stimulus. According to the American Kennel Club, the most important duty of the trainer is to give the reward the instant the aroma is identified. "You must feed the dog at the source of the odor," the AKC Scent Work guidelines specifies. As training continues, the stimulus moves from the hand to the floor, then across the room, and finally to hidden spaces that the dogs must search carefully to find.

"When you're training puppies to be sniffer dogs, you don't say, Well, puppy, when you smell this, what do you think of?'" says Dr. Bill Simpson, who instructed me, as well as more than 25,000 professional tasters with his AROXA taster training technology. "No. You give them the stimulus and reward them when they get it right. And that feedback loop will make them get better."

That is the theory Bill uses to train tasters, and what makes the AROXA classes feel much different from exercises in conventional tasting groups. There is very little open discussion of what we might be tasting. The format is more like the dog training procedure. First, we get familiar with the stimulus aroma, and then we get the "reward" when we can identify it. In this case, the reward is the momentary jolt of pride that comes with each correct identification.

In taster trainings like this, the stimulus aroma is an isolated flavor compound. These are called reference standards, spikes, descriptor flavors, aroma compounds, reference spikes, flavor kits, or standard molecules, depending on which industry or specialty you're working in. Some of these standards are edible, like the ones Bill invented. His nanotechnology technique encases pure flavor compounds so there is no need to adulterate them with a stabilizer. The pure flavor standards come in capsules that look like pills from a pharmacy. Other reference standards are stabilized in alcohol, oil, or glycerin. These standards may be in sniffer vials, like the popular Le Nez du Vin collection (which contrary to the name makes standards for mediums beyond wine including coffee, bourbon, Armagnac, and standard aromas). Other flavor standards, especially those isolated in alcohol, can also be both smelled and consumed.

Akin to the dogs' training regimen, Bill started us off with associating the stimulus taste and aroma with its name and meaning. While holding the specific compound under our noses, sniffing, swirling, and tasting it, Bill described its origins and common associations. In fact, the tasting method Bill taught in this class is similar to the one I taught you in chapter 4. You can envision myself and my classmates sniffing the compounds in all different ways, blowing out our noses, plugging our noses, sipping, blowing again, while he talks over our activity. This process of familiarizing ourselves with the stimulus was repeated for each reference compound—pleasant compounds like vanilla and iso-amyl acetate (fruity banana) and challenging aromas including hydrogen sulfide (rotten egg).

For me, the most memorable compound in this class was damascenone. This is a not-so-common note that sometimes turns up in beer. Bill told us that tasters often associate it with berries, black tea, or stewed fruit. Yet, as I smelled it, I realized I was picking up on tinned cranberry juice (specifically the individually canned cranberry juices you might mix with vodka in a plastic cup on a sticky bar top during spring break on the Florida coast). Bill continued his spiel on damascenone, emphasizing that levels are dependent on the ingredients in the beer. I sniffed cranberry. He said the intensity of damascenone increases with age. I tasted cranberry. When he noted that damascenone can be pleasant, I thought of fruity aromas and Spring Break memories. Damascenone. Cranberry. Listen. Smell. Remember. Then, we had to taste without the background explanations. He presented us with several unmarked cups, and we had to identify the flavor spike in each one. I assumed there would be a learning curve as I got accustomed to testing this way. To the contrary, on our first test, I identified every cup correctly. Tasting some cups, I could even hear Bill's voice in my head saying the compound's name out loud.

Logan and the whiskey panel trainees also had tests like this, but the flavors they were studying were extremely similar, so similar that most people would assume they were identical. How did he learn to separate the bourbon aged for eight years and bourbon aged for fifteen years? It's all about repetition. He tasted the same whiskeys repeatedly. He tasted them alongside mentors already on the panel. He tasted them alone. He tasted them with a trainer. He tasted them after aging in the bottle, aging in the barrel, diluted with water, tainted with foul substances. Then he tasted them as part of an exam. Almost all trained tasters gain their chops in this way; they repeat the same monotonous exercises with the same set of flavor targets until they know them so well that identification is no longer a guessing game, it's a natural reflex. Over and over again, Logan practiced until he had to use only his nose to ace all the tests, including the dreaded triangle tests. Unlike the standard identification tests I underwent in Bill's class, a triangle test isn't about recognizing a flavor but recognizing a difference between two flavors. The test consists of three cups, two are filled with the same liquid, one has a subtle difference. It's the taster's job to select the odd cup out. This task is harder than you think! Try it with two cups of Bud Light and a cup of Coors Light. Or a single Pepsi in the company of two Cokes. Even a test with two Wheat Thins and a low-sodium Wheat Thin is a difficult prospect. The tests Logan had to face were much more difficult than these examples.

"Every single test was given in black cups, to make sure we were relying just on our nose and taste," Logan recounts. "Triangle tests, identification tests, contamination tests, nosing tests." If he was unsuccessful in any test, he would be thanked for his time but wouldn't return for panel training.

Gian Luigi Marcazzan's students fly from all around the world to study with him in Italy. They spend between three and five days fully immersed in the sensory aspects of unifloral honey. Just like Logan and me, the honey students spend their days sniffing and swirling, talking about what they smell and where those flavors may have originated in the honey making process. Gian has eighteen different kinds of honey produced by bees that have access to only one type of flower.

"Some of the honeys are very different and you can smell the flower they are made from, but some are almost the same and the only way to recognize the difference is repeat, repeat, repeat," Gian tells me. His students may taste honey up to seven hours per day when class is in session.

"It's difficult to describe the different characteristics because we can sense so many more odors than we have words for," he added, "so it's repeat, repeat, repeat until you know the honey so well you don't need a word to describe it. You just know it."

In this way, smelling a particular bourbon and then blurting out its brand name is as natural a reaction as swinging a leg when a doctor strikes your knee with a rubber mallet. At the end of this chapter, I outline how to replicate some of these repetition tastes at home to build strong flavor references for yourself.

"It got to the point where I could smell a glass poured for me at a bar and know immediately if they were serving me the brand I ordered," Logan says. "That's the only time I've ever felt like a snob. It's like I know that I paid for a glass of Rock Hill, and that's not in this glass."

It takes serious practice to build enough confidence in your tasting skills that you trust them more than you trust the bartender. That level of confidence is required to be inducted onto the tasting panel at what is widely considered the most award-winning American distillery of all time. To be one of a handful of palates entrusted with the responsibility to protect the reputation of more than two hundred years of making bourbon, the panelists have to really know their flavor references.

You probably won't need to know any references this well. No one is staking their reputation on your palate, at least not yet. But still, building out a personal collection of flavor references is one of the great rewards of thoughtfully tasting. And it doesn't need to be this regimented. In fact, it can be absolutely delightful and as exhilarating as starting your first collection as a child. Think back to your first collection. It may have been pressed flowers picked from the backyard or rocks from around the neighborhood. Whatever the medium, it is a profound discovery that you can gather a small menagerie of possessions to build a collection. You can study each item, noting their similarities and differences and determine which ones are really special and which ones just exist as part of the collection. Once you're a collector, every walk to school is a chance to expand your assortment of pebbles. Soon enough, you have a shoebox full of your treasures to show the babysitter when he comes over. Collecting tastes is like this; even a mundane meal becomes a chance to get the thrill of adding to your collection.

In her book *Garlic and Sapphires*, Ruth Reichl recounts a tedious dinner with a man who fancies himself a wine expert. She is immediately annoyed by his overly precious interactions with the sommelier, but her perception changes mid-meal when he shuts his eyes before sipping the wine. He takes small, quick sips and shared what he was tasting: "Violets," he says.. "Silver. A cool brook babbling in a forest. Sunshine on rippling leaves." Her dining companion explains that he's "attempting to build a mental wine encyclopedia he can recall at will."

Her former bore of a dinner date becomes fascinating to Ruth and she listens as he continues.

"When I first taste, I like to concentrate and just let images come. It helps me remember. Try it yourself."

Ruth closes her eyes and takes a sip of wine. "Grapes," she thinks. "Chardonnay. A bit of oak."

It's clear the man had ample practice capturing and expressing flavors found in wine in his own personal style. Ruth had less experience with this exercise and pulled flavors mostly related to wine generally rather than stretching for specifics. Neither was right or wrong, and as Ruth keeps practicing, she would establish her own style for describing wine flavors, too. In this case Ruth's dining partner might've been acting like a bit of a snob, but he does seem like he is having fun adding another flavor to his mental wine encyclopedia. It doesn't require being a snob and examining flavors should be fun; that's why I don't like the idea of a mental flavor collection being an encyclopedia. There is a little thrill that comes with adding a new flavor to your life using the tasting method. Who feels a thrill constructing a new entry in an encyclopedia? There's nothing inspiring or vibrant about adding another page to a dusty reference book. Rather than an encyclopedia, I think of the collection of personal taste references as a wardrobe. Our clothing closets contain at least a few treasured garments donned for special occasions or ratty but cherished sweatshirts worn for good luck. If you're like me, your wardrobe also includes a few things that don't bring you so much pleasure. A dress I spent too much money on that remains a half size too small comes to mind. You'll run into these clunkers on your flavor journey, too, new tastes that don't sit right, that you'd sooner return if only that were possible. But those are part of your flavor references, too. The beloved and the mundane, all of these garments in a closet come together to show your personal style; even the way they're arranged says something about you. Each time you taste or smell something new is an opportunity to expand the wardrobe of flavors in your memory. It's not limited to things you can eat or drink; you can add flavors you can't consume, too. Flowers (like powerful Casa Blanca lilies), landscapes (fresh rain on a country road), and situations (climbing into a bed with fresh linens) all deserve a place in your sensory memory. Obviously, you can't perform the full tasting method on fresh laundry, but taking in your surroundings combined with a few deliberate sniffs while saying the name of what you smell is enough to purposefully add it to the mental collection.

Everything from the minty pop of the after-dinner candy to the strong smell of gasoline at the truck stop is a potential flavor memory, so in order to have a grasp on them all, they must be organized into mental categories. Each person remembers flavors by grouping them in a way that makes sense to them. Similar, once again, to the way you might arrange a wardrobe. Clothes can be organized by season or sleeve length. Or maybe everything is grouped by color with purple tank tops, eggplant sweaters, and mauve pants intermingling within their category. Maybe all the tops go to the left and all the bottoms to the right with dresses in between, and that cursed too-tight cocktail dress tucked away in the back.

My personal flavor wardrobe is organized around where I might run into the particular flavors in the world. There are spice cabinet flavors and bakery flavors and lawn flavors and forest flavors and zoo flavors. (Think you don't need a zoo flavor section? Give blue cheese a sniff and think again.)

As you start to collect flavor memories, you'll need only a few basic categories to place them in. My students tend to group them like that outdated food pyramid: fruits, vegetables, fats, breads and cereals, dairy, meats and nuts. Maybe this arrangement will work for you, too. Eventually, your collection will expand, and you'll need to fit banana and artificial banana (like banana candy) in the same closet. Maybe they do both belong in fruit. Maybe one belongs in natural flavors while the other is in artificial flavors. Or they could both belong in the yellow category. In the next chapter we'll explore our associations between color and flavor.

You can build and arrange these categories as you collect flavors. So, if you're asked what you taste in a wine on a dinner date, you can go to the "plants" section of your memory to pull out *geranium* or *rose* instead of the typical *grape*.

It may be that learning about the way someone else organizes their flavor memory inspires you to throw out your system and restructure it. This kind of inspiration is one of many reasons that tasting with other people is beneficial. Group tasting can expand your vocabulary and shift your perspective on the flavors you sense from any dish. Discussing something as simple as salsa with the right group can be eye-opening. While you wait for your margaritas and entrees, have everyone taste the salsa and identify its strongest flavor. Then share the flavors you picked. Different palates may identify chili, onion, lime, or oregano as the most prominent ingredient. (Many traditional recipes use oregano instead of cilantro. Did you know Mexican oregano has lemon and citrus undertones while Italian oregano tends to be more grassy and minty?)

In professional tasting circles, asking questions and sharing tasting notes are imperative to communication. One coffee taster told me that Russian coffee tasters use the term *lalaberry*, to denote what she considers blackberry flavor. "You have to hear a term you don't know and then ask, or else you'll never really understand," she said.

You already know that we each live in our own individual taste world, so in matters of taste the aphorism, "There's no such thing as a stupid question," rings especially true. Go ahead and ask people to explain what they mean when they say something tastes like *pyrazines* (a technical wine tasting term) or *Tim Tams* (an Australian cookie). The answers will go toward expanding your flavor collection.

Tasting in groups has its benefits, but it's also important to avoid being biased by other people's opinions. Especially when it comes to tasting something for the first time. First tastes are really important. The taste of something naturally creates the memory for it, like my taste of damascenone in Bill's class. What you notice in that first taste becomes the definition of the flavor for you. This definition can be augmented by subsequent tastes, but never fully erased. We'll talk more about these memories in chapter 12, but for now, while you set out on your collection of new tastes and smells and flavors and textures, please don't screw it up for yourself.

One way to screw up a first taste is summed up aptly by culinary raconteur Anthony Bourdain, who described so many things in the world of food aptly, during a short rant about all the reasons that truffle oil is terrible: "It's evil and it has no relationship to truffles at all. It's an industrial solvent basically and a truffle is a beautiful, beautiful, beautiful thing. But if everything you eat that you think has truffle in it is jacked with truffle oil, when a [real] truffle comes along you will be totally oblivious to it." (*MUNCHIES: The Podcast*, December 23, 2016.)

He goes on to compare the expectations set by overpowering industrial-strength truffle oil to the expectations set by porn. He emphasizes that you'll never appreciate the magnificence of the natural thing if you're expecting the pumped up artificial version. A metaphor that perfectly encapsulates appreciating flavor the Bourdain way.

To be clear, I am not saying you need to go out and buy the most expensive ingredients and taste them all to set your reference memory (although, wouldn't that be fun?). I am saying that for your first taste you should endeavor to try the real thing, not an artificial version of it. If you've never tasted a papaya, a scoop of neon-orange papaya sorbet is not an ideal way to taste it the first time. Neither is a papaya mango green tea, where the flavor is part of a mixture. These are not going to give you an accurate reference for the flavor of papaya. Does this mean you should deprive yourself of the glowing orange sorbet beckoning to you? No! But when you taste that neon treat, take a moment to say to yourself, "This is papaya ice cream." And tuck it away in that section of your mental flavor closet as blue raspberry.

Another way to screw up the first impression of a flavor is tying it to a bad memory. Here's the truth: a flavor that made you barf is likely always going to make you want to barf. It's a result of our sensory memory functioning properly. This flavor clearly upset the delicate balance of your bodily functions and therefore is not invited back to the stomach . . . ever. Barfing is not the only way to create a bad flavor memory; you can do it intentionally, too. One way to do this is through an exercise that the pros call "off-flavor training" and I call "why-are-you-teaching-me-to-dislike-this-flavor training." Avoid at all costs adding any flavor to your collection under the context that it is "bad," a "taint," or a "flaw." A negative first association with a flavor is very hard to shake. It's like putting a shirt you hate into your closet, knowing you'll never wear it, even if an occasion calls for it. Every time you're looking for something to wear and you thumb past that terrible shirt on the hanger you remember how annoyed you were when you first got it. An example of this negative first association would be tasting a wine with barnyard (funky, musty, hay-like) flavors and learning those flavors are a flaw indicating that the wind is infected with wild yeast. After learning about this so-called flaw, you would always consider funky wine defective. So when natural wine, which showcases flavors from wild yeast, rises to popularity you can't enjoy it. You've considered those flavors "bad" for so long that a single whiff of barnyard and your brain reacts with "flaw."

Years before I learned to thoughtfully add flavors to my tasting vocabulary from Bill and other instructors, I had to commit six "off flavors" to memory to pass my Certified Cicerone exam. These are the flavors quality-assurance panelists (trained tasters who assess the final beer before it goes to market) are conditioned to recognize. The presence of these so-called "off flavors" can signal a mistake in the brewing process. Dimethyl sulfide (DMS) smells like creamed corn, and it's a sign that the boil on brew day was too short or sluggish. Buttery diacetyl signals incomplete fermentation. Acetic acid that tastes of sharp vinegar indicates stressed yeast. The list goes on. . . . Pure samples of "off flavors" are available for purchase, so I could practice sniffing cups of beer adulterated with these aromas to prepare for the exam. But these kits cost around sixty dollars, and I'd already spent more than two hundred dollars to sign up for the test. I figured I had a good sense of smell and I could identify aromas like corn and butter and certainly vinegar on exam day.

During the off flavor identification portion of the exam, I nosed a cup and assumed it must be the diacetyl, the compound described in all the study guides as "movie theater butter." I understood why people would call this scent butter, but in the context of the beer it wasn't really buttery, it was sweeter. Was it caramelly? Was it more like buttery toffee? After a few thoughtful sniffs, I determined it was enough like the buttered popcorn–flavored jelly beans that the correct answer must be diacetyl. And right there, under the stressful conditions of taking an exam, my flavor memory for diacetyl was imprinted: buttered-popcorn-jelly-bean flavor in my beer equals off flavor. My mind still signals "Beer flaw! Beer flaw!" whenever I smell diacetyl, although this buttery flavor is not always a mistake. The flavor profile of Czech lagers is partially defined by diacetyl. Soft buttery chardonnays simply reek of it, so do some aged cheddars. And guess what? People adore all those things and the flavor of diacetyl! Low levels can impart a pleasant velvety texture to wines and beer as well as trace caramel flavors that have a light amount of it. Yet many American brewers have a strong negative reaction to even a tiny amount of diacetyl because it is associated with being an off flavor. The buttered popcorn aroma is an ugly shirt in my flavor closet that I try on over and over again and I really wish I could like.

Designations of "flaw" or "off flavor" are not the only labels that will get in the way of appreciating flavor. Sulfur compounds can be stinky; that's why they are used in literal stink bombs and as an additive to natural gas to alert us to potential leaks. But these compounds are also essential to the aromas of grapefruit, strawberry, tropical fruits, and fermented beverages like wine and beer. A trace amount of sulfur can be interpreted by our brain as an indication of freshness. Confronting these negative labels will also make you a better taster of the world. Rather than immediately disliking a new food and banishing it to the back of your flavor closet, ask yourself what you don't like about it. Is it the context you tasted it in? Does it remind you of another flavor? Is it that you're nervous about trying something new? Refusing to label any flavor as "bad" forces you to ask interesting questions that go beyond tasting.

A Sake Samurai (yes, a very real and very prestigious title!) tells me that in sake judging in Japan, TCA (the "corked" flavor discussed in chapter 2) isn't considered a flaw. The Japanese master sake makers can sense it, but for them TCA is part of sake's profile and doesn't have a negative connotation. This can be tough for judges from other parts of the world to wrap their minds around. It wouldn't be difficult to accept TCA as just another tasting note if they hadn't already classified it as a flaw. A 2001 study found that we react differently to the same aroma when it is given two different names. The same mixture of acids was presented as either "vomit" or "Parmesan cheese." Participants' ratings of how much they liked the aroma changed drastically depending on which label it had. The Parmesan aroma was rated as generally positive or neutral while the vomit aroma was rated as definitely negative.

Furthermore, when it comes to food trends, yesterday's "flaw" is today's chic flavor. Natural wine has those wild barnyard flavors that winemakers tried to avoid for centuries. Hazy IPAs flipped decades of efforts to make beers brilliantly clear on their heads. Ya dong, a version of moonshine infused with harshly bitter herbs, has made it from the street stalls of Thailand alleys to being savored in gold plated cups at fashionable cocktail bars. Fermented flavors, always considered a "flaw" in coffee, are now coming in vogue. If you had already marked those "flaws" as negative flavors in your sensory memory, you wouldn't get to enjoy the innovation around you.

In this chapter, you've learned about the importance of repetition in building a mental collection of flavor references. You've considered how you'll categorize these memories. You've examined the significance of first tastes and you're wary of adding anything with a negative connotation to your flavor collection. Now, you're ready to get out there and collect flavor memories. Here I'll outline a few exercises to help you discover new flavors and amass an extraordinary wardrobe of flavors to try on.

THE REPETITION EXERCISE

As you can see from Logan, myself, and the honey tasters, the most reliable way to permanently add something to your mental flavor collection is through repetition. Once you've tasted something so many times that recognizing its flavor becomes second nature, it becomes a reference you can pull out when tasting other things, say a wine on a dinner date. Rather than saying wine tastes like grapes, you can sense the fruitiness and relate it to one of your mental reference standards, for example blackberries or sweet cherries.

This exercise starts with repetition and ends with a quiz, the same method Dr. Bill Simpson uses. It doesn't require any specialized flavor references or tools, and it's a task that is possible to practice either alone or with other people.

Step 1 Gather your tastants. This step can be as simple as grabbing a few jars of spices from the pantry or going to the store to purchase different fruits. Three to five tastants is an ideal number for beginners.

Step 2 Prep your tastants. It is important that all of the tastants are in the same type of container or jar. For spices in matching jars, this step is already done for you. For edible tastants like fruits (or cheese, or nuts), cut each tastant into equal-sized cubes and place them into small bowls or ramekins that are the same size. In this step, you're doing your best to erase any difference between the tastants other than their flavor. The goal is to have the jars or bowls feel exactly the same when you close your eyes and lift them.

Step 3 The tasting method. Perform the seven-step tasting method outlined in Chapter 4 on each of the tastants. While performing the tasting method, say out loud the name of the tastant, describe what it reminds you of, and mention any facts you know about it. An example of what you may say while smelling a jar of cinnamon would be, "Cinnamon, cinnamon sticks. Cinnamon reminds me of the holidays and mulled apple cider. Cinnamon comes from Indonesia. Cinnamon." Repeat steps 1–3 on each tastant two or three times and focus on tying the words you speak to the flavors you smell and taste.

Step 4 The sniff-only assessment. Once you've run through the full tasting method on each tastant, the next step is to go down the line of tastants and assess each only using smell. This process is more rapid than the tasting method. Simply give each tastant a few different smells, maybe a moving sniff, followed by a short sniff, and finally a long sniff. All along continue to say the name of the tastant aloud.

Step 5 The aroma quiz. If you have a tasting partner, you can take turns closing your eyes and handing each other bowls or jars to smell. If you are practicing alone, close your eyes and mix the bowls or jars around on the table so you don't know which tastant is which. Then, reach for one bowl at a time. Smell the aroma of the tastant and guess which of your tastants you are smelling. Even if you are tasting alone, say your guess out loud. Then set the jar or bowl down to your right. As you guess through the remaining tastants be sure you place the used bowls or jars in order so when you open your eyes, you can check your answers. Try not to open your eyes between guesses.

Step 6 Repeat. A few days or a few hours later, try the quiz again without performing steps 1–4 first. Were you still able to identify all of the tastants? Which tastants were the easiest for you? Which were the most difficult? For difficult to identify tastants, consider finding a new story or memory to say out loud when you practice or creating a new memory to help you recognize the taste. For instance, if you have a hard time differentiating cinnamon and clove, try making cookies using only clove as the spice or putting cinnamon in your morning coffee every day for a week.

HINTS:

- This exercise is designed to help you build flavor references, the reliable favorite shirt of the flavor wardrobe that you return to over and over again, so your tastants should be basic and straightforward. Think cubes of mango, not spiced mango chutney, or smelling pure cinnamon, not a pumpkin spice blend. For more complex tastants like wines, teas, or jams with multiple fruit flavors, use the side-by-side exercise below.

- Take the spoken words up a notch by recording a voice memo for each tastant and playing it while you taste. Playing the audio allows you to focus on tasting while listening to the notes rather than multitasking by both tasting and speaking. Making these voice memos and then tasting as they play is how I prepare for tasting exams.

THE SIDE-BY-SIDE EXERCISE

THIS EXERCISE WILL HELP YOU IDENTIFY FLAVORS IN A MIXTURE AND also build flavor profiles for complex tastants like wines, spirits, coffees, and specialty products. I find this exercise especially enlightening when tasting items I think I know very well, for example, tasting three beers: a German Helles (should be the least bitter), next to a Czech Pilsner, next to a German Pilsner (should be the most bitter). You may do this with different apple varieties (are you sure Honeycrisp is your favorite apple?) or several kinds of wine, or even a smattering of ice creams.

The idea is to objectively taste and find the differences between each item through observation, rather than relying on definitions of what the different beers, wines, or ice creams "should" taste like.

Tea is a good medium to start with because there are so many teas that are generally considered "green tea," but they have vastly different flavor profiles. One green tea can be earthy and herbal like damp mint leaves while another is floral with touches of lemon oil. Sampling a single green tea makes it hard to pick out these nuances, but when there are two teas next to each other, you have a chance to discern the differences.

> **Step 1** Gather your tastants. All of the tastants should come from the same category. If you're not a specialist in the category, it's helpful to make sure the tastants have marked differences. For example, don't get three different teas labeled "Sencha green tea"; instead, try a sencha green tea, a gunpowder green tea, and a jasmine green tea. Once you know teas well, you can try tasting three highly similar teas.

> **Step 2** Prep your tastants. Once again, make sure all tastants are the same temperature, in the same container, and cut or poured to the same serving size.

> **Step 3** The smell comparison. Sniff each tastant. Say aloud the name of the tastant and the primary aroma you notice in it. For example, during a tasting of green teas you might say, "Jasmine green tea, flowers," or "Sencha green tea, grassy."

> **Step 4** The clarification. In a tasting of similar items, you may describe the dominant flavor in multiple tastants with the same word. For instance, if you mentioned that more than one green tea smelled grassy it is time to clarify the difference. Does one grass aroma seem more muted? Maybe, that one is dry grass and the other is fresh cut grass. Or it

could be that after you take another sniff, the aroma of one tea seems more smoky, like burnt grass, compared to the other that is like true green grass. It's okay, even encouraged, to change your mind about what is the prominent flavor of each tastant as you closely study the aromas.

Step 5 The multi-tasting method. Now, perform the tasting method on your tastants all at the same time. So, you will perform the see step on tastant 1, tastant 2, tastant 3, etc . . . and then move on to the sniff step for each of the tastants, and so on.

Step 6 Synthesize the differences. We always synthesize as the final step of the tasting method, but take this time to consider how the things you're tasting differ. One green tea will be the sweetest, one will be the most tannic, one will have the most intense flavor.

Step 7 The definition. Taste each tastant again and say out loud the name of the tastant, the primary flavor of the tastant, and how it compares to the other tastants. For example, "This is Sencha green tea. It smells of green grass, it has a more green fresh flavor than the other teas, and it has the longest aftertaste."

HINTS:

- The above outline is the dependable way to add the flavors of the items you're comparing to your flavor memory. However, this exercise doesn't need to be so formal. It can happen anytime you're tasting multiple items of a similar category. At a wine bar, you can compare your current glass to the previous wine you had. Or if you eat many of the same item, for example a morning banana, you can compare the way today's fruit tastes different from yesterday's.

- Don't become discouraged. When you're starting out, it is hard to put the differences between tastes and smells into words. Even if you can't verbalize them, pay attention to the differences you sense in the flavor profiles. Over time, you'll get better at describing precise shifts in flavor.

THE TASTE-AS-YOU-COOK EXERCISE

This exercise has less structure than the others, but it is still one of the best ways to collect specific flavors and add them to your mental flavor wardrobe. As you prepare a dish, smell and taste every element individually (but skip uncooked ingredients e.g. raw eggs, meats, seafood) and taste the entirety of the dish after each addition. If you were caramelizing onions, taste both the cooking oil and the raw onions before you add them to the pan. Then taste an onion before you add the salt. Finally taste them after they've caramelized.

Doing this simple taste-as-you-cook exercise will create flavor memories for ingredients in both their raw and cooked forms and may help you discover the true character of some common ingredients. Vanilla extract is part of the majority of dessert recipes, but have you ever tasted it on its own? Standard cooking butter and canola oil have a similar flavor when tasted cool straight from the refrigerator or pantry.

HINT:

- Try changing the order you add some ingredients in simple recipes. Make a vinaigrette by adding oil, vinegar, then mustard, followed by salt; next time add oil, mustard, then salt, followed by vinegar, tasting as you go. Did you notice the flavor profile of your dressing change? What does the vinegar add other than sourness?

THE 20 QUESTIONS EXERCISE

THIS EXERCISE FOR COLLECTING MEMORIES TO OUTFIT YOUR FLAVOR wardrobe requires a partner. It's another way to incorporate thoughtfully tasting into everyday activities.

Tonight, or the next time you plan to go out, order a drink for the person you're with and in turn, ask them to order your drink. You will have to get your server to play along and keep the drink orders a secret. I've found telling them you're surprising each other and pointing to the drink on the menu keeps the secret without being a hassle for your server. Once the drinks arrive, taste and play 20 questions until you correctly guess what's in your glass. A conversation could look like this:

"It tastes fruity; is it tropical fruit?"

"No, but you're on the right track with fruity."

"Apples?"

"No."

"Berries then?"

"Now you're onto something."

"And there is a lot of carbonation and sweetness. Oh, it's cherry?"

"Yep."

"Oh my gosh, you ordered me a Shirley Temple?"

"Yes!"

HINTS:

- Take note of the questions you use to narrow down what could possibly be in your glass. The initial three to five questions tend to be category-based questions. As in the example above, the questioner clearly has a mental category for fruits designating whether they are tropical or non-tropical. The way you naturally whittle down possible answers is an indication of how you subconsciously group flavors.

- You don't necessarily have to close your eyes for this one, but try not to pay too much attention to the appearance of your drink. As you'll learn in the next chapter, what we see can really mess with what we taste!

You aren't limited to drink orders with this game, order each other dessert or pick up a random item from the grocery store. Drinks are simply a low stakes order that make it easy to incorporate a little tasting into a night out.

———⬤

KEEPING YOUR MIND AND PALATE OPEN TO NEW FLAVORS MAY EXPOSE you to some funky tastes, but in the end, exploring and expanding your flavor closet is never a bad thing. Several years ago, to celebrate my husband's birthday, I booked an omakase meal. Omakase is a style of serving sushi based on the chef's choice. The chef shapes each rice ball with his hands, carefully tops it with fish of his choice, and hands it directly to diners, who should eat it right away. Some chefs will place the fastidiously prepared pieces of nigiri directly into the diners' hand while others place it on a plate for them to eat.

This sort of direct access to the chef is nothing less than heaven for a taster shaping their flavor collection. We were able to clarify what made the raw tuna higher grade and what we should look for in a good piece. (Fatty pieces cut from the lowest part of the tuna belly, otoro, are more expensive and should melt in your mouth like cotton candy. Lean tuna, called akami, can be judged on its quality by its lack of fishiness and overall clean taste rather than any specific flavor.) We found out that ebi (shrimp) are the sweetest and creamiest in late autumn when they eat more to prepare for the winter. At the end of the meal, we were able to order a few extra pieces of nigiri from the chef if we were still hungry. We weren't hungry anymore, but we were having fun, so we asked Chef Toshio if he had anything we had never tried before, something that would be totally new to us. He looked at us quizzically, but he had just spent a little over an hour answering our questions and watching us nose each piece before delicately placing it on our tongues with our eyes closed. I think he could tell we appreciated his skill.

"Okay, it is very different," he said, and paused, piquing our interest. "Do you want to try crab brain?"

Kani miso is called crab brain, but it is actually only *partially* crab brain. It is a mixture of all the organs and other nonwhite-meat parts of a crab mixed together into a paste-like concoction that has the texture of whipped cream cheese with a little grittiness. Rather than feeling like sand caught in an oyster, it's like soft grits of chestnut shell. At first, the flavor is sweet, then it transforms to be a bit like a bitter mineral chalk, with a hint of dark grassiness similar to very, very dry parsley. It's not exactly pleasant. But it is memorable. And it was a new flavor for my collection. And it's a moment I'll never forget. So often at a bar, when you ask the bartender to "surprise me," they'll give you a tame cocktail. They have no interest in making you a new drink if you send their creation back. I can safely say kani miso, that gray-green paste reminiscent of wet concrete placed thoughtfully on a beautifully formed rice ball, was anything but tame.

We have been back to Tanoshi Sushi many times and had the pleasure of dining with or close to Chef Toshio. I haven't tried crab brain again, but its flavor reference is still very clear in my memory. In late 2018, Chef Toshio passed away. I'll never forget the flavor he gifted me with. It's weird and specific and it's in my collection forever.

CHAPTER SIX

BLINDED BY THE SIGHT

"OH GOD, THAT WAS HARD," THE CHEF WHO IS THE WINNER OF MULtiple James Beard awards tells me. "All I was doing was second-guessing myself. It was so much pressure."

This wasn't the pressure of an overcrowded restaurant on opening night, or even the stress of a newspaper review. This pressure was brought on by a lone piece of fabric: a blindfold. Chef Rick Bayless had made it all the way to the penultimate episode of *Top Chef Masters* without a single misstep. After fashioning street food out of offal and cooking a gluten- and soy-free vegan meal for actress Zooey Deschanel, it seems like the producers couldn't invent a test that would shake the experienced chef. But all it took was one unassuming piece of fabric to have him shaking in his shoes.

The four chef finalists would have to taste twenty simple ingredients without using their sense of sight, hence the blindfold. It's an intimidating challenge. One of Rick's competitors, Michelin-starred chef

Hubert Keller, said, "I feel nervous about the challenge. The sense of sight for a chef is very important because you eat first with your eyes. It is a very difficult challenge."

Hubert was right; all the chefs struggled. Michelin-starred chef Anita Lo thought hummus was tahini paste. Hubert identified chervil as parsley. To Michael Chiarello, mascarpone tasted like sour cream.

Rick had a rough start, immediately identifying hoisin sauce as ranch dressing, and cubed mango as plum. "I know when my chefs at home see this, they are going to make lots of fun of me." He sighed. Even with items like corn, almonds, and maple syrup in the mix, out of twenty possible points, the winner among all of these "master" chefs identified just seven foods correctly. Six correct answers were enough to place Rick in a tie for second with Anita, who said to the camera, "It was really nice to tie with Rick, who I know has a great palate and is really an incredible chef." She sounded relieved.

This episode is one of those very satisfying moments for a TV viewer. Sitting comfortably on the couch, they are certain that they'd do better at this challenge of identifying ingredients blindfolded. A basic blindfold isn't enough to turn the dark, salty tang of hoisin into the dill-flecked taste of ranch! It's an ego boost to think they are smarter than the well-known chef floundering on the television. But before viewers go too hard on Rick (or his competitors Michael and Anita, who passed on the hoisin sauce completely and refused to make a guess at all), let's do a little experiment to imagine what it might be like standing there in his chef shoes. This challenge requires no timer, no food samples, no blindfold, and not even a celebrity judge to tell you how you've done. All you need is your mind.

Ready? Clear your mind and imagine the flavor of a green bell pepper. Only that flavor. Summon the sensation of exactly what you taste when you bite through the skin of a fresh green bell pepper. Do you have that flavor held in your mind? Hold it there and count to five.

Next, imagine you're eating green bell pepper in slices. In your mind, conjure the flavor you sense when eating a single slice. Has the flavor changed? Hold on to it as you count down from three. Three, two, one. Now, open your eyes. You did close your eyes, didn't you? Most people will close their eyes at least twice during that exercise. In order to remember a flavor, we'll automatically picture the food that gives us that flavor and close our eyes to get a clearer picture. I never asked you to visualize a pepper, but I'm certain you did anyway. Tying the concept and memory of particular flavors to sight is a natural inclination because it is how we categorize everything else in our life. Birds, clothes, trees, our family members—we know what they are when we see them. Some of the names we use for foods are tied to their appearance: star fruit, blueberries, Buddha's-hand. If you add grapes to your shopping list, you'll jot down red or green grapes rather than sweet or tart grapes; their actual names—Flame Tokay grapes (red) and sultanas or Thompson seedless (green)—never come to mind. Before we taste a flavor, we see what is about to go into our mouths. Our mind constructs a cause-and-effect relationship: there's a tropical, starchy, sweet flavor in my mouth. The last thing I saw was a mango. Therefore, we conclude that this starchy, sweet flavor is from the mango. Take that visual cue away. There's still a sweet, slightly starchy, definitely fruit flavor in your mouth. Was the cause mango, or was it plum, like Rick guessed?

"The fruit, I didn't have an idea what it was," Rick says. "It flipped me back to thinking just how much I rely on my eyes to narrow down the flavors." Of course, if he had seen it, even if it did taste like plum, he would have known the orange fruit wasn't a plum. Once he saw the color, his mind would think through what orange fruits the sample could be, and likely come up with mango.

It's like that children's card matching game, the one that begins with twelve cards face down. Each turn, the child can flip over two cards in search of a match. The dog matches with the doghouse, an umbrella matches a rain cloud, etc. Tasting behind a blindfold, we'd all, even lauded chefs like Bayless, be reduced to playing our own mental card matching game with our flavor memories. That green pepper image you inadvertently conjured in your mind's eye is one card in the pair. The green pepper taste, that slightly bitter, grassy flavor you experience, is its match. However, that taste is also a match for the pyrazines in some red wines, and it's not all that much different from the match for green peas. Without a blindfold, it's indisputable that the flavor is coming from a pepper, not a pea, or a glass of wine. With the blindfold, that clarity is gone. Now, one card sits on the tongue. The other, the visual to match that taste, is somewhere in the mind. I can imagine Rick flicking through the mental images frantically testing each idea: *Is this the match? Apricot? No. Papaya? No. Nectarine? No. Plum? Sure!*

In their work, chefs never need to taste their ingredients blind. In fact, it all goes back to what his competitor said when they were confronted with the challenge: "You eat first with your eyes." It is chefs just like Rick and Brooke Williamson who create the strong tie between what we see on the plate and our expectations for what we will taste. Brooke rose to fame on the *Top Chef* series and has racked up more victories in the show's signature blind tasting challenges than any other "cheftestant." At her three California restaurants, Brooke always considers how flavor matches the visual on the plate. "I try to never present a dish to people that needs explaining," she says. "I really want the food to speak for itself."

A new dish on her menu at Playa Provisions is a simply grilled chicken with chili orange sauce. But just having heat in the sauce wasn't enough. "I wanted [diners] to be able to see the chilies," she says. "I added a touch of Korean chili flake and some Fresno chilies. So you can see that the heat is there. The flecks of chili are visual in the sauce."

This visual trigger that subconsciously sets flavor expectations is a form of the concept known as priming. Visual priming is a phe-nomenon where seeing one stimulus influences a viewer's response to a subsequent situation, without the viewer's conscious awareness of the influence. An example of priming at work would be seeing a lemon on a can of soda and rating its citrus flavor as more intense than you rated it before seeing the can. Chef Brooke is priming her diners: See this chili. Now, you'll taste this chili.

Our expectations are primed on the dinner plate, but even more so in the wineglass. "We think red wine and white wine are so dif-ferent," says Rick. "At staff tastings we've had people close their eyes completely, taste wine. And we'll say, 'Okay, is it white or red?'" He pauses for dramatic effect and a giggle. "And lots of people had trouble figuring that out."

On the table, a white wine triggers thoughts of light citrus and tropical fruit, and pairs with fish. Red, on the other hand, draws out thoughts of boldness, berries, tannins, and pairs well with red meat. Even if that isn't how the two categories actually taste. A famous wine-tasting study published in 2001 was reportedly a "cheeky little test" that proves "wine 'experts' know no more than the rest of us," as Adam Sage put it in an *Independent* article. The study, by Frédéric Brochet (at the time a PhD candidate at the University of Bordeaux II in Talence, France) and his colleagues, was summarized to show that "wine experts" were unable to tell a white wine dyed red with flavorless coloring from an actual red wine. Because the "experts" described the dyed white wine with typical red wine characteristics, they demon-strated once and for all that wine tasting was, in effect, a bunch of junk.

This study has always fascinated me. Are visual cues so powerful that they can completely obscure the cues of smell and taste? Perhaps driven by my own defiance of the concept, I dug into how the study was conducted. Frédéric had fifty-four of his oenology students— practiced tasters but still students of wine, not experts in wine (ah the exaggerations of the media)—conduct two routine tastings of a red wine and a white wine. At the tasting, they were given a list of common wine descriptors and asked to match those descriptors with each wine, or add their own words. In the first tasting, the red wine was a 1996 Bordeaux made from cabernet sauvignon and merlot grapes and the white was a 1996 Bordeaux made from sémillon and sauvignon grapes.

One week later, the students returned for a second tasting. They were once again presented with a red wine, a white wine, and a list of descriptors. This time, the list of descriptors consisted of words they chose at the previous tasting. It was their own words they had used to describe the red or white wine the prior week given back to them in alphabetical order. The task was the same: assign the descriptors from the list to either the red or the white wine. Little did the students know that the wines they were assigning descriptors to were actually the same white wine, except one glass had been colored with a flavorless red dye. Yes, the wine students were successfully tricked and, overall, still gave the dyed red wine far more red wine descriptors than the white even though they were describing the same wine. And so, the top-line takeaway was born: you can trick "wine experts" with dye; tasting is BS! But a nuanced look at the results reveals something more interesting.

The number of "red wine terms" used to describe the dyed-red wine shrank by 35 percent compared to those used in the first tasting (of a real red wine). This indicates that the tasters were less confident in selecting descriptors. That inkling is, in my mind, confirmed by the fact that the number of "white wine terms" used to describe the white wine also shrank by roughly 15 percent compared to the first tasting. It's like the tasters had an idea that something was wrong, and the descriptions weren't matching up, but the influence of the visual color cue was too strong to fight. Rather than exhibiting that wine expertise is meaningless (and once again I have to point out that these were undergraduate students studying wine, not a bunch of Master Sommeliers!), this study shows how much weight we give visual cues even when they stand in contrast to our intuition. As the saying goes: seeing is believing.

Perhaps if the oenology students were given a *Top Chef* blindfold to wear during their taste test they would have performed better. In fact, had there been any indication that the wines may have been tampered with they certainly would have paid closer attention to their tasting notes. Instead they defaulted to their expectations set by visual priming and past experience.

The priming expectations set by color don't end with wine, though there is the most scientific research dedicated to this phenomenon in relation to wine. When I teach blind-tasting classes, I conduct a test to prove to my students just how much they rely on their sight. I call it "the half blind." The exercise goes like this: I tell every other student to close their eyes. Each eyes-open student has an eyes-closed student on either side. Once eyes are shut, I pour a sample of a beer that appears dark but has the flavor of a light lager (this is traditionally called a schwarzbier if you'd like to try one yourself). Everyone tastes the beer (which by this point you know means ortho- and retronasal sniffs followed by a swirl and sample of it). The eyes-open crowd writes down their top three tasting notes on a sheet of paper. Once they are done writing, the eyes-closed crew, one by one, says their top three tasting notes out loud. The eyes-open group usually looks completely perplexed as words like *bread*, *cereal*, and *herbal* are listed. Then the eyes-closed students are allowed to open their eyes and read the descriptions written by the eyes-open group. They see words like *coffee*, *campfire*, *burnt bread*, and *ash*. Each group pokes fun at the other, especially as couples and friends tend to be split down the middle.

"How could you taste coffee? There's totally no coffee!"

"Yeah, well, I don't think 'cold' counts as a tasting note."

I explain that both groups are right and both groups are wrong;

there are very subtle chocolate and caramel notes that can be hard to pick up on without the color cue, but those dark flavors are never harsh like burnt bread or bitter like dark coffee in a schwarzbier.

Visual priming is not the only form of priming. The triggers that lead to misidentifying a flavor or conjuring a phantom one can be much more subtle. During our whiskey tasting Ben asked me, "Do you get the cucumber in this one?"

I sniffed and swirled a little bit, took a whiff of my shoulder as a palate cleanser, and sniffed again. "Ugh, I'm not getting it," I told him, feeling a little dejected. "Maybe I'm not sensitive enough to these aromas to find it under the caramel."

"No, no, there isn't any cucumber." He laughed. "Sometimes that works, though; people will just say, 'Oh, yes, wow. Fresh!'"

Ben's suggestion primed me to find cucumber in the glass even though it wasn't there. I have a very strong reference in my mental flavor wardrobe for cucumber, so his suggestion wasn't enough to sway my palate. But a less experienced taster could easily be misled.

Written tasting notes on food packaging are another form of priming. Brooklyn Brewery's Black Chocolate Stout doesn't have any actual chocolate in the recipe, but the name helps consumers find the chocolatey notes from the roasted barley in the beer. Tillamook's Maker's Reserve cheese tastes like a quality white cheddar with classic nutty and dairy flavors. It is only once you read the description about the cheese that those notes transform to be very clear flavors of hazelnut and custard.

We don't even need written flavor descriptions for a package to prime our taste buds; simply seeing one number is enough: the price. Numerous studies have proven that we don't just *think* wine tastes better when we know it is more expensive, it literally tastes better. Areas of the brain associated with pleasure and reward show greater activity when test subjects taste a wine they are told is more expensive. This benefit in brain activity occurs even if they had just tasted the same wine but were told it costs less.

Sometimes you don't need to be primed by price, tasting notes, or your tasting partners' suggestions. Sometimes the flavor suggestion can come from within your own mind. Especially when tasting under pressure.

Master Sommelier Fernando Beteta was under this kind of pressure during the tasting portion of his exam. He breezed by the theory and service sections of the exam, but he kept tripping up when he had to face the blind tasting. On his fourth (and final!) attempt at the tasting exam, he realized he needed to pay attention to the difference between his thoughts and what he was actually sensing.

"I learned you can't put anything in that glass," Fernando says. "You might want to. You might think if it just smelled a little more this way it would be a classic example." For instance, if a red wine on the exam presents with an aroma of pyrazine (like olive tapenade or roasted pepper) it's tempting to seek out flavors of new oak and jammy blackberries that would make the wine a classic California cabernet sauvignon, even though they aren't really there. That's what Fernando means about putting flavors into the glass with your mind as opposed to sensing them objectively. To find success in blind tasting you have to quiet the brain enough to observe the wine like a scientific subject: without expectations or bias. Then, you have to catch your thoughts when they are trying to play tricks on your senses.

In order to help blind tasters avoid these mental pitfalls as they deduce what is in the glass, certification bodies like the Wine & Spirits Education Trust and Court of Master Sommeliers have created their respective "deductive tasting grids." A grid functions as a tasting worksheet to guide students through each aspect of a wine, from appearance to aroma to palate to conclusion. (To see examples of tasting grids, visit howtotastebook.com/grid.) The goal of filling out each section of the grid is to force a slow and objective tasting process that individually covers each aspect of a wine, spirit, or sake—like intensity of aroma, sweetness of palate, and length of finish. The tasters will make anywhere from nineteen to thirty-five observations along the way. This deliberate, systematized assessment keeps wine tasters from rushing to conclusions like the above example of jumping from pyrazines to cabernet sauvignon.

Once these data points have been collected using the grid it is time to use deductive reasoning to determine what exact wine they are tasting, hence the name "deductive tasting grid." Deductive reasoning is a thought process that uses a series of premises that build on one another to arrive at a conclusion. For example: All rose bushes have thorns. This bush is a rose bush. This bush must have thorns. With one incorrect premise, deductive reason can go very wrong. A single fallacy destroys the whole chain of logic. In this case, all rose bushes do not have thorns; the Smooth Prince Hybrid Tea Rose is thornless and as lovely as any other rose. Therefore, the conclusion, "This bush must have thorns," is incorrect. In the tasting grid, this may come down to recording a wood aroma as French oak when the aroma was really American oak, which would lead you to conclude the wrong wine through deduction.

When the process of deduction goes right, the mental calculus to reach the correct conclusion plays out like another children's game: Guess Who? Instead of cartoonishly drawn faces on each panel of the board, there are all the various wine styles (or beer, or sake, or cheese, depending on what you're deducing in the blind tasting). Using the sensory information from the grid, panels are eliminated one by one. For instance, if it's a red wine, go ahead and knock all the white wine panels down. (No, no one is tricking you with a vial of red dye on the Sommelier exam.) You wrote medium plus tannin on the grid, so flip down panels like low tannin Beaujolais. It tastes like American oak, so topple all the images of French wines. If all goes according to plan, there will be one panel remaining. A wine that perfectly matches the evidence collected on the grid. The wine style on the panel will be the wine in your glass.

Now all you have to do is repeat this deduction process involving dozens of sensory criteria and hundreds of potential styles of wine six times, for three whites and three reds. In twenty-five minutes. So, four minutes and ten seconds per wine. And did I mention that the Master Sommelier candidates are playing this mental board game while describing the wine out loud to the judges?

Even armed with a deductive tasting grid and a strong collection of flavor memories for each wine style, it's enough pressure to make any taster anxious. Fortunately, most people will never need to hone this skill. But for the small group of people who do (usually in pursuit of a professional certification or top honors on shows like *MasterChef* and *Top Chef*), blind tasting is as much about mastering the palate as it is about mastering the mind.

Chef Brooke Williamson's blind-tasting performance is legendary in the *Top Chef* series. She blew away the competition, beating out her closest competitor by five correct identifications. Even though she didn't need the point, she would have scored one more if she slowed down and listened to her palate.

As a timer ticked down, Brooke was flying through the little glass bowls filled with mystery ingredients and racking up points for correctly identifying cucumber, okra, clam, and pistachio. "Sherry vinegar, next," she asserted, handing the glass to judge Padma Lakshmi. "No, wait! That was balsamic!" But with the word *next*, she had locked in her answer. It was too late, and she lost that point. After finishing her twenty tastes Brooke lowered her blindfold and simultaneously blurted out, "Gahhhhh, it was balsamic, wasn't it?"

Padma smiled with a hint of a nod.

"You can't second-guess yourself, that's the most important thing." Brooke tells me she thrives under pressure, which is why she loves the pace of the kitchen as well as the pace of reality cooking shows. She not only holds the title of Top Chef, but she's also the first-ever winner of the Food Network's *Tournament of Champions*. Keeping a clear head and moving precisely when tension is the highest is her secret to excelling at these challenges, and what her competitors couldn't quite grasp. According to Brooke, the people who said "totally insane things" behind the blindfold were all overthinking. "Someone called 'butter' as 'flour' or something like that"—she laughs—"but his rationality was that it tasted like some kind of dough. The minute you start rationalizing, you're not using your instincts."

Brooke says second-guessing yourself is the death of a blind taster, and the Master Sommelier candidates would agree.

Fernando Beteta says of the first three times he took his Master Sommelier exam, "I was doing things I knew were wrong, doing things like going back to change my answer on a glass after I had already moved on," he said. "But there was so much pressure. You work all year for this."

By the fourth time he faced the six glasses on the blind-tasting portion of the exam he was ready to relax and observe them objectively. On that final attempt he said he sat back, crossed his legs, and told himself he would go with his initial conclusions and not overthink them. And with that mindset, he passed the hardest wine exam in the world.

Jonathan Eichholz tells me he's coming up with a similar plan for his second attempt at the Master Sommelier exam. "The first time I took it there was so much pressure," he tells me over lunch in Midtown. "I was like, *I have to do this. I have to get through this test.*"

I related to the anxiety Jonathan felt in the blind tasting. During one of the tasting portions of my first attempt at the Master Cicerone exam, I felt self-doubt rising upon my first sniff of a beer sample. Suddenly, I couldn't smell a single identifying aspect of the beer. Panic mounted and it felt like a physical sensation of buzzing in my skull that blocked me from accessing my objective senses. I was trying to recognize the beer style through sheer willpower rather than calmly evaluating my sample the way I had hundreds of times before in my studies. This act of giving into anxiety is a recipe for blind tasting disaster—the kind of disaster Jonathan would do everything in his power to avoid.

"Honestly, I've been doing a lot of yoga and looking at art," he said. "I have to know that if I don't pass it, I'll be able to take another attempt. And I'm still me. You have to be able to forget about the pressure."

Jonathan also has a plan for how he'll approach each glass, and if he follows it, there won't be any room for uncertainty to mislead him.

"What I will do is get that wine on my palate. Smell it and taste it before I start talking to the judges about sight," Jonathan said. "That way, while I'm doing this performative thing, I am deducing the wine in my head."

He tells me that appearance points are the easy points. He has the opportunity to collect himself mentally while he runs through the appearance section of the deductive tasting grid. When the time comes to enumerate aroma, taste, finish, and eventually call a style, he'll be calm, cool, and collected.

That's where the yoga and plan for a relaxed approach come in. Every candidate for the Master Sommelier exam will have some sort of game plan going into the tasting. These hopeful sommeliers in their tailored suits assessing fine wines are like super yachts gliding gracefully through the ocean. Everyone on board sees luxury and well-groomed furnishings and hears the classical music piped through each of the lavish rooms. But that music is playing to obscure the hundreds of decibels of noise created by the boat's massive engine. And in the control room, out of the guests' view, lights are flashing and pistons are pumping in barely organized chaos. The engine room, of course, is the sommelier's brain. Candidates like Jonathan will explain the eight parts of the tasting grid focused on appearance to the judges while simultaneously analyzing the wine's body and structure in their mind. See, engine room roaring, yacht gliding by.

Blind tasting doesn't need to take place in a high-pressure environment. It's also a great exercise to help you explore the nuances of your own palate. This is one reason that Chef Bayless, who went on to win *Top Chef Masters* that season, thinks that not only is the blind-tasting challenge a fair assessment of a chef's skills but also that those skills are very necessary. And they seem especially necessary when it comes to winning the title of Top Chef specifically. In the nine instances that *Top Chef* has aired a blind-tasting challenge of some kind, the contestant who goes on to win the season finished in the top three all but once (beloved Chicago chef Stephanie Izard won her season even though she finished dead last in the blind-tasting challenge).

"At each one of my restaurants we're tasting all the time." Chef Bayless says a new menu at Topolo, his refined restaurant with a fixed tasting menu, will go through a half dozen tasting sessions before the public ever gets to look at it. There are two tastings once the dishes have been developed to perfect them and decide to put them on the menu copy. Then another tasting with the sommeliers. Another one with more staff. Then a tasting specifically to decide pairings. All of these tastings are done without telling his staff exactly what is in the dish. It is not until the grand finale tasting that the menu is presented with the descriptions and the pairings to all of the staff. During all of those tastings, Rick and his team are looking for feedback about flavors that are hard to understand or feel confusing or seem out of place.

"You can't work here if you're egotistical about your dishes," says Rick. "If one person along the way says, 'I don't know what's going on with this dish, but it's got a finish that reminds me of cherry Jolly

Ranchers.' We'll start over completely. I don't want anyone tasting cherry Jolly Ranchers in my food." He says he personally might not taste the cherry candies in the flavor profile, but he'll still go back to the drawing board with the dish because taste is subjective and occasionally, he is the odd one out. Staff regularly tells him he's put too much garlic in a dish. He loves the flavor but must not be very sensitive to it because his chefs will say, "No more garlic, please. I think you're right on the edge there."

That learning from his staff tastings has extended to other parts of his empire, especially recipe writing for his website and cookbooks. "I learned that I love garlic, I love it, but other people might be put off by it. I had to stop putting in my recipes three or more cloves of garlic," Rick explains, "because I'll use more, but three might even seem like a lot to some people."

If you're not afraid to learn where your biases lurk, try blind tasting. Maybe you've always spent more money on wine to get only the best Grand Crus grown in France. A bottle from your local vineyard would probably offend your fine palate so you skip drinking wine when you can't source it from France. But taste them blind next to each other with a calm mind, not attempting to determine which is which, and you may be surprised at the one you select as a favorite.

This was the exact premise behind the iconic 1976 wine tasting now referred to as the Judgment of Paris (although at the time it had a less grand moniker, the Paris Wine Tasting). The proprietor of the highly regarded Parisian specialty wine shop La Cave de la Madeleine was one of the earliest advocates of tasting wine before you buy it. He was also an Englishman. As such, Steven Spurrier wasn't overly romantic about the concept of French wine and when he started receiving some startling good red wines from California, he was open to the fact that it may, in fact, be better than the stuff made in the Bordeaux wine region in the South of France. Unfortunately his patrons were very much French, and even though they could admit the California wines were tasty, they were not quick to buy them in place of their French counterparts. And thus, a publicity stunt was born. Steven, and his American business partner, Patricia Gallagher, gathered nine highly regarded judges. A group consisting of sommeliers, winemakers, restaurant owners, and wine writers would taste French and American wines side by side. They would use their expert palates to grade each wine, and the vineyards on one side of the Atlantic would be proclaimed the winner while the other accepted the fate of a loser.

Although the inspiration for the event was publicity, just one journalist showed up that day because the outcome of the competition, if it could even be called that, was obvious to all the French news outlets. Wines were poured, sniffs and thoughtful sips taken, notes and scores fanatically written, and results calculated. One country had taken the whole event, having the best-scoring wine in both the red flight and the white flight. That country was the United States. California specifically. Hysteria ensued. One judge demanded that she get her scorecard back lest her comments fall into the hands of the media and tarnish her reputation. How could she have given that American swill such high marks?

The chardonnay from Chateau Montelena was the winningest white, and for reds it was the cabernet sauvignon from Stag's Leap Wine Cellars. A bottle of the 1973 vintage of each wine is housed in the Smithsonian's National Museum of American History's collection designated as "Objects That Made America."

Without tasting these treasured wines blind, the Judgment of Paris would have played out just like any other wine event. The typical structure of a wine tasting is ripe with opportunities for priming, both visual and otherwise. Winemakers would stand to tell the story of their vineyard and the wine, followed by the tasting notes (sometimes in language so florid the tasting feels more like a poetry reading than a tasting event). Finally, they'd sit, and attendees would sip, discuss, en-joy, and move on to the next winemaker. The United States wouldn't have a chance in one of these events. No matter how inspiring their backstory, at this point the oldest wineries in California were just over one hundred years old. These newbie vineyards couldn't hold a candle to the centuries-long traditions of vineyards that have existed through wars and floods and famines. And tales of wine cellars among cata-combs and hand-whittled corks. Judges and attendees would hear the legends bordering on myths of the French wineries, clink their glasses, and revel in the fact that they were savoring a tradition that dates back to the times of the Romans. But blind tasting allows judges and somms alike to assess the quality of the wine and form an opinion without the burden of history or hierarchy. Only once they've made a decision is the answer revealed.

So a couple of fancy-pants French men and women declared the United States the superior maker of grape juice. Should anyone else care? What special powers are judges endowed with to determine bet-ter, worse, and just okay? And that score sheet one judge so desperately sought to conceal her true assessment of the shameful United States wines, did the numbers she happened to write down actually *mean* anything? Or did they just feel right? Let's talk about that next.

PART THREE

USING YOUR TASTING SKILLS

CHAPTER SEVEN

CRITICS, JUDGES, AWARDS, AND GRADES

YOU KNOW THE INS AND OUTS OF IDENTIFYING FLAVORS, SO HOW DO you know when you'll be qualified enough to go bite for bite with the judges on a reality show like *MasterChef*? Or give a restaurant a five-star seal of approval? Or score a wine out of one hundred à la Robert Parker? When can you be the judge of whether the coffee from the fancy shop is truly a specialty or only a notch above the Folgers in the breakroom? We attribute superpowers to judges, critics, and graders, but are their tasting abilities superior to those of mere mortals? Perhaps. Are their opinions the definitive word on the quality of a beverage or food? Well, not so fast.

How do reviews by critics diverge from awards by judges differ from scores by industry experts? Let's look at how tasting affects these awards and grades and who the tasters are that determine them. We'll begin with critics. Adding numbers and stars to critics' reviews makes opinions feel objective, as if the subjective analysis by taste buds can be objectively quantified. But stars, ratings, and awards can be deceiving. For one, it's not always clear exactly what criteria is being judged. The Michelin Guide is one of the most respected restaurant-ratings body among both chefs and consumers (although it is not without bias or fault). The anonymous inspectors who decree star ratings from on high insist that their decision is based only on food.

"A Michelin Star is awarded for the food on the plate—nothing else. The style of a restaurant and its degree of formality or informality have no bearing whatsoever on the award," an anonymous Michelin inspector said in a Q&A on the guide's website.

The statement clarifies some of the criteria used to make star decisions: outstanding cooking, quality of the ingredients, harmony of flavors, mastery of techniques, personality of the chef as expressed in their cuisine, and consistency both over time and across the entire menu. Seems a bit hard to quantify. I'm not sure how you could put a number to how much harmony is in front of you. And is the personality of the chef really part of the "food on the plate"? The write-up continues on to add this confusing line about the wine list: "Restaurants who are serious about their food tend to also ensure they have an interesting wine list to complement it, so that element usually takes care of itself."

So does the wine factor into the star rating or not? The inspectors insist that quality of service isn't a factor. But as we know, slow service means cold food, and cold food simply doesn't express as much flavor as it would at the right temperature. Furthermore, the Michelin Guide defines each star tier as: one star signifies a very good restaurant; two stars signify excellent cooking that is worth a detour; three stars signify exceptional cuisine that is worth a special journey. (If you're wondering why the guide uses travel as a qualifier in their star ratings, remember, this highly regarded guide was originally a marketing ploy to sell Michelin tires!)

Michelin may be the most mysterious guide, but other critics don't give much context for their ratings, either. Before the *Los Angeles Times* did away with their star ratings in 2012, their stars considered "food, service and ambience, with price taken into account in relation to quality." Other outlets hold on to ratings while shifting away from stars. In 2018, *New York* magazine converted its star ratings to a hundred-point rating system that was premiered by critic Adam Platt as "our rating scale, from 1 ('unfortunate') to 100 ('nirvana')." One assumes many things go into experiencing nirvana (some of them are not available in restaurants at all; perhaps this is why their highest rated restaurants still get ninety-nines). On the reviews themselves, the score is clarified: "The rating scale of 0 to 100 reflects our editors' appraisals of all the tangible and intangible factors that make a restaurant or bar great—or terrible—regardless of price."

For those still using a starlike grading system, there are creative takes on the concept. In Philadelphia, Craig LaBan created a Liberty Bell system for reviewing restaurants. The "bells" are really based on one thing: Craig's assessment. He says the establishments he has awarded four bells (the highest available rank) "are places that capture a moment in time, a unique magic at the table, and have proven it over years of consistency with a continued growth that shows they're still evolving as living restaurants," and went on to admit, "there is no checklist of criterion involved—I just know it when I feel it."

It seems these ratings are largely based on gut and experience. So, you're thoughtful enough about tasting to pick up this book; I guess that makes you ready as anyone to dole out some stars.

Surely awards presented at competitions judged by experts rather than individual critics aren't quite as arbitrary, or are they?

As a homebrewer, I've entered beers in several competitions. One of the most frustrating aspects of the judging is when my entry gets rated inconsistently. How could the same beer get full marks for aroma at one competition and a measly seven out of twelve at the next one? I have always chalked the numbers up to better beers in the flight I'm up against or a judge's personal dislike for the style of beer I entered. But retired oceanography professor and active winery owner Robert Hodgson decided to put some numbers to the regular occurrence of mismatched scores for the same product in wine competitions. What he found was not encouraging. To understand why his results were troubling for competition entrants and organizers, let's talk about how these competitions are structured. Industry competitions for judging chocolate, tea, wine, cheese, coffee, beer, and even granola bars are run in generally the same way. First, entries are carefully stored and organized into groups to be presented to judging panels. These groups of entries are called a "flight." At the California State Fair competition (where George Hodgson conducted his studies), flights consisted of thirty glasses. This number shifts from competition to competition. At the International Wine Challenge (IWC), Michael Tremblay, a senior sake judge, tells me that the flights typically range from ten to fifteen samples. These flights are presented at an ideal serving temperature to judges panels. Each panel has a leader, who is usually the most experienced judge, and anywhere from three to ten more judges depending on the size of the competition. Once the flight of samples is given to the panel of judges they all taste them individually at the same table, so, according to Michael, "you can taste at your own pace. You can try things; you can come back to things . . . And we wait for everyone to make their marks." Judges mark notes and scores on their individual score sheets.

Then the panel chair, in this case Michael himself, goes around and asks each judge about their marks for each sake. This includes which medal they awarded each sake or if the sake was "out," meaning it wouldn't receive a medal. "Sometimes everyone's in consensus and we move on to the next sake, and sometimes it's more we need to taste together as a group to make a determination."

Michael says since judges come from varied backgrounds this discussion is important. It can help rein in enthusiastic newbies who give high marks to mediocre sakes, or it can keep the ultra-qualified from being too harsh.

"Once I had a PhD scientist from the National Research Institute of Brewing who studied yeast on my panel," he says. "It was fascinating to hear his point of view, but he would say, 'This one is out! The yeast died here.' And no one else could perceive it."

These conversations, led by the lead judge, determine the final overall score submitted by the panel. It is the time for judges to work together to reach "a balance between what consumers would like and what is technically flawed and maybe acceptable," according to Michael. The panel chair records the final score for each of the samples (in this case, sake) and the panel begins their next flight. Michael and the other judges at the IWC will taste and score around 120 samples a day. And now back to Robert Hodgson's mission to test the veracity of wine competitions. In his most damning study—or the most revealing depending on how you feel about wine competitions—Robert scrutinized the reliability of the judges at the California State Fair wine competition (the oldest commercial wine competition in North America). Organizers served the judges the standard thirty samples in a typical flight, but for the experiment three of the glasses were poured from the same bottle. One would hope that the expert judges would award identical scores to all three of the duplicate wines because they were, obviously, the same.

After four years of collecting this data, Robert's analysis found that only 10 percent of judges were able to score the identical samples within a four point range (the range of one medal) consistently. Ninety percent of judges awarded a glass of wine one medal and just minutes later evaluated the exact same wine and awarded it a different medal. In a market where "gold medal bottles" have the potential to make more profit for the winemaker, this is a vast discrepancy.

The results are beguiling, but Robert's data didn't take one factor into account that would help the judges' consistency. Instead of recording the panels' final adjusted score marked after the discussion led by the lead judge, Robert's data is based on the initial scores marked by individual judges. In his paper he wrote, "Based on the discussion, some judges modify their initial score; others do not. For this study, only the first, independent score is used to analyze an individual judge's consistency in scoring wines."

It's still baffling that judges wouldn't simply give the same wine the same score, yet it does seem that competitions are designed to safeguard against individual inconsistency. The lead judge is there to cajole wayward tasters into adjusting their scores in the right direction and reaching a group consensus. When the judging process is working, the experts' experience comes together to fairly grade the entries. To that end, a 2008 study out of Australia found that wine judges evaluating red wines were more consistent and more accurate when judging in panels of three than they were judging independently.

Robert didn't solely focus on the judges' performance in a single competition, he also gave attention to wine competitions at large. In his influential 2009 study he performed a statistical analysis of 4,167 wines and their entry and/or performance in thirteen competitions in the United States. His oft-quoted conclusion found that of the 375 wines that were entered in five competitions, no wine received a gold five times, or even four times. In fact, 106 of the wines won a single gold medal out of five competitions. You know, it only takes one award to print it on your bottles for potential customers to see! Of the six wines that were awarded three gold medals all three were also awarded at least one "no award" or a bronze medal at another competition.

Robert's statistical work on wine judging is best known (and weaponized by some media outlets) for questioning the validity of so-called expert wine judges and the awards presented by their palates. But he is clear: "I'm not intent on debunking the whole idea of tasting and judging wine," he told *Wine Spectator* in 2013. "On the other hand, the tasting and judging of wines in the setting of a wine competition, in my view, leads to meaningless recommendations."

(I couldn't help but notice that the website for Robert's own winery, Fieldbrook Winery, lists a few awards, including "Gold Medal in 2019 Humboldt County Fair" for his Rosato de Sangiovese. I suppose those award titles must mean something.)

There are a few reasons not all gold medal awards are created equal. First, judges come to these competitions with their own ideas of quality. (Judges often come from many specialties within their industry, including critics, producers, distributors, and restaurateurs.) If expectations for what is considered excellent, or gold medal–worthy are not set, judges will rely on their own biases to guide the points they award. Some of these biases are smoothed out in panel discussions; however, some are not, as shown in Robert's work. Second, there are disparate specialties and audiences for each competition. Therefore, the inconsistency of scores and awards may have nothing to do with the judges' palates but instead the context they're judging in.

Every day there are a multitude of competitions judged throughout the United States. The Beer Judge Certification Program's official competition list has as many as twelve sanctioned and judged competitions on a single day. There are regional, statewide, countrywide, and even international cheese-grading events. Between homemade pies judged at state fairs and the chili cook-offs, barbecue competitions, and professional-level cocktail competitions, there are thousands of opportunities to judge by taste each day. These flavor face-offs are graded by judges with supposedly expert palates. But are all judges approaching their products with the same qualities in mind?

I asked dozens of judges what they look for in the item that would take the crown in a competition. "Originality," one chocolate judge

told me, while another said it was definitely "high-quality ingredients."
A master bourbon taster said, "Harmony," but a master distiller said,
"A clear beginning, middle, and end to the flavor profile." An olive oil
sommelier said, "Bitterness and pungency," and an olive oil quality-assurance panelist said, "Bitterness and pungency." Seems like the olive
oil industry is on the same page.

Just as every judge has their paramount qualities in mind when
they search for the first-place entrant, each competition dictates scoring
scales and parameters differently, depending on the audience for, and
breadth of, the competition. Some of the largest competitions in the
world have a very narrow focus—like the IWC, the largest sake challenge in the world that Michael judges annually. Michael and many
other judges professionally assess sake as their job. He teaches Wine &
Spirits Education Trust certifications as well as acting as the Sake Samurai and sommelier at Ki Modern Japanese + Bar in Toronto, Canada.
"While judging, we've been reminded, these awards are for consumers,"
he says, "we're not judging the brewery. We're not saying is the sake
flawed or not flawed. It's about, if you gave this a gold medal, would they
[consumers] be happy with it?" The IWC denotes on its website that its
judging procedure is superior to other competitions because every wine
is assessed for its faithfulness to style, region, and vintage on at least
three separate occasions. All of these tastings occur completely blind,
and judges are not provided with pricing or producer information.

Meanwhile, another large competition, the USA Spirits Ratings
competition (which also has entry categories for wine and beer), insists
their scoring system is a superior measure of customer interest because
they take all aspects of the product into consideration. Each entry is
given a quality score out of one hundred, a value score out of one hundred, and a package score out of one hundred. These three marks are
converted into a weighted overall score with the quality score getting
twice the weight of the other marks. It's obvious to see how a well-made

wine with rudimentary packaging would come out of these two competitions with markedly different scores.

But sometimes the distinctions between competitions are more subtle.

Sharyn Johnston judges tea at prestigious competitions all over the world and as of 2017 was named the head judge of the Tea Masters Cup, a multifaceted competition that takes place in twenty countries. "The first thing you have to think about when coming into judge is, what part of the world are you in," she says. "For example, judging in Sri Lanka or India, it's a lot of judging black tea against black tea against black tea, and they're judging for wholesale buyers. That is completely different than a competition aimed at the retail market."

With her global palate she established a tea competition, the Golden Leaf Awards, in her home country of Australia. She's clear with her judges that the goal is to award teas that are high quality and will appeal to the palates of Australian consumers. "High astringency, for example, that is not going to suit the average person who buys a tea online or comes into a shop and buys a tea in Australia," she says. "But in China, they do a five-minute boil on a green tea to judge it. They want to bring out the astringency because that is what they are used to. In China you might resteep a tea all day."

These subtle differences are discussed by the judges beforehand: the ideal characteristics they are looking for, how tea will be prepared for judging (factors like the length of steep and tea-to-water ratio), and the meaning behind each medal rank. Then the judges are left to assess the samples with their audience freshly instilled in their heads.

"Another thing I decided to do with my competition is get very specific with the categories," Sharyn says. "That way they're being measured equally next to each other and it's not as hard to compare." The Golden Leaf Awards has four different entry categories for oolong teas alone, then there are the seven categories of non-matcha-variety green tea. This division into precise categories makes sense for the judges and competition organizers, and it can also allow innovative products to break into the industry with an award.

"I remember I tried this sake and it was really interesting, really dank, and tasted different," Michael says, "but I had to mark it out. I was like, this just doesn't fit in the category; I can't score it." This happened at the U.S. National Sake Appraisal that has just four entry categories. "I later found out that it was based on a recipe that was four hundred and fifty or five hundred years old. And the brewer is paying tribute to that. And I thought, *Oh, it should be a specialty thing.* Because when you take that context out, I don't like it."

He says those sorts of bottles put him into a philosophical debate about the need to commend makers doing things that are innovative, without giving them the same award as other sakes. "Because if a consumer tasted that and thought it was supposed to be a medal-winning junmai [category of sake], they would think, *What the heck is wrong with these judges?*"

If there is one thing all the judges seem able to agree on, including the judges in Robert's studies, it is what is not good. Of the 375 wines entered into five competitions in his study, there were twenty-five instances of the wine scoring within the same five-point range across the board. All twenty-five of these wines fell within the no-award range and the bronze range. Michael agrees that there are far fewer debates about sakes that are considered "out" of the medal range. In fact, judges are so sure when a sake has clear flaws that there is a designated table where judges can tag the less-than-stellar examples with their issues and judges can taste through them at the end of the day.

"It's a treat for us," says Michael. "You teach about these faults in sake, but it's really hard to come by examples. And the table will have everything, all kinds of microbial issues and spoilage." He says it's one of the best learning experiences he gets out of judging.

This high rate of accuracy at finding faults and flaws is ultimately what our sensory system is built for: identifying flavors that we've labeled as "dangerous" to us. When a judge is able to identify a fault in a wine, for example very high levels of pyrazines (those green bell pepper vegetal aromas that are okay in some wines but not all), they can immediately mark that as a "no award." But if they identify pleasant fruity notes (esters), a moderately drying mouthfeel (tannins), and subtle vanilla flavors (possibly from barrel aging), there is no formula to determine what the score should be; it's all up to how the judge is feeling and what the other tasters on the panel think.

Some competitions use prescriptive scorecards to aid judges as they make their decisions. By breaking the overall score into smaller sections and specifying a weight for each attribute the subjectivity is reined in. Even if a judge absolutely hates the color of a wine, for example. "Color" on the UC Davis 20-Point Scale only counts for two points out of a total twenty. The Beer Judge Certification scoresheet allows judges to award up to five points of a potential fifty points for the mouthfeel of a beer. One assessment sheet for the International Olive Council International Competition for Extra Virgin Olive Oils has seven of out of one hundred points dedicated to "olive fruitiness." (To see these scoresheets and other examples visit howtotastebook.com/scores.) These worksheets force the judges to make many thoughtful choices while grading a wine, beer, or olive oil, instead of making an immediate snap judgment. They also provide the entrant with context for their decision. An olive oil producer hoping to add a gold medal to the label will be able to tell right away if "fruitiness" is holding her back.

Commodity judging or "grading" is a more technical version of the competition judging procedure that does away with these subjective uncertainties. This grading is performed by highly trained professional assessors because their evaluations determine the price the product can fetch on the market. Competition judges strive for fairness so the consumer has a better idea of what to buy and the producer can market a quality product. Graders, on the other hand, must have indisputable objectivity because their score determines the label a product can carry on store shelves. A coffee scored more than eighty points by a Q Grader can be labeled a "specialty coffee." (These are the coffees purchased by the specialty shops charging more than five dollars for a cup of drip coffee.) Without the sensory rating by a qualified taste panel that has been officially recognized by the International Olive Council (IOC), olive oil cannot be denoted "extra virgin." Milk Graders make sure dairy is high quality and safe for consumers when it hits store shelves.

These tasting certifications require extensive professional experience and investment. To become a coffee Q Grader one must pass twenty-two tests over six days to prove that they have the sensory prowess and coffee knowledge to definitively grade coffee on the most objective scale possible. The nearly weeklong undertaking to get certified costs more than $2,000. The first three days are a workshop on theory and a chance to practice all the tests. The rest of the time is dedicated to testing. It takes three days to proctor these exams because of the strain they place on the candidates' palates. They need to be able to identify thirty-six common coffee aromas, the differences between four organic acids, take triangle tests based on coffee origin, and perform the ritual coffee-tasting method called "cupping" on twenty-four samples.

Candidates' innate tasting abilities are also tested, not exclusively their palate for coffee. For example, one small part of one test consists of nine identical glasses of what looks like water. Candidates must identify which three are sweet, which three are sour, and which three are salty. And then, within those three sets, they must rate each sample on its intensity of that flavor. Some tastes are added at such a low concentration that they are barely perceptible. That intensity scale is essential to their function as a Q Grader because graders must be calibrated with one another. If the same coffee is sent to graders in locations across the world it is expected that the final grade will be within points of each other. It's not just a question of *Is this sour, pretty sour, or not sour at all?* When one Q Grader rates a cup as having a 7.25 intensity of acid, other graders need to know exactly what that level of acid means.

"It's about adding that objectivity," says Shannon Cheney, the director at Coffee Lab International, who has more than twenty-five years of experience in the coffee industry. Consistent grading is imperative, so much so that unlike many professional tasting designations, coffee Q Graders must be recertified through a calibration evaluation every three years. "Anyone can assign a number to something. Or when you have the vocabulary, anyone can be poetic about their experience," says Shannon, who is a certified Q Grader for both robusta and arabica coffees, "but when you go through these protocols, you're certified to say, 'Yes, I can call these things out.' And other people that are calibrated with you are identifying them the same way; that's how you learn to take out the subjectivity. [But it is] sensory, so there's always a little bit of subjectivity."

Shannon, as well as fellow Q Graders, still judge in certain industry competitions that are run in a similar structure to the consumer-focused competitions Michael judges. But the competitions she takes part in tend to have an audience of wholesale coffee buyers, roasters, and industry insiders rather than anything a customer is aware of at the coffee shop. Once certified, Q Graders evaluate the quality of a coffee in order to assign it a grade. Grades more than eighty points allow farmers to earn more money for their crops. Even when grades come back lower than expected, the extremely knowledgeable graders can provide feedback to farmers so they can learn where there are flaws and how to improve the coffee.

Assessing the quality of a wine or spirit or chocolate bar takes into consideration what the winemaker or distiller or confectioner did to the raw materials in order to make their final product. Sometimes they blend grapes, add colors, or sugars, or natural sweeteners. They decide how long to age something or if it should be entered into a competition fresh. A judge has to decide if they like these decisions, if the choices of the maker resulted in a higher quality end product. These sorts of judgments are different from competitions like Cup of Excellence, where certified graders like Shannon are the judges. Cup of Excellence is self-described as "the premier specialty coffee competition that discovers amazing coffees and rewards the farmers."

"When you're dealing with a raw ingredient, like coffee or cocoa, you're looking at the base quality of what nature created that people could only influence," says Shannon, "so we can see the root causes of flavor in the agricultural practices themselves."

Shannon and her colleagues don't judge the lattes and flat whites the barista makes for you in the coffee shop but instead the qualities of the beans themselves. Unlike the competitions that Robert included in his study, where it is unclear whether medal-winning producers directly profit from their accolades, awards presented to farmers result in an immediate increase in their earnings.

"The farmers can potentially get a better premium for their crops that they put into the competition," says Shannon. "That is a kind of competition I think is very interesting and rewarding for everybody involved."

So, can you do what Shannon and her fellow Q Graders do? Maybe, eventually with a decade or so of specialized training. What about your local state fair competition? If you think you've practiced tasting enough, throw your hat in the ring! Just don't forget to listen to the wisdom of the chair on your panel. Want to assign stars to some restaurants? Go for it; you'll be as rigorous as anyone else doing it.

CHAPTER EIGHT

ONE PLUS ONE MAKES SEVEN

"**P**UT MUSTARD IN YOUR BROWNIES."

I smiled, unsure what to say. Was this a joke? Or was it a test? Was he proposing an outlandish ingredient pairing to see what I would say?

"No, I'm serious. It's like chocolate and coffee, only instead it's chocolate and mustard. The mustard throws in some acid and a little contrast," says Chef Brandon Collins, an official mustard sommelier.

This title had me suspicious at first. I mean, can you just be a sommelier of anything now? But Collins has more than 275 years of history to back him up. His company Maille has records of its founder Antoine-Claude Maille mentioning in writing that each of his stores should have a dedicated mustard sommelier in 1747. Brandon undertook an intensive ten-week training in France to earn this designation. During that time, he learned about all the varieties of mustard seed (there are more than three thousand species, but we eat only three), what they should taste like, and how they affect the final mustard flavor.

"Without really high-quality seeds, you can't have a classic Dijon mustard." Brandon tells me flavor gives away the seeds' condition instantly: When you eat a high-quality seed "there will be some bitterness but it's still pleasant, like broccoli rabe. You don't want it to have any burnt bitter flavors." Dry mustard seeds alone have an exceedingly bitter taste; it's not until they are mixed with a liquid that they reveal the pungent spice they are known for.

The liquid component of classic Dijon mustard is verjus, the acidic juice of pressed unripe wine grapes, but modern Dijon mustards use various white wines and vinegars to achieve this sour grape character. The balance between fiery mustard seeds, salt, and tangy verjus determines the flavor profile of the resulting mustard. It can be sharply tart and biting or smooth and slightly sweet. These qualities determine how that mustard will work with other ingredients in a recipe. Like, say, a recipe for dark chocolate fudge brownies.

Brandon isn't some mustard geek trying to sneak the stuff into every dish. He had nearly two decades of experience as a chef after graduating from the Culinary Institute of America before becoming North America's mustard sommelier. As a younger chef he would sometimes use a dozen or more flavors to achieve the complexity and balance he wanted. "Now an ingredient is only there for a specific reason; sometimes you still need ten or more, but my dishes are simpler overall." He adds, "Building a dish is always going to be about balancing the flavors. With mustard, I'm thinking about acid, some sweetness, some bitterness, and heat. But that has to work with saltiness and fat and the flavors in other components of a dish."

Brandon's mustard brownies rely on the relationship between the recipe's ingredients: bittersweet chocolate, plenty of sugar, creamy butter, and bright punchy mustard. In this case they come together to invigorate the cocoa flavor, intensifying it and making the chocolate seem richer on the palate without being too heavy.

Chefs like Brandon use their understanding of the relationships between the basic tastes to build creative dishes. Salty, sweet, umami, sour, and bitter tastes interact by enhancing or suppressing one another. Once you're familiar with these interactions, combinations like mustard and dark chocolate are more intuitive than shocking.

SALTY

SALT ENHANCES SWEETNESS. THAT'S WHY STARBUCKS CLAIMS IT'S THE sea salt and turbinado sugar in the caramel sauce that makes a Salted Caramel Mocha Frappuccino an "explosion of flavor." This interaction is also why the rim of a margarita glass is garnished with salt. The salt elevates sweetness from the orange liqueur and highlights any sweetness from the lime.

Salt reduces bitterness. So, the salted rim of a margarita will also help balance the bitterness inherent in lime rinds. My favorite tip from the endless hours of food TV I've watched comes from Alton Brown's *Good Eats*: a tiny pinch of salt in your coffee mug will do just as much to neutralize the bitterness of coffee as all that sugar we're used to adding. Instead of taking your morning caffeine with a side of sugar high, keep some flaky sea salt within arm's reach of the coffee maker. Salt reduces bitterness because of the manner in which sodium bonds with taste receptors. Low-sodium salt alternatives never seem like genuine substitutions for the real thing because they're missing the sodium bonds on the tongue.

All around, salt can be thought of as a flavor enhancer. It literally makes foods taste more like themselves, pulling out their flavor. Scientists tell us that this happens for a few reasons. The first is that sodium is blocking bitter receptors, allowing the gustatory system to perceive other tastes without the unpleasant nagging of bitter compounds plugging up our systems. Salty bacon is found in so many brussels sprout recipes because the salt diminishes the sprouts' natural bitterness.

Another explanation for salt's all-around flavor acceleration: salt creates a liquid flavor jacket on the surface of many foods. When salt is sprinkled on food, especially foods that are damp and/or warm, it starts to draw flavorful juices to the surface through the process of osmosis. A thin layer of flavorful salt solution encircles whatever you're about to eat. This layer of flavorful liquid goodness is packed with compounds ready and waiting to come in contact with your tongue and fly up the retronasal passageway to your olfactory bulb. I had a friend in high school who used to eat tomatoes like apples, taking a bite straight from the pale red flesh and then shaking salt onto it before going in for another bite. The sight is etched into my memory because at the time I thought it was so revolting; now I think of it as a stroke of genius.

SWEET

ANOTHER WEAPON IN THE BATTLE AGAINST BITTERNESS IS SWEETNESS. We see it in our coffee, our chocolate bars, and forming the crystalline candied crunch on what would otherwise be a bitter dried orange garnish in a cocktail. It is there in all of those instances for one reason: sweetness reduces bitterness.

Sweetness is boosted by both salt and umami. Scientists found that participants tasting various seafoods noticed an increase in sweet intensity when the fish was dosed with umami compounds, even if the umami itself was too subtle to taste. Remove the umami-licious glutamates and the sweetness was measurably dulled. As I said before, salt pumps up the sweet. That's why most desserts will have at least a pinch of salt in the recipe. And many will mention you can use a little more as a garnish. Us tasters know that crunchy sea salt garnish is hardly a suggestion; for the most flavor, it's a requirement.

Sweetness reduces sourness. Ultra-sour candies rolled in over-the-top sweet powder are the obvious demonstration of this relationship. The grown-up version is the simple syrup or orange liqueur in a sour margarita. Adding sugar won't completely eliminate sour taste but it will bring it into balance. Add packet after packet of sugar to that excessively tart lemonade and eventually it will be drinkable. Sometimes nature does the balancing for itself; for example, a tomato would have an unbearable level of acid without its natural sugars (and a tomato's healthy dose of umami boosts that sweetness even further).

A 2010 study found that, in general, when tastes mix, sweetness resists suppression. When mixed in equal parts with bitter, sour, salty, or umami, sweetness will be perceived as the dominating flavor. With this in mind, go slow when adding packets of sugar to balance something sour or bitter; the sweetness level will increase quickly.

UMAMI

AS THE MOST RECENTLY DEFINED BASIC TASTE, THE UNDERSTANDING of umami is constantly evolving. Even though umami is an essential part of some of the oldest known dishes, experiments aimed at testing its relationship to other flavors are few and far between. One thing is certain: every other basic taste suppresses the perception of umami. The intensity of umami in a dish will always, by definition, be low and easily overpowered by other flavors. This fleeting quality has nothing to do with the flavor profiles of umami-rich foods like kombu, tomatoes, mushrooms, or Parmesan. Instead it might be tied to our taste receptors for umami. In his book *Flavor*, author

Bob Holmes recounts a working theory by Paul Breslin, a professor in the Department of Nutritional Sciences at Rutgers University and a member of the Monell Chemical Senses Center: "Our umami receptors max out at low intensity, so we're physically unable to experience *very* umami in the same way we can taste *very* salty or *very* bitter . . . Thanks to our perceptual apparatus, umami can never be anything more than a subtle sensation." You can quickly identify a dish that is too salty or too sweet by a single taste. No matter how many spoonfuls of MSG you dump into a dish, you'll never take a bite and think, *This is too umami.*

Because of this theoretical maximum intensity threshold, it's not helpful to think of umami as a note competing with the other basic tastes. Umami is best considered as a way to elevate complexity in a dish or round out other flavors with a savory quality. In order for a dish to have clear, dominant umami flavor it should have low-intensity levels of other flavors, like the yokan dessert from Chapter 2.

SOUR

Acid adds brightness or cuts umami. Fish sauce and lime are a classic combination. When a soup might be too round or smooth from umami savoriness, lime comes through and brightens the whole thing up. It's like turning on a light bulb in a dark velvet-laden lounge; the ambiance can still be sultry and soft, but the light bulb allows you to see the edges of everything and keeps the furniture from blending together in the darkness. In the same way acid balances sweetness and richness. The song "[Put the Lime in the] Coconut" comes to mind. Cloying coconut milk, syrupy with fat, can feel heavy with richness even when whipped with a blender into a drink or dessert. But a squeeze of lime cuts that density and lets some light shine through between thick clouds of saccharine coconut milk. The brightening effect of a splash of citrus juice or vinegar is almost always welcome.

BITTER

BITTER IS THE MOST VARIABLE OF THE BASIC TASTES WHEN IT COMES TO taste-on-taste interaction, or taste pairing. We have twenty-five taste receptors dedicated to sensing bitterness; for this reason, some scientists believe, and chefs tend to agree, that we can taste different "kinds" of bitterness. For example, the pleasant "broccoli rabe" bitter and the harsh burnt bitter Brandon mentioned when it comes to mustard seeds. This might be one reason for bitterness's general unpredictability in pairing.

Bitterness is suppressed by saltiness. Pretzels and hoppy beer are commonly served together because they form a perfect taste loop. A sip of bitter beer is tamed by a salty pretzel. Some of the flavor nuances of the beer are raveled when the salt suppresses bitter hop compounds. After that salty bite, you're ready for a sip of thirst-quenching beer, and the loop starts over again!

Generally, when a low concentration of acid is present, adding bitterness to the mix enhances the perception of sourness. Something can go from subtly tangy to noticeably sour and harshly bitter. For this reason, people often consider sourness and bitterness to clash. However, with a deft hand and understanding of how bitterness can enhance sour flavors, sour/bitter interactions can be delicious. This combination is common in Asian cuisine as well as cocktail mixology. Oddly, these two flavors are the most likely to be confused in new tasters. This phenomenon, called sour-bitter confusion, baffles sensory scientists and has only been observed in English-speaking countries. The working hypothesis is that people in these countries simply aren't exposed to sour or bitter flavors often enough to recognize them individually.

Bitterness reduces sweetness. When coffee is bitter enough, you can add a whole spoonful of sugar and not notice a great reduction in bitterness. However, an overly sweet vanilla ice cream is nicely tamed by a bitter dark chocolate shell.

KNOWING HOW ALL THESE FLAVORS INTERACT, THE MUSTARD-IN-brownies suggestion made logical sense. But I remained skeptical. It was too bizarre, and the gulf between spicy sharp mustard and rich, fudgy brownie seemed too wide to bridge with the fact that acid cuts sweetness and salt enhances all flavors. However, I tried Brandon's mustard brownie recipe from the Maille website, and I also added mustard to my own brownie recipe. The result in both cases was surprisingly great. I wasn't an ideal test subject; I wanted the brownies to work. Maybe I was unconsciously missing any "off" flavor. Fortunately, I was heading to my semiregular meetup with the perfect experiment participants: a group of three friends who I first met when I was cast on a Food Network show that focused on blind tasting. The four of us never made it to air, but we bonded over both our taste obsessions and the slight at being left off the show. In the group was a cheese specialist, a recipe developer, and a bartender, all with curious and trained palates.

In order to make this a true experiment, I made three batches of brownies, identical except to one I added a tablespoon of espresso powder and to another a heaping tablespoon from a fresh jar of Dijon mustard. I baked the brownies in muffin tins for easy transport. The mustard brownies had blue paper liner cups, the coffee brownies had purple liners, and the plain had purple polka dots. With brownies in tow I headed off for the Wild East, a brewery in Brooklyn.

Once everyone was settled with pints and we'd caught up a bit, I busted out the taste test.

I had everyone rank the brownies from sweetest to least sweet and then tell me their favorite. The results for the least sweet brownie showed two votes for blue (mustard brownies) and one vote for polka dot (plain). Everyone agreed the purple cups (coffee brownies) were the sweetest. Then the real moment of truth: which brownie was their favorite? Two people voted for the blue cups as their favorite of the three.

Then I told them what the secret ingredient was.

"Noooo!"

"Shut the front door! Whaaaat?"

"Wait, why did you do this?"

"You know I did sense a—I wouldn't say dryness, but a saline in the blue one. . . ."

"So, the purple were what again?"

Safe to say, no one detected the mustard on their first taste. We munched on the remnants of the experiment and talked about our upcoming projects and whether a beer should have to be specified as "sour" on a menu. Then we headed to a barbecue spot around the corner to share some late-night meats. Written on the chalkboard menu was a message: "Try our World Champion Mustard BBQ Sauce." I did try it, and I can confidently say it did not taste like brownies.

CHEFS LIKE BRANDON USE THESE BASIC FLAVOR INTERACTIONS TO PAIR ingredients within a dish, and they are also the guiding principles behind pairing foods with beverages or other foods! Food-on-food pairing is how I ended up in western Oregon under a flock of flying loaves—well anywhere else they'd be called blocks of bright orange cheese. The entryway to the Tillamook Creamery was bustling with families heading toward the lines in the cafeteria where, yes, everything is cheesy, or making their way up the steps to the self-guided tour of the cheese-making facility. I was expecting a rustic-farm vibe from this more-than-a-century-old cheese maker, but the interior is full of sharp angles and impeccably clean glass.

"Oh yes, back when I started, we didn't have any of this," says Jill Allen, director of product excellence at the Tillamook County Creamery Association, as she motions to the modern interiors and flying cheese loaves suspended from the ceiling. She's been with Tillamook for more than twenty years, and I can't imagine her effusive passion about cheese has waned at all since she started. Jill heads up product excellence at Tillamook, which means she watches over the sensory team that ensures quality assurance as well as the quantitative descriptive analysis (QDA) panel made of staff volunteers. But once a year she has the ultra-fun responsibility of working with Tillamook's executive chef, Josh Archibald, to define the paragon flavor matches for each of Tillamook's products. Tillamook has an aging program called "Maker's Reserve." Each year these cheeses are reassessed for their pairings because their flavor profiles shift as they age. A cheddar that is bright and tangy when it was produced in 2013 can taste rich, nutty, and tropical by 2023.

"You should see the table," one of the Tillamook employees says as he recounts Jill and chef Josh's epic pairing day. "It's lined with like hundreds of things, and they are walking in circles around it tasting all of them."

The table is loaded with standard cheese plate fare like jams and nuts and charcuterie, alongside unexpected items like oysters, kombucha, vegetables of all kinds, ciders, fruit juices, and pâté. Jill and Josh need to determine a sweet pairing, a savory pairing, a wine, a beer, a cocktail, and a nonalcoholic-drink pairing for every cheese. In all of these pairings, they want their cheese to be the star of the show.

This brings me to the first rule of food pairing: know your centerpiece. Which element, ingredient, or specific flavor should be highlighted in your pairing? Once that question is answered, all the other decisions can fall into place.

Food pairing rule number two: Match intensity. Establish the flavor intensity of your centerpiece. Does it have bold flavors that prompt you to say "Whoa!" on first bite? Or does it have a light, delicate intensity? Since we're highlighting cheddar with Jill, all of the potential pairing items should have less intensity than the cheese. "I have been able to pair with a hot sauce before, but the cheese has to be able to handle it," Jill tells me. "A mild or medium cheddar won't work because the hot sauce will overtake it.

"For the 2013 I pulled a stout, something heavy to go with the strong profile of a really aged cheddar." The 2020, just a baby compared to this decade-old block, has a mild pilsner sitting nearby. Today Jill and I are tasting three of the Maker's Reserve vintages that will be released in 2023. And another extra-special cheese.

"I brought this back from the Somerset region of England. So, it's cheddar made in Cheddar, England, in the gorge." Jill beams. "I'm very careful about who I share my cheese with, but I really want you to taste this."

On the table there are two long wooden boards each lined with the four cheeses, three beers, and a handful of accoutrements like olives and crackers and candies and jams. We are going to do our own, much smaller version of the pairing day she and Chef Josh have each year. Pairings between foods and drinks, or foods and foods, are built around four broad categories. I call them the four Cs: Complement, Contrast, Cut, and Create.

COMPLEMENT

I REFER TO THE COMPLEMENT INTERACTION AS THE "THAT MAKES sense" pairing. It's expected that vanilla ice cream and thick caramel sauce will come together to highlight dairy creaminess and overall sweetness. Strawberry iced tea and strawberry pie go together? Well, you don't say! But just because complement pairings are easy to figure out doesn't mean their flavors are dumbed down at all; they can be some of the most satisfying combinations.

Jill describes the Tillamook 2017 Maker's Reserve as having bright acidity, so it pairs with a fruit that has bright acidity: raspberries. The cider she and chef Josh selected to pair with the 2017 follows this trend: it's raspberry cider. Another example of complement pairings are her official pairings for the Hickory Smoked Extra Sharp White Cheddar. The smoky cheese is complemented by grilled sausage, toasted walnuts, and grilled tropical fruit, which all have their own smoky notes. What we're looking for is a complementary note that ties the pairing together.

However, the reasons complement pairings work aren't always immediately obvious. Researchers from the Department of Food Science at University of Copenhagen spent weeks meticulously dissecting the molecular compounds that make champagne and oysters a popular pairing. They found that both the bivalves and the wine aged on its own yeast (also called "on lees") have subtle umami compounds that complement each other. Umami may not come instantly to mind on the first taste of either, but it is the connector that makes the matchup work.

CONTRAST

THE CONTRAST INTERACTION RELIES ON OPPOSITE TEXTURES AND/OR flavors.

Jill brings together a roasty, dry stout with aged cheddar for a Contrast pairing that highlights both. The cheese feels creamy in my mouth, but the stout finishes bitter and dry on the palate, even bordering on a little astringent. The contrast between creamy cheese and drying stout emphasizes the velvety mouthfeel of the cheese. Without the contrast provided by the stout, the cheese might have felt like any other cheddar. The second element at work in the pairing is roast flavors. Notes of coffee and dark chocolate in the stout contrast with the sweet dairy notes in Jill's cheese. My notes on the pairing say "sea salt caramel" while Jill's flavor note is "dulce"—a pretty close match! As a trained taster, it is always exciting to see your senses are in tune with other professional tasters, and clearly this stout pairing is doing an excellent job highlighting the sweet and salty flavors of the cheese.

A final note on Contrast interactions: Chefs will add contrasting texture elements to the other types of pairings as well. Crunchy honeycomb over a soft honey-infused ice cream is a complement pairing with an element of texture contrast. Since crunch is such an enticing element, especially for Americans, many dishes with a creamy or soft texture will incorporate some kind of texture contrast to keep our attention.

CUT

THE CUT INTERACTION DOES EXACTLY WHAT THE NAME SOUNDS LIKE: one part of the pairing acts like a knife and cuts through a major component of the other element. This type of pairing is usually based around cutting down the impact of fat, spice, or sweetness. The sharp coolness of mint cuts through the thick, sweet, creamy profile of white chocolate. This interaction is why peppermint bark is such a hit. The chocolate doesn't seem too rich because the mint cuts through all that heaviness. A big dose of honey drizzled over a super-hot pepper jack works in the same way; sweetness would cut the burn of the peppers.

But Jill and her team don't want their rich smooth cheeses to be cut by anything! That's the opposite of the cheese being the star. Brandon, the mustard sommelier, on the other hand uses his star ingredient to cut through all kinds of things. He tells me he swears by another dessert pairing (this time the brownies are not invited): "I really love to take the old-style mustard and put a spoonful of it over a really good quality vanilla ice cream. I'm telling you the bitterness, that kind of sweetness, that little bit of sour all play extremely well." He smiles and continues: "The mustard cuts right through the sweetness and creaminess of a really good high-fat ice cream and brightens everything."

CREATE

JILL PICKED OUT A COUPLE OF NEW ITEMS TO PAIR WITH THE CHEESES before I arrived this morning. She's palpably excited to try them alongside the cheeses she knows so well. "I know that green olives work well with the 2020, but this intrigued me." She grins as she points to a jar. "These are citrus-infused. So we will see!"

This final pairing interaction is the most whimsical. It's hard to pin down the exact mechanics of how a Create interaction works; it always feels like a little bit of magic. You taste two elements separately but when you taste them together somehow a new flavor appears. Sometimes the new flavor has to do with a story already in your head. Served side by side, a really jammy American red blend wine and house-made peanut brittle come together to create a peanut butter and jelly sandwich on the palate even though all the elements aren't there. Other Create pairings are less romantic, like the way very ripe peaches occasionally summon almond notes when they meet goat cheese. Jill seems to have stumbled on a Create pairing by adding a new element to her olives.

"When you taste the cheese with this citrus-infused olive it really intensifies that bright note on the back side. So it's kind of fun. It's different." She says "different" in the tone you use when you tell your friend their experimental one-man show was "interesting." The pairing isn't bad. If Jill wasn't interested in maintaining the core nature of the 2020 cheddar's character it would actually be pretty breathtaking. The citrus of the olive found some lactic tang hidden in the relatively young cheese to create a citrus note that falls somewhere between lemon peel and orange oil. I would have never picked out a fruit note of the cheese by itself. And the olive tastes more of stone fruits than citrus fruits on its own.

"It's interesting how accompaniments can pull out different flavor profiles and strengthen them," says Jill.

Even if this isn't going to be the official Tillamook pairing for the 2020 Reserve cheese, she's still geeking out on flavor.

———————

COMPLEMENT, CONTRAST, CUT, AND CREATE ARE NOT HARD-AND-FAST rules because when it comes to pairing there are no hard-and-fast rules. There are many instances of pairings that feel like they should work and they don't. And there are matches that seem unhinged (white chocolate and caviar, anyone?) but will make an unforgettable combination. Pairing, just like everything about tasting, is subjective. It's not a pure science. That's not to say no one has tried to make it a science. A company called Foodpairing built a database that matches foods based on their chemical compounds. The idea is that ingredients that share a large proportion of their aroma profile will pair well together. It makes sense: the most popular pairings are based on the Complement interaction; they use a shared flavor to bring the pairing together in harmony.

The Foodpairing database is built based on the ideas of the pioneer of the science-driven pairing movement, Heston Blumenthal. He is best known as the chef at The Fat Duck, where he was one of the earliest chefs to adopt and promote another mash-up between science and food: multisensory cooking. He discovered the peculiar but wonderful interaction between white chocolate and caviar working on a dish for The Fat Duck. His curiosity about that pairing started it all. He enlisted a scientist friend to figure out what makes the pairing work. Turns out that fish eggs and cocoa butter share a flavor compound, trimethylamine to be specific. The duo set out to revolutionize the way dishes and menus were built. Their "food pairing hypothesis" recommends pairing ingredients based on their chemical make-up. By 2002, the food pairing hypothesis had transformed into "the food pairing theory." Now, Heston claimed it was the number of aromatic compounds that two ingredients share that indicates if they will make a good pairing. The more shared compounds, the better the pairing.

But it turns out flavor compounds do not determine if two foods work well together, human noses, taste receptors, and minds do. Because the Foodpairing database built on this theory produced strange pairings that obviously do not work. According to the software (which chefs can access for a monthly fee), coffee, chocolate, and garlic are a winning combination, as are asparagus and cherry. Um . . . yuck!

As I've already established, culture and individual experience play a larger role in what we'll accept as a successful pairing than the molecules hovering around the food itself. And as such, Heston has denounced his food pairing theory and his role in popularizing it. In 2010 he wrote about it for the London *Times*: "I now know that a molecule database is neither a short cut to successful flavour combining nor a failsafe way of doing it . . . " he continues, "that two ingredients have a compound in common is a slender justification for compatibility. If I'd known then what I know now, I would probably never have tried this method of flavour pairing."

I suspect Heston felt he had to make this proclamation simply because so many of the pairings his theory suggested failed.

There are three major ways I find that pairings fail: they're an Intensity Mismatch, a Clash, or a Wash.

An Intensity Mismatch is easy to spot; one element erases the other completely. A salty T-bone steak with a mountain of butter will eviscerate the delicate apple and brioche notes in champagne. Syrupy balsamic vinegar reduction conceals any flavor contribution from mild milk chocolate.

A Clash happens when two elements come together and fight each other. The dry roast of an Irish stout fights against the funky cream in Roquefort blue cheese, leaving behind an almost metallic flavor. High-iron red wines clash with oily fish, and result in a long unpleasant aftertaste.

A Wash is the hardest pairing mishap to identify. It happens when adding one element to another seems to take flavor away. As opposed to brightening a rich chocolate torte, a glass of high-acid Chablis quietly disappears into the dessert while dampening its overall cocoa flavor. It's as if the cocoa flavor was washed away. Attempts at Complement interactions are the most likely to result in a wash. Adding a scoop of blueberry jam to blueberry yogurt mutes the berry flavor in both.

Another pairing Jill brings out results in a Wash. She offers me some strawberry champagne jam. It's another potential pairing element she's trying for the first time with me. We each scoop a little jam on its own. "I like it," I say, "I'm not sure if it tastes exactly like champagne, but it tastes more interesting than strawberry jam."

She thinks the jam will complement the sweet caramel and nutty notes in the cheese. Tasting each of them alone, it seems like a solid Complement pairing. But tasting them together, the abstract champagne flavor became even less clear.

"Honestly, I've never tried this pairing together, and I'm not exactly thrilled with it myself," says Jill with an evident look of disappointment. "For me, it deadens the 2013 [cheddar]. It was so . . . just beautiful on its own. The jam mutes the cheese. I'm not thrilled about that." Both the jam and the cheese managed to have less flavor when you combined them, the polar opposite of what happens when you make a successful Create pairing.

Jill sits with her disappointment for just a second and then adds, "You know, I think this is why people should put together cheese boards and just have the most fun with it. Something might not work, but who cares? It's fun to talk about it and just experience all the different flavors and textures"—now she's smiling—"like this! I love comparing notes with other tasters."

THESE ARE THE GENERAL RULES WHEN IT COMES TO FOOD PAIRING. THE taste interactions are based in solid, though sometimes still shifting, science. The four Cs of flavor interactions are not so well defined. They're guidelines born out of collective wisdom and experience. As Heston discovered, food pairing is too subjective for hard and fast rules. With practice, you'll be able to avoid pairings that result in an Intensity Mismatch. But even the most thoughtfully conceived pairings may end up being a Clash or a Wash. The most critical thing, when it comes to food pairing, is that you enjoy the pairing. Because when it comes to pairing, there are no correct answers. Around each major holiday we read headlines such as: "How to Pair Whiskey and Halloween Candy"; "The Best Wines to Drink with Peppermint Bark"; "Here are the Cheeses that Match Your New Year's Champagne." I know about these articles because I've been asked to write them. And the writer will always have a logical reason for their pairing. However, you're eight chapters into this book and you know if there is one thing tasting is not, it's logical! Take these guidelines as an opportunity to experiment. See if you agree with the writer, but don't be afraid to toss their recommendations out the window in favor of your own pairings.

A beverage director told me in the chilly marble bar of his restaurant that he didn't think food should ever be eaten with cocktails because the alcohol level numbs the palate. And yet people love to drink a bartender's creation as they dine. A brewer told me to ignore what I'd heard because he was 100% confident that there was no beer style that paired well with tomato sauce. And yet Pilsner and pizza is a classic combination. In New Zealand, a hotel owner told me eating fruit with marmite would ruin it. And of course, I had to try it as soon as she was out of sight. (Not for the faint of heart, but not bad, if you ask me!)

This chapter can help guide you, but you can also follow your own cravings and creativity. Toss out the conventional wisdom that food and beverage should be paired based on price point (the logic behind expensive champagne and caviar). Pair your caviar with cheap potato chips and your champagne with takeout. Forget the old adage "what grows together goes together" and be like young talented individuals across the food landscape bringing cultures and traditions together through pairings. People like Jack Beguedou, a whiskey expert and the creator behind one of my favorite Instagram accounts: Hood Sommelier. Jack founded a traveling event to merge the two things he is most passionate about: American whiskey and African food. Afrofusion is part dinner party, part dance party, and all guided by Jack's thoughtful palate.

"You know, when I go to a party and we're having jollof rice and wings and pineapple, we're drinking whiskey with it. But it's usually a single malt," he says. "So my idea was I wanted to get people to drink bourbon." When he first suggested bourbon to his friends they would say, "Oh, that's too sweet, that's a white people drink." And when he told people he knows through the bourbon community about African food, they always brushed it off as too spicy, or raised their eyebrows at the idea of eating goat. In reality, those two objections prove just how well the two would interact with each other. Food that's "too spicy" is ideal to balance a drink that is "too sweet." Jack says if both of these groups know one thing, it's good food and drink, so he was determined to get them in a room together. It finally happened in Omaha, then again in Louisville, and he has big plans for Washington, DC. At Afrofusion events, Jack serves a series of courses matched with straight bourbons or bourbon drinks. He sees one pairing as the core of the event. "Rice is the heart of African cooking. And I take jollof rice—you know rice cooked in a tomato stew seasoned with basil, anise, all the spices you think of—and then we'll top it with goat meat or beef. What do I pair with that? The staple of bourbon cocktails: the old-fashioned." Jack's old-fashioned uses spicy chili bitters in place of the typical Angostura, which boosts the overall intensity to meet the rice dish. Then there are the vanilla and caramel flavors of the bourbon that add the impression of balancing sweetness to the pairing. To accent that sweetness, Jack adds "a dash of cocoa on top of the old-fashioned, to get everything to meld together." Here his guests are eating the most quintessential African dish with the most quintessential bourbon cocktail, and they taste great together.

"You know, I was surprised when I first started floating the idea, how many distilleries weren't open to it. They seem so innovative, but like ten of them said no," Jack tells me. Heaven Hill partnered with Jack on his events and each consecutive Afrofusion balloons in size. "It was supposed to be forty-five maybe fifty people, but there's more than sixty people now and I think we will have to make it even bigger."

I'm not surprised Jack's event draws an ever-growing crowd. Trying unexpected foods and drinks together is a thrill. This kind of pairing shows you exactly what you've been missing by sticking to conventional wisdom. The unconventional yet delightful matchup between African food and American bourbon is a lot like putting mustard in your brownies or quirky elements on a cheese board. These creative matchups remind us that flavor is all about exploring. But what is the point of exploring if you can't find the words to describe our adventures?

CHAPTER NINE

A POET OF THE PALATE

"THE SERVICE WAS GREAT AND THE LIGHTING WAS JUST RIGHT. ALSO the sounds were not too loud so we could talk to each other . . . I remember ordering a steak, and it was just flavored so right and tasted so good, I think I could have ate two of them. It was a very pleasant meal, and I had a great time."

"When I ordered a pepperoni pizza and a Buffalo chicken pizza at one of my favorite places. I couldn't decide which one to order, so I ordered both and ate most of both of them."

"Every Christmas Eve my Italian grandfather and Greek grandmother would cook a meal consisting of creamy carbonara with bacon pieces and homemade spinach pie and sausage. It was always amazing."

These three responses came from Americans asked a single question: "What was the best meal of your life?" Paul Rozin, professor of psychology at the University of Pennsylvania asked two hundred Americans that question during his research on cultural attitudes about food. He says these responses, which he presented at the 2012 MAD Symposium in Copenhagen, Denmark (*mad* is the Danish word for "food"), were representative of the answers he received.

Paul was surprised how little description of actual food made it into many of the recountings of what was meant to be the best meal of Americans' lives. He wasn't asking about the best conversation, or the best date, or the best lighting in a restaurant, but the best meal. Where were the descriptions of the food?

This lack of descriptors when it comes to food is not uncommon. The most enthusiastic recommendations for restaurants usually include some combination of the words *good*, *delicious*, *pretty*, and occasionally a *flavorful* thrown in there. We know that we enjoyed a meal, but we have a hard time describing why or exactly what we enjoyed about it.

Eleven Madison Park, a three-Michelin-star restaurant in Manhattan, has one of the most expensive tasting menus in a city jam-packed with expensive tasting menus. Diners willing to pay for a meal that starts at $335 per person before drinks, tax, and tip are motivated to remember their extravagant feast. I went scrolling through social media captions and blog posts tagged with Eleven Madison Park to see how patrons recounted their experience of eating at the restaurant once voted best in the world. Excluding all the "Best meal ever!" and "Happy Birthday/Anniversary/Engagement" captions, the descriptions of a tasting menu at Eleven Madison Park don't diverge far from the answers given to Paul Rozin during his study.

> "Exquisite presentation and cuisine! The food was incredible for me but not my partner who was affected by the sodium in the food."
> "I can't figure out how to describe the meal I experienced at Eleven Madison Park last night, so I'm just going to put two words right here: inspired and inspiring."

"We are big foodies so the first thing we did while planning our trip to New York was book Eleven Madison Park. . . . it did NOT disappoint!! It's a full vegetarian tasting menu that was out of this world!"

"When it comes to us thinking back to this meal, we both actually thought about the bread first, which goes to show how good it was. It was quite unbelievable how they were able to create such a great vegan croissant bread."

At least there is mention of a specific dish that made the meal remarkable, but the portrayal of the memorable bread relies on generic positive terms, *good*, *great*, *unbelievable*. One of those Eleven Madison Park reviews goes as far as to admit the difficulty in describing their food experience. And with the proliferation of food and restaurant content on social media, this lack of sensory vocabulary is more apparent. Bloggers and passionate foodies need the right words to capture what they eat, drink, and savor, in order to stand out on crowded platforms. They're on the hunt to increase their vocabulary around food.

I always ask students what inspired them to sign up for my blind tasting classes. Sometimes they're couples looking for a fun date night. Other times they are hopeful whiskey, wine, or beer professionals looking to pick up on tricks to improve their blind-tasting approach. Occasionally they're a food photographer or blogger seeking wisdom on how to describe what they taste even when they don't know what it is.

One New Zealander in class told me he had an Instagram account that showcased pictures of breakfast and brunch foods.. He had close to one hundred thousand people following his breakfast adventures but his inability to describe the taste behind his posts vexed him.

"I feel like I can only say *cheesy* or *sweet* so many times," he told me. "Like bacon, egg, and cheese sandwiches—they're good if they're cheesy, and maybe, like, not greasy?"

He struggled to describe why the foods he shared stood apart from other food experiences. This blogger was not alone; most people never learn to effectively communicate what they taste. That's why for the first couple of glasses in each blind tasting class, students usually can't think of anything to say other than "This tastes like beer."

Once I clue them in that beer is barley-based, just like the bread they eat, more interesting words emerge: *toasted wheat bread*; *fresh-baked pizza crust*. Once they know about the barley connection, the students can judge whether the beer tastes more like cooked pasta, golden biscuits, or burnt bread. Soon, phrases like *warm oatmeal with raisins* are met with nods of agreement. By the time class is over, the breakfast blogger was ready for his next post with words like *caramelized*, *toasty*, *savory*, *rich*, *fresh*. Cheese melting over his sandwiches could be salty and mild (American cheese) or sharp and tangy (goat cheese). Buns were *crispy* or *buttery* or *supple* or *crusty*. Sauces could be *one-note* or *complex*, they could have *pops of texture* or be *velvety smooth*. You will leave this chapter armed with techniques and tools to help you find specific, provocative words to describe what you taste and communicate it to others.

First, I'll show you thought exercises and professional tools to help you identify what you taste. From there, you'll be able to produce a basic description of the flavor you taste. Then we will build on a basic description with tone, emotion, and story to portray your sensory experience in a way others can authentically relate to. Before this starts to sound too much like a creative-writing class held in the basement of your local middle school, just know that there is a simple template to organize all of this, which I'll share later in the chapter.

"What am I tasting for?" beloved chef and cookbook author Samin Nosrat asks a Parmesan maker on her Netflix series *Salt Fat Acid Heat*. She wants to know what should change in a cheese as it ages. The cheese maker explains that over time the cheese will transform from tasting like fresh milk to displaying rich dairy flavors and sweet nuttiness. A well-aged Parmesan will have crunchy crystals of tyrosine, in fact a Parmesan that has been aged forty months is a "fireworks parade" of crispy tyrosine crystals. That's what Samin should search for in each nibble of cheese.

Samin was lucky to be accompanied by the cheesemaker while endeavoring to identify flavors in Parmesan. Without a professional in the field by your side, how could you know what flavors to look for in a cheese? A good place to start is with the ingredient list. In the case of cheese, the flavors come from milk. So the most basic flavor terms used to describe it will reflect the spectrum of dairy, from fresh to aged. The spectrum will start at bright, fresh cream, or sweet young butter and continue to thick whipped cream, rich cultured butter and finally through to hard salty cheese or waxy salty rind. Wine, which is made from grapes, has a flavor spectrum that consists of fruit and plant attributes as well as some characteristics from the wood used in the wine-making process. Common basic wine terms include berry, stone fruit, floral, oaky, and vanilla. For beer brewed from barley, flavors are reminiscent of bread—lightly baked, toasted, or burnt. On top of that, beer is seasoned with hops, which display qualities of growing things like herbs, grasses, trees, and fruits.

This approach works for some items but it can be too basic. After all, there is only one ingredient in winter squash. It's winter squash. But the squash can display notes of nuttiness or custardy dairy flavors depending on the proteins, starches, acids, and other compounds in its chemical makeup. The spectrum of flavors related to these chemical attributes isn't intuitive, and we're once again left grasping for words to describe the squash other than the rudimentary *sweet*, *good*, or *delicious*.

The most prevalent tool available to assist with uncovering and identifying these tastes and aromas is the flavor wheel.

The first widely used flavor wheel was the wine aroma wheel de-

veloped at the University of California, Davis, by Ann C. Noble, a professor in the department of viticulture and enology. Her creation is a
visual way to display the ingredient spectrums previously discussed
as a round diagram. Ann's wheel consists of eleven broad categories
of common flavors used to reference wine: fruity, floral, spicy, herbaceous, nutty, caramel, woody, earthy, chemical, oxidized, microbiolog-
ical. These categories make up the central hub of the wheel. Within
each of the eleven broad categories are subcategories with words that
splay out from the central hub like spokes of a wheel. The fruity category, for example, contains the subcategories of citrus, berry, tree fruit,
tropical fruit, dried/cooked fruit, and other. Within each subcategory
there is another, smaller set of spokes that make a third ring. These are
specific flavors or foods. For example, within the tree fruit subcategory
there is cherry, apricot, peach, and apple.

Ann selected each word from a collection of wine descriptors con-
tributed by UC Davis students and wine industry professionals. These
descriptors are meant to tie the complicated chemistry of wine aromas
to ordinary, everyday flavors that are familiar to Americans. For example, ethyl hexanoate, an ester produced during wine fermentation,
is described using apple, pineapple, or simply "fruity" from the wheel.

The elements listed on Ann's wheel can readily be found in a standard American grocery store, things like raspberry or clove or asparagus. Even tar from the "chemical" section of the wheel can be found in
the store parking lot. Ann wanted to use common flavors because she
set out with a mission to make describing wine objectively like a scientist a straightforward endeavor. The wheel is purposefully devoid of
words that are biased (e.g., *unpleasant*, *luxurious*), esoteric (e.g., *tannic*,
rancio), or abstract (e.g., *sunshine*, *lusty*). Notice that the eleven categories are all ways to label specific aromas. There is no classification for
"flaws" or a "texture" category containing words that would describe
mouthfeel like *chalky*, *dry*, or *creamy*.

Ann banished all of these hedonic words from the wheel because she wanted to see them banished from the wine world as well. Since the 1980s, when she first premiered the wine aroma wheel, she has seen a great deal of success on this mission. Her simple and direct way of describing flavor was quickly and unanimously adopted. Winemakers used it on their labels, reviewers started using the terms in their critiques, sommeliers used it in their pitches to diners. Gone were the days of "luscious tannins from a good vintage," instead wines had "big dark fruit flavors of blackberry and dark cherry accented by notes of spice and tobacco."

After the wine aroma wheel popularized this way to visualize flavor, copycat versions popped up across myriad specialty-food industries. This structure of concentric rings starting with broad categories and fanning out to singular aromas has been copied again and again to exhibit the flavors of general foods like chocolate or coffee as well as very specific items like winter squash. There are even flavor wheels for individual ingredients, like the malt aroma wheel, to describe a small set of flavors within beer.

Every unique wheel provides guidelines of what flavors to look for in each sip or bite. Stringing a few of the words from a flavor wheel together become a basic flavor description.

Now, we can imagine Samin tasting the artisanal Parmesan cheese in Italy and instead of speaking to the cheese maker directly she could reference the aroma wheel for hard and semi-hard cheeses. She would be able to pick out the fresh cream and boiled milk characteristics in the younger cheeses and the hazelnut and hints of caramel in the aged ones.

Look at these flavor wheels below that focus on hard cheeses and beer. Many of the categories around the hub of the wheel are similar. For instance, both wheels have a category for "fruit(y)" flavors. Remarkably, for such disparate food items, some of the specific descrip-

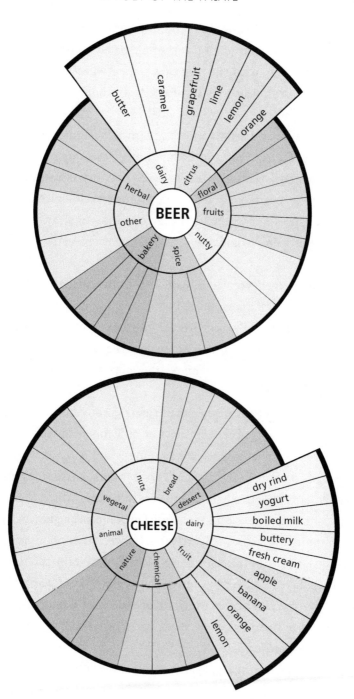

tors are also the same: orange and butter sit around the perimeter of both wheels. Orange is not a flavor immediately associated with hard cheese, but maybe with the help of a tasting wheel you'll discover it there! (Visit howtotastebook.com/wheels for more examples of flavor wheels.)

These flavor and aroma wheels are invaluable tools for beginners tasting specialty products for the first time. However, not every flavor wheel is created by a thoughtful professor, scientist, or research association. As more examples of flavor and aroma wheels are created across many industries and specialties, they continue to stray further and further from Ann's original goal of creating an objective description tool.

Now there are flavor wheels with "off-flavor" categories. (We talked about the many pitfalls associated with categorizing a flavor as an "off flavor" in Chapter 5.) I've seen wheels with an entire category dedicated to a list of the five basic tastes. Some wheels even offer modifiers like *intense, delicate, dull*, or *unbalanced*, the subjective words Ann created her wheel to avoid.

Another flaw of flavor wheels with less rigorous creators is the color scheme. Colors don't necessarily have an attachment to the words written upon them. The original wine aroma wheel is made with muted colors that correlate to the category. Fruity words are in soft pink, and vegetable words are in a light green. Less thoughtful wheels have dairy flavors in intense blues and tree fruit flavors in near glowing yellow, a color normally associated exclusively with citrus. This mismatch primes you to follow the color down the wrong flavor path.

This color discrepancy was part of the inspiration for another tasting tool that has taken off in the world of chocolate: Taste With Colour: The Chocolate Tasting Flavour Map created by Hazel Lee, a food scientist and chocolate judge.

Rather than tasting chocolate while looking at the lexicon on a flavor wheel, Hazel's strategy is to first taste the chocolate and be aware of what color associations arise in the mind's eye.

"For me, I just see the colors first in my mind, and then the word or the flavor comes after that," Hazel says. She realized her mind was less suggestable when conjuring a color before looking at the flavor wheel or the judging guidelines.

She set out to create a tool to aid in realizing flavor this way. From far away, the map Hazel painted appears to be an intuitive color spectrum with shades of green and brown melding into yellows that fade before turning into reds, pinks, and purples. It is something that could hang in an art school as a study on color. It's not until you get close to it that you see the dozens of flavor words written over the colors. Her philosophy of color and flavor clearly resonates with other tasters because her original hand-painted watercolor map is now a print that has been translated into eight languages and is sold in specialty shops around the world.

To use Hazel's map, first let the chocolate melt on your tongue, close your eyes, and see what colors or visuals come to mind. Once a color emerges, maybe it's a vivid red hue, you can go to the corresponding color on the Taste With Colour map. Each section of the map lists flavors that naturally occur in chocolate that are associated with this color. In the case of red, some of the flavors listed are dried cherries, prunes, fig, red wine. The most vividly colored of these descriptors is dried cherries, it's up to you to decide if that is what you're tasting or if it's the slightly less intense shade of prune.

"Look I see licorice as black, but some people might see it as a brown shade," Hazel says. "The map is really just presenting a concept to help people zone in on themselves and to see what connections the flavors have, what they bring to mind."

Hazel says that the dynamics of a flavor wheel can be distracting. For example, she wonders if the words and categories can be arranged in any order. As a scientist she feels that there must be, or should be, logic behind placing flavors opposite or next to each other. She reasons that the categories that touch should be similar to each other. These thoughts about the logistics of the wheel itself have nothing to do with making sense of what you're tasting; they're just distractions. And the enemy of fruitful tasting is distraction.

In order to avoid as many distractions as possible, Hazel doesn't even rely on words when she teaches Taste With Colour classes. She sets out paints, paint brushes, and chocolates for the students. Then, she will have them taste the chocolate without describing it at all. Students then use their painting supplies to capture what they taste on small squares of paper using only colors and abstract shapes. Dark bitter chocolate may be painted in browns or harsh reds using jagged lines while sweet milk chocolate may be translated as shades of pink in pleasing swirls. Instead of the student's thought process moving from flavor to color to word, she allows them to explore flavor through impressionistic imagery. An astonishing outcome of this methodology is the revelation that her students not only paint colorscapes that are very similar to one another but they're also similar to the shapes and colors some chocolate brands use on the packaging of the bar the students are tasting.

She asks me to wait for a second and scurries out of sight. When she comes back she's holding a large frame filled with thirteen small rectangular paintings about the size of an index card arranged around a central wrapper from an artisanal chocolate bar.

"This one I just love because the paintings are so similar to the actual packaging."

The paintings were all golden waves and circles with accents of faint pink and some of almond-hued streaks. The packaging itself was magenta with tight swirls of golden and orange.

"This is why I try to do workshops with chocolate makers: to get them to think about their packaging, because, look, the colors obviously communicate with the customers."

By encouraging her students, and chocolate makers, to think of colors first rather than words, Hazel has unknowingly helped them circumvent a psychological phenomenon that prevents us from accurately remembering our sensory experiences. It's called verbal overshadowing.

Verbal overshadowing as a term was first coined by Jonathan W. Schooler as part of the results of a study on humans' ability to remember faces. He had his subjects watch a video of a robbery. Half the subjects then verbally described the robber while the other half did a nonverbal control task. When it was time to identify the robber in a lineup, the subjects who gave a verbal description earlier in the study were markedly less accurate at identifying the correct person than the control group.

This occurs because when we give a description of a sensory experience and later attempt to recall that experience our memory of the words we used to describe it is stronger than our memory of the sensory inputs of the experience itself. In the case of the subjects identifying the correct robber, those who had transferred a visual experience into a verbal memory tapped into their verbal memory rather than their visual memory when looking at the lineup.

Dr. Schooler and his coauthors and collaborators continued to look for other sensory experiences that could be affected by verbal overshadowing such as recalling colors and abstract figures; naturally, tasting wine was an optimal test case. In his paper cleverly titled "The Misremembrance of Wines Past" he compared non-wine drinkers, wine drinkers with "intermediate" experience, and wine experts. Participants had to drink a red wine and either give it a verbal description or perform a control task, then select the wine they had previously tested out of a lineup of three. The middle group, which enjoyed drinking and learning about wine but had a fledgling vocabulary tied to describing it, were the most affected by verbal overshadowing. They were familiar with wine flavors, but weren't yet proficient at connecting those flavors with words. When they said their pedestrian description of the wine, it replaced their memory of what they tasted. These verbal memories were at the forefront of their minds when it was time to select the wine by taste. In contract, experts who had described wine flavors numerous times were able to separate the sensory data and the verbal description in their memory. So, when they smelled and tasted the wine again they were able to easily identify it.

It may be that Hazel's approach with shapes and colors is the perfect bridge between developing a sensory memory and having a reliable sensory vocabulary. Tying flavor to a visual and then that visual to words helps combat the default of turning a flavor into a verbal memory.

Stringing words together from a map or wheel will produce a basic sensory description of a flavor, but using those basic descriptions to depict the wines on a beverage list or nightly specials on a menu wouldn't do the job of engaging customers. The explanations we see at restaurants and in stores have more finesse to them, sometimes reading like little vignettes of poetry rather than a sales pitch.

A beer described as having notes of "fresh-from-the-oven ladyfingers topped with candied orange rind," ties directly back to the *fresh-baked bread* and *orange* words on the corresponding flavor wheel. "Freshly turned garden on a spring morning," is a fancy twist on the *grass* and *earth* words from the perimeter of the tea flavor wheel.

By pulling the basics from the flavor wheel, pairing them with our personal collection of references, and combining them with experiences, we can start to form more evocative summaries of what we taste. We understand that candied orange peel and orange have the same primary flavor, but one is more specific and intriguing than the other. Beyond being intriguing, we place greater value on a beer described as tasting like an artisan pastry than one compared to a generic loaf. Multiple studies have shown that words associated with high-end products—words like *steak, elegant, truffle,* and *velvety*—are more likely to be used in reviews of expensive wines while basic words like *good, pizza,* and *tropical* are consistently found in critiques of cheap plonk.

And the price we're willing to pay doesn't only hinge on the association between the word and quality; we're also subconsciously more willing to pay for longer words. Another study showed that wine reviews with an average word length of seven characters rather than six characters represented a wine that people were willing to pay $2.60 more for per bottle.

It's proven that we'll pay more for longer words, but not every tasting description is meant to increase the bottom line. In fact, intimidating seven letter words may be enough to keep people from trying something new. Carin Luna-Ostaseski, founder of SIA Scotch Whisky, takes a straightforward approach when describing her product. Her goal is to reach an audience she calls "scotch curious." In her opinion people who aren't familiar with scotch often associate it with big bold flavors of smoky peat and burning alcohol, but that characterization isn't always true.

By controlling the blend, Carin created a scotch whiskey that displays notes of vanilla, caramel, and lemon zest up front with just a touch of smoked vanilla as a tertiary characteristic. She says she settled on the blend because it brought up memories of a carnival with caramel popcorn and caramel apples and funnel cake when she nosed it. A fun, welcoming carnival is exactly the type of environment she wanted to evoke as opposed to a smoky, dark, leather-clad lounge, which comes to mind when sipping many scotches.

Once she knew her whiskey tasted approachable, smooth, and slightly sweet with no alcohol burn she had to go about getting people to buck their ideas about scotch and try something new.

"My philosophy was, let me choose some descriptors that are a little bit more general, a little bit more safe," she says. "I'm not dumbing it down. I want people to be like, I like vanilla. I like caramel. I'll try this."

While Carin keeps her tasting notes cheerful and straightforward (the SIA bottle currently reads "SIA awakens the nose with a hint of vanilla and caramel, followed by a touch of citrus honey. Enjoy!") some of the whiskey reviewers who write about it veer into the whimsical. She's read comments that contain flavors like marshmallow fluff and sliced banana.

"The one that really got me was 'lead pencil!' I thought, *What is he talking about?*" Carin says with a vestige of an eye roll. After rereading the review, she called her importer, who told her some people use 'lead pencil' to indicate a flavor of iodine in the smoky notes of scotch whiskeys. "So what he means is that smoky alcohol or distillate flavor."

Saying an abstract term instead of what you really mean is the opposite of Carin's uncomplicated approach. She speaks to people in terms that they understand so they won't be intimidated by her product or the scotch category.

Aldous Huxley's 1944 novel *Time Must Have a Stop* contains a passage that encapsulates this idea that thoughtful descriptions don't need to be outrageous to be effective. It also happens to be my all-time favorite depiction of the taste of champagne, specifically a 1916 vintage from Louis Roederer. The main character, Sebastian, is working to ingratiate himself with his wealthy epicurean uncle. When Sebastian takes a sip of the champagne served at dinner he thinks to himself that it had the taste "of an apple peeled with a steel knife." But he doesn't share this thought with his uncle; instead he says that it tastes of "Scarlatti's harpsichord music," a comparison that delights his pompous uncle.

The first description rings true. It elegantly plucks two common descriptors for champagne, found on the wine aroma wheel, apple and metallic, and brings them together in a way that is evocative and tactile. The peeling away of skin with a sharp knife is reminiscent of the sharp tartness of the apple and prickle of carbonation. This accessible description is like the cheerful carnival of caramel corn in Carin's whiskey.

The second description, the one that he gives to please his uncle, feels contrived and pretentious. This comparison to a prolific Italian composer's music has no innate meaning to the common man. In fact, it may mean nothing at all to his uncle, either, but it pleases the wealthy uncle because the abstract analogy demonstrates they are in the same social class: the ones who enjoy fine champagne as much as fine music. Occasionally, when you come across a tasting term that doesn't seem to fit, it's likely that the writer is using it to indicate that they are an "insider" of a certain class. (Scotch experts in the case of lead pencil, wealthy elite in the case of harpsichord music.) These jargon terms cause more confusion than clarity.

Writers of literature like Huxley are so adept at portraying sensory experiences like the taste of champagne because they are trained storytellers. As it turns out, lengthy words and interesting descriptions make us open our wallets to buy something, but a description written as a story will make us dig still deeper inside them.

Two French researchers noticed the price of Grand Crus from Bordeaux had enjoyed a "strong increase" in recent years. They decided to investigate what was driving the change in value perception. After analyzing the 132 chateaux members of Union des Grands Crus de Bordeaux the researchers determined "the price increase is not explained by the objective value of these products but rather their symbolic position and image evoked of a world of luxury." Specifically, the research-ers found that stories, especially those that covered how the wine was made and topics about the winemaker, reliably correlated with an in-crease in wine price.

Another study presented the same three wines to subjects in three different situations: under blind conditions with no additional infor-mation (like the tastings in chapter 6), a tasting with basic information about the sensory attributes of the wine (think of this as a list of words from a flavor wheel, words that apply to the specific wine), and a tasting with sensory attributes as well as background history about the winery itself and the quality of the grapes. Across all three wine samples the tasting with the description that combined sensory information with storytelling consistently evoked higher expectations before tasting the wines, increased overall liking ratings, and substantially boosted will-ingness to pay when compared to the blind condition, with the basic condition landing in between. Without a story to tell after the tasting, a wine is just a wine, a bourbon is just a bourbon, and a chocolate is just a chocolate.

These stories don't need to be told by the artisan makers them-selves to effectively increase the value perception of a specialty product.

In a tasting of "China's Famous Teas" at the Jin Yun Fun Tea Shop in the Flatiron neighborhood of New York City, tea master Olivia care-fully brewed me a cup of tea. The leaves in this cup that had been hand-plucked from trees that were more than eight hundred years old. For the previous five teas in the tasting Olivia told me about flavor notes like fresh bark, or white flower stems while I sipped the tea. The teas were all expressive and graceful but not especially profound. As I in-haled the steam from this sixth-round cup of tea she said, "You can smell all the things the trees have smelled, you will taste all the things the tree has seen in eight hundred years."

At the risk of sounding dramatic, I have to say that I couldn't take a sip right away because I had a bit of a knot in my throat. Without being able to explain it exactly, I knew what she meant. The tea smelled of brown and green at the same time. There was a scent of rich clay, like earth but with springtime sun-showers and freshly sprouted grass. It was a cup of bewitching contradictions, and the only way to describe it was to say it smelled like eight hundred summers, eight hundred winters, seventy thousand rain showers, hundreds of thousands of sunbeams swallowed up by a tree and given to me in a cup. This short story about the age of the tree that provided the tea leaves combined with her succinct description of what I would taste made the cup unforgettable.

This is the last element that helps descriptions of taste feel authentic: words that are collected from our other senses and emotions. A good storyteller creates depth within their story by using words that capture colors, palpable sensations, and feelings. These kinds of words and emotions added to a description can make it more relatable and vivid without it getting too whimsical.

Spicy peppers and burning alcohol can be angry. Bubbles from carbonation can be zippy and lively. Bright citrus flavors can be cheerful, while the earth and ash of charred mushrooms is somber. The vocabulary doesn't need to be limited to emotions; Olivia effectively used personification to emulate the taste of the tea. Shards of broken toffee can dance on the palate just as sweet and sour flavors can be dance partners. An aftertaste that lingers for minutes is lazy in your mouth.

Remember, the goal of stretching our minds and our vocabulary is to better communicate what we love and share it with others. Before we dive into the process for describing taste, take a second to reflect on this and accept that no description will work perfectly for everyone. The range of experiences out there is vast and varied, and it is impossible to be universally relatable, but we can try our best. By incorporating objective flavor notes (like those we find on flavor wheels), thinking of our audience, embracing story, and using words that depict emotion and tactile sensation, we can come close!

On to this description template I've been promising you. To begin, your description should be three to four sentences. Any longer and you risk opining; shorter descriptions may be too brief to have real meaning. Start off with a few words on what the item you're trying to describe looks like. The concepts of French plating: texture, color, and volume, are a helpful guide. Observe the food or drink you are describing. Is the most prominent aspect of its appearance its texture, its color, or its volume? An aged Parmesan cheese that crumbles into rocky shards is texture, a bright pink Cosmopolitan cocktail is color, and a salad that towers inches off the plate is volume.

After developing a visual description, move on to the primary aroma you sense using a word from a main ingredient or a flavor wheel. This goes back to the tasting method when you identified the most prominent flavor in what you were tasting. For the aged Parmesan, the primary aroma may be inspired by a word on the flavor wheel like "nutty" or "buttery." The primary aroma in the Cosmo cocktail would come from one of its ingredients, probably the tart, bright cranberry juice. Take this a step further and consider what condition that primary aroma is in. Use that to modify the primary aroma. Is the hazelnut flavor rich? Or candied? How about that cranberry note in the cocktail? Is it fresh cranberry or cranberry jam? Some suggestions are *fresh-picked, dried, juicy, cooked, stewed, bold, warm, flat, canned, cooling, bright,* or *intense.*

Once you've identified the primary aroma, sprinkle in some of the secondary and tertiary aromas as well as the basic tastes. Are there more evocative synonyms for the words you pulled from the flavor wheel? Maybe *unbaked pizza crust* is a more descriptive way to say *dough* or *toasted walnuts* works in the place of *nutty.* Be sure to expand on how these peripheral notes interact with the primary aroma. Maybe they compete with it, or they are almost obscured by it. They could exist in harmony or dance together, or maybe they simply mingle.

The next step is to consider the texture you feel in your mouth and nostrils. You could be feeling a creamy sensation or it could be *drying, chalky, aggressive, zippy, puckering, furry, fragile, crunchy, soft, delicate,* or *numbing*. It can help to compare the texture to familiar items that exist outside of dining. Some textures are reminiscent of fabrics—satin, suede, or leather—or natural items: prickly like pine needles, breakable like clumps of dry sand, crisp like freshly fallen snow.

Finally, think about how the flavor is making you feel. The sensation could be energizing, rich, surprising, calming, meditative, horrifying, scary, or so joyful you wish to exalt.

Appearance, aroma, flavor, mouthfeel and emotion come together to create a basic description in this fill-in-the-blank style template. Simply place your own words within the brackets.

This [color/texture/volume] [item] [item category] smells of [modifier] [primary aroma] mingling with [secondary aroma] and [secondary aroma]. On the palate it is [mouthfeel] with flavors of [one of the five basic tastes] [primary flavor] and a [mouthfeel or flavor] on the finish. It reminds me of [emotion/pop culture reference/other version of this item].

In reference to the Cosmopolitan cocktail, the completed template would look like this:

This bright pink Cosmopolitan cocktail smells of bright cranberry mingling with fresh lime and subtle orange. On the palate it is tangy but not puckering with flavors of sweet cranberry and a little alcoholic warmth on the finish. It reminds me of the Cosmopolitans the characters drink on a lively night out on *Sex and the City*.

After you practice using this template, you can break away from it and use words that appeal to specific audiences. For example, are the people you're describing the flavor to familiar with the item? Is it something you're recommending or not so much? Let's take one of the finest blue cheeses I've ever tasted, the Bayley Hazen Blue from Jasper Hill Farm in Greensboro, Vermont, and go through a more in-depth description process. Here are my perceptions: The colors are the most prominent visual attribute. It's a deep-cream-colored block with veins and patches of dark blue/green throughout. The most striking flavor is of hazelnuts, followed by grassiness and clove or anise spiciness. I would say the hazelnut flavor is a toasted hazelnut, and the grass is dry and hay-like. Then there's the fact that the texture of the cheese is akin to fudge that is like buttery satin in the mouth. Between the creaminess and the nutty sweetness, the cheese is a little sensual, luxe, and seductive.

My fancy but short-and-sweet description would read: "From the hills of Vermont, Bayley Hazen Blue is a creamy off-white cheese flecked with blue green veins. A sweet, toasted hazelnut flavor is grounded by hay-like grassiness and spice cabinet notes of anise and clove all mingling with rich cream. It's easy to be seduced by the soft fudgedy texture and flavors that are complex but not too intense for the blue cheese wary."

Using this method can help you expand your ability to describe what you taste. Instead of calling a Czech pilsner "a light and refreshing beer," you can describe it as a strikingly brilliant deep golden lager capped with frothy white foam that lingers for the entirety of the pint. Delicate notes of butter melting over fresh-baked bread are complemented by the fleeting aromas of dried herbs and grasses that come from Czech-grown hops. Brisk and bubbly, the beer disappears from your palate as soon as it's swallowed, leaving it clean and refreshed, ready for each consecutive sip until you're left with only an empty glass and a quenched thirst.

And the next time a menu or recipe promises you "an incarnadine lagoon so richly savory, memories of seared filet mignon float to the forefront of the mind with bright pops of basil grown under a Tuscan sunset refreshing the palate just in time for the next bite," you can work backward from the description to realize you'll be dining on meat sauced with red wine and herbs. Equipped with this description template you're ready to jet off on your next exotic food or drink experience. And when you're asked, "How was the trip?" You'll have a riveting story about what you smelled and tasted in place of the uninspired answer, "The food was so good!"

PART FOUR

TASTING LIFE

CHAPTER TEN

TRAVEL LIKE A TASTER

MARTHA STEWART IS BEST KNOWN FOR BUILDING A MULTIMEDIA EM-pire based on homemaking content—and maybe also for her five-month stint in prison. But I—and I suspect at least a fraction of her nearly four million Instagram followers—stay up to date with her for another reason: the absolutely engrossing saga of the brazen misbehaving peacocks that rule her farm. She is constantly coming to their defense in captions, and reminding her followers that the correct term is *peafowl* because she has both males and females on the property! Turns out I'm a sucker for peafowl antics.

While I can appreciate most of her non-avian posts, there are some that simply make me cringe. I honestly love her selfies, and her picture-perfect plates are aspirational. However, I simply cannot stomach the insanely elaborate meals she serves on her private jet. Vine-ripened, fresh-from-the-garden tomatoes, hefty scoops of osetra caviar, and thinly shaved smoked salmon all disgraced. On more than one occasion, upon seeing one of her "plane food, not plain food" posts I have audibly wailed, "Martha! No!!!" All that good food going to waste. You see, there is no environment more hostile to our senses than an airplane. Even Martha's plane, which from the pictures looks very comfortable, has the three hallmarks of sensory destruction. First there is profoundly dry air. The air in the cabin is recycled through filters, rendering it exceptionally clean (a boon for our hopes of making it to our destination without contracting a new disease) and also exceptionally dry. Humidity in a typical airplane ranges from 5 to 15 percent, depending on how tightly people are packed together. (Yes, there is one disadvantage to flying first-class, uncomfortably dry skin!) For context, the daytime humidity in the Mojave Desert ranges from 10 to 30 percent, depending on the season. These arid surroundings in an airplane wreak havoc on the moist lining of our nose first, and with extended exposure our mouths and eyes will also dry out. We rely on mucus and saliva to put flavor compounds in contact with our taste and odor receptors. In conditions where we are short on both, only the most fragrant foods and beverages have any flavor at all. A 2010 study conducted in an airplane simulator found that perception of light and fresh flavors decreased across the board while in flight, but spices like cardamom, lemongrass, and curry were still apparent. Kiss that subtle difference a once-a-year summer-garden-grown tomato offers goodbye.

Dry nostrils are just one issue fighting the appreciation of delicate vine-ripened tomato flavor; the nasal passageway is also narrowed by swelling due to low cabin pressure.

"It's like having a cold," the research team's leader from that same 2010 study told German News outlet Deutsche Welle shortly after it was published. "When you have a cold, all your nasal mucous [tissue] swells up and you have reduced odor and taste perception." And for the record, this unexpected inflammation also happens within our delicate sniffer every time a storm comes rolling in (storms are low-pressure systems). The lockdown during a hurricane is not the time to break out your finest añejo tequila. In this case, the silver stuff and a heavy hand with the lime juice will do.

The few flavor molecules that successfully make the treacherous journey through narrowed dry passage to the olfactory bulb will still seem bland thanks to the final wicked sense killer in the airplane trifecta: loud and constant background noise. The sounds of a plane engine might seem like a low hum, but in reality, passengers are exposed to 85 decibels of sound for the entirety of the flight. That's roughly the equivalent of a continuously running food blender or the sounds of traffic outside a car window. Sounds this loud are known to dampen our sensitivity to salty and sweet foods. Go ahead and save one of the speculoos cookies flight attendants hand out on your next trip to eat at home. When you taste the crispy golden-brown biscuits in a quiet environment, they pack a stark sugary punch that we don't experience on the plane.

One curious result of the loud background noise on planes is that it seems to make us more sensitive to some savory flavors. The researchers from the 2010 study even hypothesized that's why so many people order tomato juice on planes and nowhere else. The balance of the drink is shifted; tomato's natural sweetness takes a back seat to its umami qualities. And since our overall sensitivity to flavor is reduced in an airplane cabin, the vegetal flavors of the juice seem less intense. Tomato juice may be one of the only beverages offered on a flight that really tastes like something rather than a whisper of its on-ground persona. My go-to order of ginger ale is affected in a similar way. I can't stand the sweetness of soda on the ground, but in the sky the drink seems more ginger-forward and less sweet.

Martha's fresh-from-the-garden tomatoes were surely wasted on a cabin full of friends and colleagues who were dried-out, stuffy-nosed, and had dulled senses. Martha, some advice if you're reading this: enjoy a champagne toast and some caviar in the airport before you take off. Then serve an umami-laden menu of Bloody Marys and bacon, egg, and cheese sandwiches in the sky. The same advice goes to you: pack savory snacks like beef jerky or Parmesan crisps if you want your in-flight treat to have any flavor, and save the luxuries for after you land.

Once your feet are safely on the ground outside the airport, the effects of the flight are still with you. The first thing you should do if you're on a tasting journey is drink lots of water to try to replenish your mucus and saliva supply. To get serious about replenishing your tasting powers, you can pack a travel humidifier. Mine weighs only a couple of ounces and is small enough to fit in a standard cup holder. It's definitely worth the minor inconvenience to pack it. Sometimes your hotel will be set up perfectly to hack your own quasi-humidifier. If the heater and/or air-conditioning unit has a flat top (something level enough that you can drape a towel over), you can simply wet a towel, wring it out to even out the moisture and make sure it doesn't drip, and drape it over your unit. The air blowing into the room will carry a little moisture with it, plus the moisture evaporating off the towel generally will provide a tiny humidity boost.

Beyond tossing the travel humidifier in the suitcase or rigging up our DIY version, there are more things you can do ahead of a trip to make the experience tastier.

Paul Rozin is an eminent cultural psychologist and professor at the University of Pennsylvania. Of his more than one hundred published research papers, many of them have been dedicated to meals and pleasure both experienced and remembered. His work specifies three types of pleasure that can be gleaned from a dining experience: the pleasure of anticipating the event; the pleasure of experiencing it; and the pleasure of remembering it. With proper planning you can maximize all three types of delight on a vacation.

Before traveling, I tend to make reservations at particular restaurants well ahead of time and study the menu, plotting out exactly which dishes I'll order, what I'll try to persuade my husband to split with me, and the drinks I'll pair with my choices. This routine is heavy on anticipatory pleasure. During the weeks, sometimes months, I spend looking forward to the meal and all the flavors that will come along with it, my anticipation continuously grows. Logically, one would think that experiencing the carefully planned meal, finally tasting the flavors I had planned out, would be the pinnacle of pleasure, but Paul tells me that maximizing anticipatory pleasure can lessen the actual experienced pleasure of a meal. It's like I had already lived through the meal twenty times in my mind, so living it the twenty-first time in real life is nothing special.

This thought is reminiscent of my reaction to the Blue Hill at Stone Barns carrot. More than just thinking about the carrot dozens of times between making the reservation and actually eating it, I saw this carrot on TV and I heard a restaurant critic describe the carrot in words that can only be categorized as effusive. I sat in my booth at the restaurant itself looking forward to the carrot. Did the real carrot stand a chance of living up to the carrot I anticipated? It did a pretty good job. But I have to wonder what my experience would have been like if I wasn't expecting the dish. How would I have reacted to a single unadulterated carrot served alone on a beautifully crafted ceramic plate?

The surprise and delight I experienced in that moment of the carrot's appearance would be the second type of pleasure: experienced pleasure. To maximize this type of enjoyment while traveling, leave room in your itinerary to take suggestions from locals you meet on your travels or the servers at restaurants you previously reserved. Walking into a situation without any expectations will surely provide the kind of experienced pleasure that comes up unexpectedly, but to cement the memory of that pleasure you need to order something new when you get there.

"If you order a dish you know and like, you get a certain anticipation and enjoyment of it," says Paul, "but you aren't creating new memories; you're creating another memory of something you have had before and know that you like."

Say you're obsessed with pão de queijo, the tapioca flour–based cheese bread snacks that puff up to have a crusty outside and soft but chewy inside. You make sure to order them everywhere you see them available. You've had some great ones and some forgettable ones, but you're counting down the days until you land in Brazil and you can have the real authentic thing, the genuine article. Sitting outside Pão de Queijo Haddock Lobo in São Paulo with a basketful of freshly puffed cheese snacks, you won't be creating a new flavor memory. These real Brazilian-made pão will be lost in the long and continuing procession of pão de queijo in your life. Fortunately there is a simple fix to this minor memory mishap.

"So, I sort of try to split the difference myself. Most meals are more than one thing," Paul says.

In this case he suggests asking someone who works there what's good on the menu. You're all but guaranteed to create a long-lasting memory by ducking into the corner bar your hotel bellman suggested because he loves to nosh on some late-night bolinhos de bacalhau (fried codfish snacks) surrounded by clusters of quiet locals.

But according to Paul, ordering a new food can aggravate a common dining quandary: "The safety issue. It's a major issue with people's discomfort about new foods. If you have uncertainty about new foods, the safer the environment appears, the better you'll feel when trying them," says Paul.

An off-the-beaten-path saloon you've never heard of may not appear safe enough to some diners, so Paul recommends trying something new at a nice restaurant rather than a roadside stand.

And here, I have an unconventional suggestion: if you find yourself traveling out of the country but are apprehensive about the unfamiliar foods you may be confronted with, there are worse things you could do than go to the closest McDonald's or Starbucks. (Even if you aren't nervous about trying new foods, if you see the golden arches at a rest stop or the airport it's not a bad place to stop.) The McDonald's around the world act in the same way fast-food restaurants in America do: they take the popular flavors of the moment and convert them into something appealing for the masses. The surroundings of the fast-food restaurant look exactly the same as they do stateside, and you can convert the electronic menu to English so you can understand each and every ingredient. Voilà! A safe way to introduce you to new, local flavors. In New Zealand I had a "Kiwiburger," which came topped with sliced beets, a fried egg, and the standard lettuce, tomato, and onion. Belgium has a delicacy smothered in Belgian beer cheese and mayonnaise along with crispy bacon called the "Generous Jack." Acquaint yourself with the local flavors in an environment that feels familiar as a sort of training ground for the rest of your trip. And in all honesty, you're likely to see more locals inside Mickey D's than in any of the bars or tourist-driven restaurants surrounding the town marketplace.

Even inside a familiar and welcoming restaurant you still might be skittish about eating bloodred beets on your burger. Guess what? That's natural. Humans are naturally wary of trying new foods; it all goes back to keeping ourselves from being poisoned. The slightest sour or bitter flavor in a tiny taste of something new might be enough to turn someone off from eating the entire dish. Some people are more naturally neophobic than others when it comes to food, and that's not their fault. Researchers have found that about two thirds of our neophobic tendencies related to eating are hereditary. A child with picky-eating parents can only hope to be marginally more open to novel food experiences.

For the most risk-averse eaters, vacation is likely the ideal opportunity to try unfamiliar food (as long as it's perceived as safe!) for several reasons. "People think they're immediately relaxed because they're not at home, or not in the office, which is true, but you're also relaxed because you don't have any olfactory triggers of being at the office or being at home that create stress," says Dawn Goldworm, an olfactory expert, trained perfumer, and cofounder of 12.29, an olfactive branding company. "You're now in a new environment that doesn't have any of those olfactive triggers, so you can relax. Your brain actually really does relax."

Subconsciously, from the sensory world around us, we know we're in an environment where things may be different. Our habits have changed. We don't smell the trash cans at the end of the driveway every Wednesday morning or hear the train cruise down the tracks at exactly noon every day. The smell of our normal hand soap or dishwashing detergent is nowhere to be found. Your mind fully registers, *I have a feeling we're not in Kansas anymore.* Studies show that our taste memory, especially for flavors we remember as repulsive, is tied to a spatial or "place" memory. In new locations, the brain responses to foods previously considered negative are "more forgiving." During an especially enjoyable dinner a few thousand miles away from the landlocked shack you tried oysters in for the first time is a good time to give the bivalves another shot.

Since a new physical environment is already forgiving, combined with the natural relaxation that comes with the lack of olfactory stress triggers, we're primed to collect new positive flavor experiences while traveling. Building a healthy balance of anticipatory pleasure and experienced pleasure into a trip comes from the planned and unplanned, and both can result in the third type of pleasure brought on from dining: the remembered.

Studies have shown that flavor (specifically aroma) produces the strongest memories we'll have in our lifetime. After the age of twenty or so, the opportunity to create these sensory-triggered memories drastically diminishes. "We create the majority [of sensory memories] when we're young. Before we're born up until about ten years old," says Dawn. "As adults, we rarely have new emotional experiences. We recycle them. So that's why you don't create as many effective memories as an adult."

She says that after childhood, we'll create memories triggered by scent around milestones and major emotional events: the first time you fall in love, moving away from home for the first time, having children. "Other than that, it's when you're traveling around the world, right? With new food, new smells. Maybe it's the first time you smell diesel if you go to the United Kingdom. All of those memories are connected to new smells."

Travel is an investment of money and, perhaps more important, time, and one of the great benefits of it is these profound memories. So how do you go about capturing them? First of all, they will come naturally. If you are smelling diesel for the first time in the United Kingdom, maybe you're coming up the stairs at the exit of King's Cross station, and merely inhaling the fumes near the line of black taxis is enough to make a memory. But a little extra effort has a huge payoff when it comes to creating lasting memories of the flavors you encounter on your vacation. Perhaps the most obvious way is a technique you already engage in: busting out that camera!

Restaurateurs may collectively plot the demise of the smartphone at the table because it distracts from the attention to flavor by providing more addictive things to concentrate on, like scrolling social media or responding to email. One of my favorite stories about the backlash against phones in restaurants was a Beirut establishment that would give diners a 10 percent discount if they handed their device over to the staff for the duration of their meal. This was all the way back in 2013; I have to imagine 10 percent wouldn't be enough to tempt many diners today. But the camera function of our pocket supercomputers helps us take time to focus on what we're eating as well as a brief moment for that anticipatory pleasure Paul studies. Next time you take a photo of a food you're about to enjoy, stop and make a mental note, too, of where you are, who you're eating with, and why this moment is unlike any other. Later, when you post the image or show it to your coworkers, you'll be able to recall how you felt and what you smelled when you captured it. Memory achieved. In fact, a study from 2019 showed that if you do go through with posting an image you took during the meal it will improve your overall evaluation of the restaurant you dined at and your rating of the dining experience.

Another way to instill memories of a meal is purposefully turning the conversation to the food in front of you. "That's why sharing works well; you pay more attention to your food experience because you can talk about it," says Paul.

But this doesn't work if you're eating different dishes. "Right now, I'm working on a study to see if when people share food, they actually like each other better," Paul adds.

Talking about flavor is a way to make verbal overshadowing (from chapter 9) work in our favor. As you eat and share stories that the flavors remind you of, or remark on the potency of the local produce in whatever location you're visiting, you're effectively writing the story you'll tell later when you recall this moment. Try to use the steps discussed in chapter 9 and write the description you'd put on the menu for the dish you're enjoying and see what your fellow diners think.

Paul's research also shows that unlike other hedonic experiences, such as looking at art or listening to music, our memory of food doesn't seem to be as affected by recency. You may think back on the final song of a concert as being the best performance of the night, but unless the dessert is really spectacular, you probably won't think of it as the highlight of the meal. But the end of the meal, or the trip, can still leave a figurative bad taste in your mouth.

"I try to always mentally end any vacation before we leave for the airport," says Paul. "If you don't, you might end up saying, 'Oh the flight home was terrible,' when someone asks you how your vacation was just because it's the last thing you remember."

Using the car ride to the airport to mentally end your trip is a good idea, but there is less time to mentally end your meal before the ultimate bummer arrives: the bill. Unlike a concert or a visit to a museum, where the price of admission is long forgotten by the time the experience ends, the way we pay at restaurants invites us to do mental-value calculation before the meal has a chance to settle in our minds.

"It's easier for people who smoke," laughs Paul. "They can leave the restaurant to have a smoke or something and that is the end of the meal. Everyone else, maybe you can take a walk outside."

Going for a walk isn't always possible, but there are other ways to mentally instill the pleasures of your meal to remember in the future before the check comes to deflate any exuberance. I'm partial to ranking all the dishes and discussing which was my favorite and which was the most original. Paul thinks it's a pretty good idea, but there's really no reason to recall the bad dishes in the lower rankings if you don't want to remember them.

All of these ways to instill pleasurable memories work because of how the brain functions. In fact, they might even work too well.

"Say there's a chocolate maker in the Caribbean and he will temper his chocolate and it's perfect," says Hazel Lee, the creator of Taste With Colour. "It melts softly and is exactly how he likes it, but then it gets to England, and our room temperature the majority of the year is a lot lower than it is in Jamaica. We might think that the chocolate is a little firmer, maybe it's too slow to melt. What this means is it is just a different eating experience. Everything is totally shifted eating it over here compared to eating it where it is made."

Take Hazel's point one step further and imagine you've had the best chocolate tasting of your life in Jamaica. The chocolate has a fierce snap but instantly becomes a lavish syrup of sweet cocoa scented with molasses, toasted brioche, and the faint perfume of honeysuckle in your mouth. You fill the suitcase with as many chocolate bars as you can fit; you even bring one for the plane. (This was before you read this chapter and realized you would never, never waste this fine chocolate on a plane ride.) And when you get home and share a bar with your dog sitter as a thank-you gift, you insist she tastes some right there with you because you want to share in the serene experience of this expertly crafted chocolate. But you almost cry. Not because it's as beautiful as your first taste, but because it's far from it.

To subvert this nasty trick of the senses, edible-souvenir shopping must be a little strategic. The criteria are not too difficult; plenty of options will be available on the store shelves on Main Street, USA, in Orlando as well as the public markets in Thailand. First, you must not have tasted your prize of choice yet. Second, your item must come packaged or be from a store that offers to properly package it for you. This means the croissants on the streets of Paris must stay squarely in Paris. The same for any and all Chicago hot dogs. I once brought beignets home from New Orleans wrapped tightly in their paper bag, anticipating warming them just slightly in the oven. (I would not disrespect my cross-country treasure with the microwave.) But my cherished fried dough squares were dead on arrival; the thin veneer of powdered sugar had absorbed into the bread during travel, leaving them sad and naked-looking. I pushed forward with my plan, placing them on a lined baking sheet, but when they were warmed through, they somehow tasted both stale and greasy at once.

I will assert once again, make sure you don't choose anything you've already tasted on the trip—this includes wine, cognac, and makgeolli. This does not mean you can't bring anything home from the Italian winery in the hills of Tuscany. Just ask the person who helped you select the wines you tasted to recommend a bottle you haven't tried yet. It can be similar in style, but it can't be *the same*. Leave your glass of Chianti classico behind with the Tuscan sunset and build a new kind of anticipatory pleasure for the Brunello you've tucked in your suitcase. This strategic mission will also have you on the lookout your whole trip for items that will make ideal gifts. When I was in Belgium close to Christmas, I adored the speculoos cookie displays in so many shop windows. They even came in decorative tins that would protect them so that no airline employee, no matter how hard they chucked my suitcase, could break them.

And so you've returned, your gifts in tow ready to be shared or savored. Your memories of the new things you tried and the people who recommended them to you are firmly instilled in your mind. Once again, it's time to start dreaming about the next place you'll go and the flavors you'll find there. There is a lot to taste in this world.

CHAPTER ELEVEN

WHAT TASTERS KNOW

THIS WHOLE TIME I'VE BEEN PROMISING YOU THAT IF YOU TASTE thoughtfully, use the method, and collect some references for your mental flavor wardrobe, you'll start noticing your life change for the better. But those things take time, and you're looking for your payoff now. I get that, so here you go.

Here are the tricks and facts that all tasters know. A couple of tools. A couple of habits. A little science. Tips that make good things taste better longer and save you a couple of bucks along the way. There is a laundry list of things seasoned tasters know and do to appreciate what we eat more and savor the world around us a little better.

AIR IS THE ENEMY.

AIR: IT'S WHAT MAKES YOUR APPLES TURN BROWN, YOUR BEER TASTE like cardboard, and your wine turn to vinegar. It carries with it all the nasties floating around us every day: yeast cells, bacteria, particles of dust, and spores of God-knows-what that would be more than happy to grow in whatever moist environment you leave open for them to fall in to. Have you ever noticed that you had a carton of fresh-squeezed orange juice or jug of milk that stayed perfectly tasty far longer than the expiration date stamped on the side of it? I'll bet you sealed that cap almost as soon as you were done pouring and placed it back in the fridge immediately. No airborne beasties to spoil the milk means better tasting milk for longer.

But for the most part it's not bacteria that makes air every taster's enemy—it's oxygen. Oxygen is a highly reactive atom. It carries six electrons and is ready to snatch two electrons from almost any other atom to make a complete set of eight. This means that as soon as it enters any space, it's liable to start changing the flavor profile through oxidation reactions. Oxidation creates stale, papery, savory, musty, rancid, and, um, old-people smell. Literally. Around the age of forty our skin begins producing more fatty acids as our natural antioxidant barrier deteriorates. The chemical 2-nonenal is produced when these acids on the skin are oxidized. It smells like a mixture of greasy aroma and dirt grass, and levels emitted from humans increase with age. So yes, if you don't want your vermouth to smell like a mixture of a cardboard box and a grandpa, put the lid on it as soon as it's poured.

If your bottle doesn't have a cap that can close tightly, you should invest in a good bottle stopper. You may already have one, but make sure the seal is tight. The best ones, in my opinion, are the lay-flat champagne stoppers. They're called "lay-flat" because the arms of the stopper swing out to the sides to lay flat in line with the top of the stopper. This makes them very easy to slide into a pocket, or picnic basket, or purse. I got my favorite one in France, but I also found a pretty good version at an upstate New York cidery. Go online and search for "lay-flat champagne stopper" and you'll find a wide selection at all price points. To find a good one, you're looking for two things. First, there is a rubber seal that has a protruding nipple on it. This is what does the actual job of keeping air out, and it has to have some give. If you push into it and it doesn't need to compress for you to feel the plastic body on the other side, the thing is no good. Second, the two plastic arms that swing down over the lip of the bottle to hold the gadget in place should be pretty small. When you swing them into place over the bottle lip, you want to have to force them a little bit. This is the seal protecting whatever precious thing is in the bottle from the evils of air. You want it to be tight.

The brilliant craftspeople who manage the barrelhouse at a sherry distillery or the aging of cheese in the caves of Somerset, England, can wield oxygen as a tool. They ensure just the right amount of exposure to coax out flavors or to mellow sharp notes using the molecules' chaotic powers. But by the time their artisan wares are in your hands, oxygen is your sworn enemy. Don't leave a bottle of olive oil open on the counter. "Open, pour, close," should be your mantra. Good olive oil deserves some respect, there is a reason Ina Garten always asks for it by name!

This goes for your wine collection, too. Yes, upon opening a bottle, air is beneficial to interact with flavors in the glass and carry them to your nose, but if a bottle is opened, please drink it within forty-eight hours. The first thing you'll notice after even a couple of hours of oxygen exposure is a port-like quality coming forward, a deepening and rounding of some of the grape flavors. You might like port, so you think, *Sure, no problem.* But what you bought wasn't a port. The winemaker certainly wasn't making you a port. So please, for their sake, drink it before the oxygen has a chance to rip it apart.

HEAT IS ALSO THE ENEMY.

As I've told you, volatile molecules move more rapidly as temperature increases. This is why hot coffee is more aromatic than cold. It's how a warm cookie can entice you from across a room while a hunk of cookie dough could sit out on the counter without drawing your attention. But this speeding up of molecules also makes reactions occur more quickly, specifically those pesky oxidative reactions I mentioned. When you forget a case of beer in your trunk for a few days it's as good as cooked.

Constant fluctuation in temperature also speeds up the aging process, even if things don't get that hot. Beer kept out in the garage may be room temperature during the day and then nearly freezing at night. This constant flux speeding up then halting molecule movement accelerates the aging process. Soon that beer's wholesome bready malt flavors will shift to port-like qualities and subtle notes of papery oxidation will emerge.

Keeping that expensive olive oil right next to the oven is a death wish for the complex flavors it contains. "Heat and light are the enemies of olive oil," says Irini Tzortzoglou, winner of *MasterChef UK* and passionate olive oil sommelier. "People forget it is basically a fruit juice. It's the oils pressed from a fruit. Would you let a fruit juice get hot and then cool over and over again? No! It would go bad."

She tells me she literally feels sadness when she sees a glass bottle of olive oil next to the stove. "It will be bad, it will be rancid and lose all of its fruity flavors and health benefits." She sighs.

You heard Irini! No oxygen, no heat!

TERROIR IS A THING. BUT IT'S NOT WHAT YOU THINK IT IS.

FOR SOME, THE WORD *TERROIR* IS A CUE TO START THE EYE-ROLLING. It makes someone who moments earlier sounded informed and passionate sound like, well, a bit of a blabbering snob.

"Ah, yes, the minerality here is a clear indicator of the region's excellent terroir." *eye roll* So, are we all tasting dirt right now?

Yes and no. Terroir in the way you've likely heard of it is part myth, part marketing ploy, and a little bit of truth. The term is often translated as the expression, a taste of place. In wine, terroir is a culmination of how the soil composition, vineyard structure, sun exposure, and climate of the grapes affect the final flavor you experience in the glass. Since grapes are highly sensitive to sunlight, rain, and temperature, the wine that's produced from one farmer's vines really can taste vastly different from the stock produced on the other side of the ridge. But what that explanation fails to reveal is, this is the same for any artisanal product, especially one that undergoes fermentation.

In rickhouses, the massive warehouses that hold hundreds of barrels filled with bourbon or whiskey or scotch that age and condition until they're ready for packaging. The air is literally inhaled when it's cold in the winter and the wood contracts, and then the air is exhaled from the pressure of fermentation and expansion of wood staves. That air contains the distinctive character of that rickhouse. The flavor of the wood of the building, the air that flows in from the fields or forests outside, even the dust that settles around barrels are unique expressions of that same concept of terroir.

When it comes to shellfish, merroir is the terroir of water. The briny water that slips in and out of oysters, scallops, sea urchin, and shrimp and flavors them with the natural vegetation and minerals surrounding them. Oysters from colder merroir are saltier and smaller. The merroir of the California coast makes for huge uni (the delicious gonads of sea urchin) with a pale yellow-orange hue, while the waters of Maine produce tiny, dense uni flecked with reddish-brown colors.

Professor Juyun Lim at Oregon State University conducted a study that had cheese novices group cheese cubes by flavor. Juyun and her team told them they could make as many groups as they wanted, in order to match cheese cubes with the ones that tasted the same. Participants tasted and matched and retasted and categorized their cubes until they were satisfied that the cheeses that tasted the same were grouped together. Then they left and came back a day later with refreshed senses to confirm they were happy with their final groupings. What the participants didn't know is that they were tasting cheeses made on the exact same equipment using the exact same process, the only difference was where the cows were raised.

"And we're talking the difference of a couple miles. They were all relatively local farms," says Juyun. "When we statistically compared the panel's answers to the different cheeses, it was incredible. On average they were very good at grouping the cheeses made from milk from the same areas."

Juyun says this is the first study that proves terroir is detectable in cheese.

"This is surprising because this isn't just growing grapes from the ground and pressing them and making a wine with terroir. The grass is processed by the cow and then it is processed again into cheese. And the participants could still tell the differences."

Rather than using *terroir* as an exclusive term, a label to demarcate that this product can *only* ever be made here by this small group of people who own this land, it can be used as a celebratory term. You can taste the earth and environment in (almost) everything you eat. It's worth appreciating the ever-shifting flavors it contributes to our lives.

THERE IS GOOD IN THE BAD.

As you learn to taste, you'll start to recognize which things are good and which stand out as excellent. Even better, as you practice, you'll be able to explain why things are good. You can share your skills and passions with the people around you.

But you might also notice that there are things that don't taste so great. Suddenly you recognize the slightly burnt note in your previously beloved two-dollar croissant from the neighborhood bakery. The joy you feel tasting the near perfection of a carefully crafted risotto at a special-occasion restaurant is tempered by the fact that it put you back nearly thirty dollars. Here's the secret: you don't need to drain your bank account to go on reveling in the great tastes of life. In fact, it's not sustainable (for your wallet or your time) to seek out only the flawless flavors that exist in the world. The flawless won't feel special unless you dine on a diet of ordinary and taste some truly awful things every once in a while.

All specialists and experts evolve to understand their field can be separated into categories and have identified their "best of" in each category. The coffee aficionados have their name-brand beans that are their "best of what is available at the grocery store." The cheese geeks know that if you have to buy cheese by the prewrapped block, Tillamook's extra-sharp white cheddar is the obvious pick. My gas station beer is Sierra Nevada Pale Ale, and if the gas station doesn't have that I'll reach for a Modelo. And I'll enjoy every sip.

Jonathan Eichholz was training for his Master Sommelier exam, but when I asked him if he'd do a blind tasting of boxed wines he told me, "Don't need to. Franzia Blush is the GOAT. Nothing can touch Franzia Blush; it is the best boxed wine ever. Chill it down to ice-cold and wow."

Whiskey expert Jack Beguedou also had an immediate answer when I asked for his budget pick: "My favorite bottom-shelf is Evan Williams Bottled-in-Bond with the white label." This will run you somewhere between fourteen and nineteen dollars.

Experts are able to switch easily between recommending the best in the world and the best on the bottom shelf precisely because they are experts. Studies show that the more true knowledge a person has about a topic, the more they use that knowledge to break their topic into categories. Someone just getting into the wine game sees the world as red, white, and rosé. Surely the best rosé in those categories can't come from a box. However, experts can have a dozen or more categories within rosé alone.

Beer drinkers who considered "beer" to be a single category rated mass-market lagers as less pleasing than people who mentally separated "specialty" beer from "regular" beer, according to one study. The more categories a person had for beer in their mind, the more pleasing they found all categories of beer. Ha! People are worried that too much expertise creates snobs, but actually it is the opposite: too little knowledge creates snobs.

NERD WORDS.

TASTERS USE A LOT OF WEIRD WORDS. SOME OF THEM ARE RATHER ANtiquated, others just straight-up gibberish. Here are a few I've come across on my tasting adventures that don't make a ton of sense.

When tasting oysters, liquor is the liquid naturally inside a mixture of seawater and the oyster's natural juices. In the context of beer, liquor is the water used to make the beer. If you're talking about spirits, liquor is liquor, but a liqueur is (by law) a liquor that has been both flavored and sweetened. Speaking of liquor, "proof" is twice the percent by volume of alcohol in a spirit. So, a 90-proof bourbon is 45 percent alcohol by volume, meaning 45 percent of your bottle is pure alcohol and the rest is flavor compounds and, um, expensive water.

We all know the crust, but what is the center of the bread called? It's called the crumb, even if it's not crumbly or crummy. The texture of a cake or pastry is also called the crumb. The center part of a cheese on the other hand is called the paste. So, any part that is not the rind is the paste. And by the way, you can eat the rind. It won't always taste good but legally (at least in the United States) the rind has to be edible, yes, even the wax.

Barnyard, horse blanket, funky, rustic, stable, barn cellar, goaty, and *pungent* are all words used in place of "it smells a little bit poopy." To be clear, many things that taste excellent get a little bit poopy like natural wines, sour beers, cave aged cheeses. *Fusty* is the word to describe this aroma when they become too intense and shift from a little barnyard to full decay. Fusty is a very popular term to describe olive oil that has inadvertently undergone anaerobic fermentation. Say it with me: Funky, good. Fusty, bad.

Crema is the layer of tan or light brown foam on top of a well-pulled espresso shot. Mousse or head is the layer of foam on top of a freshly poured beer. The white froth on top of artisan honey isn't a defect. In fact, it is the prized honey foam, a layer of light flavorful honey that forms as the honey settles in its package and air rises to the surface. A wine thief isn't a criminal accusation, it's a rod-shaped tool used to draw liquid from barrels for tasting and quality assurance sampling. Lest you think you'll only find a wine thief at a vineyard, the same tool is used to sample bourbon, beer, vinegar, or maple syrup. If it's in a barrel you can use a wine thief to "steal" a taste.

A flight is three or more samples of one medium presented for tasting. There are cheese flights, wine flights, chocolate flights, and espresso martini flights; anything that can come in a glass or serving about a third of the normal size and be presented in a row can be a flight. A magnum holds one and a half liters, also known as two full bottles of wine, and is not presented for tasting unless you have a large group. A magnum may be closed with a cork and cage. The cage is the metal cap and wire that holds the cork of a wine, beer, or cider bottle in place.

Cupping is the ritualized coffee-tasting method that begins with dry whole coffee beans and ends with the tasting method, but rather than sipping java to get your tastes, it is slurped out of a specialized spoon. The world of tea has a cupping ritual of its own that also starts with observing the dried tea and ends with tasting it.

A unicorn is a rare, small batch, hard-to-find *something*. Unicorn wines might come from an especially good vintage that is hard to track down. Lines form in brewery parking lots for one-annual releases of unicorn stouts or IPAs. Basically, it's something you're always on the hunt for even if you never expect to find or taste it. Whiskey fanatics have their unicorn bottles, sushi lovers have their unicorn fish (ideally prepared by a specific chef), even unicorn bottles of balsamic vinegar exist (a twenty-five-year-aged Balsamico Tradizionale from the city of Modena).

OPEN IT. DRINK IT.

"I ONCE HAD KYLE HENDERSON, THE DISTILLERY MANAGER AT ANGEL'S Envy, sign a bottle for my fiancé's dad because Angel's Envy is his favorite. And he said to me, 'This bottle cannot end up on eBay. Make sure he drinks this.'" Ben Wald pauses to laugh. "Do you know what he signed it? 'Andy, Please drink this.' That's it. Whiskey is made for drinking; some whiskey is made for drinking infrequently, but it's made for drinking."

Ben says that Andy did follow the instructions in the inscription and has refilled that bottle six or seven times now, keeping it safely off eBay.

Ben and Kyle and I agree. There are special things out there that are sometimes sealed in glass bottles, glass jars, or—as Irini informed me is the case with the best olive oil—packaged in heavy porcelain or china, but the fact of the matter is you can't taste that special creation through the package. Someone made it for you to open, so open the dang thing! If you want a keepsake to display, you'll always have the bottle.

And please, please, please, once you've opened it, use it. I know that balsamic vinegar you brought back from Italy was really expensive, so you only want to use it at the right moment, but every moment you go on living after you opened the balsamic, that vinegar is dying. Once you've opened it, the oxygen is in there, conducting its nasty business. Now respect that craftsperson who brought that vinegar into the world and use it as soon as you can so it tastes the way she meant for it to taste.

If you feel like you don't have a way to use it go ahead and throw a freakin' vinegar party. Your friends will love it. Make a cocktail with it. And if the cocktail sucks? Dump it. That vinegar was not wasted. It was used, and it taught you a lesson. Ten times as many lessons as you would learn with it languishing in your pantry, I promise. (But next time, may I suggest stirring 1½ ounces of bourbon, ¾ ounces of fresh-squeezed grapefruit juice, a barspoon of simple syrup, and a barspoon or two of your prized vinegar with ice, then straining it into a Nick and Nora martini glass?)

Oh, you don't have friends? Fine. Throw yourself a nightly vinegar party until it's gone. Pour it on good cheese while you stand over the sink, then close your eyes and taste it. You know what, go ahead and pour it on cheap cheese. Tear off a handful of bread and dunk it in. Drizzle it on salads and ice cream and love it and use it. This love affair has to burn hot and fast.

DON'T BE A JERK.

We've all run into the guy at the bar saying loudly, "I can't believe anyone would order the rosé here. It's not even from Provence," while eyeing the crowd looking for anyone who may want to debate the finer points of pét-nat bottle conditioning. One thing I can guarantee you is that guy is not a trained taster. He might be on the way there, but right now, he's in what I call the "passionate prick" phase. (Or maybe he's just a prick all the time, I can't say.)

There's a period when you first start learning about a topic that you believe you've acquired all there is to know about that topic. Three days in the gentle mountains of Franche-Comté and suddenly you're the authority on Comté cheese. A whisper to the shopper next to you at the grocery store, "The cheese is wrapped too tightly, it will already be partially spoiled by the time you get it home," seems well intentioned; you're just sharing your cheese knowledge with the world. But thoughtful tasters know that sharing knowledge without being asked is self-aggrandizing behavior, not an act of public service.

The cardinal rule is, don't ruin it for anybody else. Got it?

CHAPTER TWELVE

TASTES TO LAST A LIFETIME

Have you heard of the "Proustian phenomenon?" It's when a taste of something can spontaneously evoke vivid recollections of moments in our lives, also known as autobiographical memories. The phenomenon got its name from a seminal passage in Marcel Proust's most prominent work *In Search of Lost Time* (originally published in French as *À la recherche du temps perdu* in 1913) where he described the taste of a madeleine cookie dipped in tea immediately changing his mood.

> *I raised to my lips a spoonful of the tea in which I had soaked a morsel of the cake. No sooner had the warm liquid, and the crumbs with it, touched my palate, a shudder ran through my whole body, and I stopped, intent upon the extraordinary changes that were taking place. An exquisite pleasure had invaded my senses, but individual, detached, with no suggestion of its origin.*

American country-pop duo Dan + Shay captured the essence of the Proustian phenomenon for a modern audience in their multi-platinum single "Tequila." The song talks about how a sip of tequila brings to life so vividly the memory of a girlfriend dancing at a bar, down to the sorority t-shir she was wearing. (Google the song and hear for yourself!) Both the twenty-first-century country music artists and the early-twentieth-century French novelist recount how the sensations brought on by taste are not quite memories but rather emotional states. They arise first as a feeling rather than a concrete recollection of facts, like when and where an event took place. Flavor memories call forward the emotional state the reminiscer was in while forming that memory. This has to do with how flavor information, especially aroma, travels through the brain.

Scent signals have a direct connection to the limbic system, including the amygdala (involved in processing memory and emotion) and the hippocampus (involved in forming memories). Scientists think these parts of the brain are responsible for assigning emotional meaning to events. Hence, by their nature autobiographical memories triggered by scent must also trigger an emotion. Rather than being simultaneous recollections, emotion and memory are inherently intertwined as one.

This functional brain area where scent memories are stored explains why memories related to other sensory stimuli like music feel different when we recall them.

A song that comes up on a playlist may trigger a memory of singing it on a spring break road trip with your college roommates. This nostalgic thought might bring you warm and fuzzy feelings. But those feelings arise after your descriptive memory of when, where, and with whom. Unlike scent, which has direct access to the limbic system, other sensory inputs like touch, sound, and sight first travel through the thalamus. Furthermore, recollections brought on by odor and taste are not only more emotional but also more pleasant than memories tied to words, images, or sounds.

Dan + Shay effectively point out this distinction between memories brought about by music and physical location compared to the emotional ones brought on by taste later in the song when they sing about how showing up in the same bar they used to frequent together or listening to the same old songs doesn't bring the same memories as tasting tequila does. The country singers capture the phenomenon succinctly. A taste of something brings on a flood of the emotional memories you formed around that taste as if you were experiencing them again. But Proust is not known for being succinct (the novel the madeleine passage appears in runs more than four thousand pages). He goes on to dissect this sensation for another thousand or so words.

The character continues to take bites of the madeleine, searching his own mind in an attempt to uncover the connection between the feelings of delight and the tea-soaked cookie. He notes that with each consecutive bite the emotions of happiness and joy permeate his consciousness, even though he is unable to discern their origin. It's clear to him that the emotions are tied to the memory of this taste, but he can't seem to pull the details out of his brain.

Then after more than ten attempts at the task, a memory snaps into focus in his mind. His aunt used to hand him bites of madeleine she had dipped into her tea on Sunday mornings when he was a child.

Proust's character was able to place the memory connected to his blissful feelings only after a lot of effort. Most of us won't spend so much time searching the depths of our intellect to discover the connection between scent and memory. In fact, most of us don't even notice the magnitude of how our emotional state is affected by the fragrance around us every day.

Dawn Goldworm recounts the time she was giving a presentation at an advertising firm. She says the audience wasn't fully engaged in the discussion of building scent branding into marketing plans, so she decided to pique their interest by inviting them to "play a game."

She asked the audience member closest to her where she grew up. Dawn tells me that what the audience of advertising execs didn't realize is there are aromas constantly triggering our senses and affecting our mood even when we don't realize it.

"I asked the woman next to me in the presentation, 'Where were you born, where are you from?'" says Dawn.

"I grew up in New York City," the woman answered.

"I dip a blotter and hand it to her," Dawn tells me, "and this expression of profound delight just takes over this woman's face. She closes her eyes and inhales again. And then she says to me, 'Oh my God, what is this? It smells like home.'"

Dawn insists it's not the scents we deliberately add to our lives like perfumes or aromatic candles that conjure emotional responses and memories. It's the natural environmental scents around us as we move through the world. The aroma she handed the woman to evoke a state of total glee was . . . gasoline.

Odor-evoked memories are autobiographical in nature, they have the power to transport you back to a former emotional state as if by time travel. We form the majority of these vivid memories during the first decade of our lives, "when everything is new and we're experiencing so many things for the first time," says Dawn.

It wasn't until Dawn was in perfumer's school that she realized she had a powerful memory connected to the scent of the perfume Coco by Chanel. "I smelled it, and I couldn't pick out the different ingredients," she says. "I was trying to think, but all I could see was my mom. I couldn't evaluate the scent objectively at all; I was just thinking about my mom." After a Proustian self-examination through her own memory, she realized this powerful reaction traced back to her childhood. She remembers her father used to bring back the perfume from Europe as a gift for her mother. Once the bottles of Coco by Chanel were nearly empty, Dawn's mother would let her have them to play with and keep in her room.

We create these odor-evoked memories less frequently after the age of ten or twelve. Later in life, we only form them around strong emotional events, like first loves, or, in the case of Dan + Shay's song, tragic breakups. We still learn and remember smells. If you don't smell lavender for the first time until you're twenty, you'll be able to identify a candle's lavender aroma when it fills the room, but this is a different kind of memory; it's at the forefront of our mind rather than our subconscious, and it doesn't change the way we feel. Like pointing to a chair and identifying its color as orange, naming the lavender aroma is just an act of recall.

The ability for mundane scents like gasoline to cue emotional states is why people with anosmia (a partial or total loss of smell) become profoundly depressed. "People think it's because eating isn't as pleasurable," says Dawn, "and that is part of it. But it is that they lose touch with all of these emotional memories, without scent they have no way to recall them."

Overall, the affect of someone experiencing anosmia for the first time is described as "flat." It's not just the positive memories they miss out on; they cannot respond to cues for stress, sadness, or anger, either. Their smell loss leaves them unable to sense triggers for comfort as well as danger.

A variety of afflictions cause the onset of anosmia, including head trauma, disease, or viral infection. The global COVID-19 pandemic thrust temporary anosmia into the public consciousness when smell loss was established as a telltale symptom of infection.

The majority of people who lost their sense of smell after a COVID infection recovered it within a year, many much sooner. Caroline Huart, an ear, nose, and throat (ENT) specialist and researcher at the Institute of Neuroscience at UC Louvain, studies the functions and dysfunctions of the olfactory system. She said there is a physiological indicator of who would recover easily from anosmia related to COVID-19.

"If the olfactory bulb volume is bigger, then your chance to recover is better," she says. People with larger olfactory bulbs, the region of the brain tied to our sense of smell, have better olfactory abilities. Olfactory bulb size is not determined at birth; it shifts and grows with use or disuse.

"We know that the sense of smell is tied to the volume of the olfactory bulb," Caroline says. "Data shows olfactory training can increase the size of the olfactory bulb." In one study, scientist measured the olfactory bulbs of students setting out to become sommeliers. After a year and a half of wine study, their olfactory bulb volume measurably increased compared to controls. The human olfactory system has "astonishing plasticity." After an injury or during an illness, the olfactory bulb shrivels but as the patient returns to health its volume will increase again.

Because we can increase the size of our olfactory bulbs through practice, there is hope for people experiencing anosmia to regain their sense smell. "Olfactory training" is a specific regimen undertaken by those attempting to recover from smell loss. They are assigned to sniff four essential oils (usually rose, eucalyptus, lemon, and clove) twice daily every day for three months. The impact of olfactory training on recovery times for anosmia has been studied for more than a decade, but the widespread fear of anosmia due to COVID-19 invigorated interest in its effects. Studies show success rate varies from patient to patient. As a non-invasive, non-pharmacological treatment plan for anosmia, the overall attitude toward this regimented training is, "Why not try it?" You can beef up your olfactory bulb and smell train at home by leaving a few bottles of essential oils by your toothbrush. Each morning and evening before you brush your teeth, smell the oils and say out loud what you are smelling. Two or three times a year, switch up your oils. Right now, I have lavender and spearmint on the counter. In the winter I like to use cinnamon or clove because, to me, they smell like the holidays.

The threat of COVID-19 continues to dwindle, but it is far from the only link between loss of smell and poor health. In fact, a 2014 study of adults aged fifty-seven to eighty-five found that loss of the sense of smell was a better predictor of death in the next five years than a diagnosis of cancer, heart failure, or lung disease. Severe liver disease was the only predictor of mortality more acute than smell dysfunction.

A team Caroline was part of published a paper that builds on this finding. It enumerates the many ties between smell loss and overall risk of mortality. Olfactory impairment is also one of the earliest symptoms of both Alzheimer's and Parkinson's disease. Once you know the close relationship between processing scents and memories in the brain, this connection is no surprise. The loss of smell is tied to malnutrition. And to poor social interactions. It is seen as a sign of future cognitive decline even in presently cognitively intact subjects. It increases the chance of injury through cooking accidents, fires, and ingesting spoiled foods. It is tied to disrupted sleeping. People with an impaired sense of smell experience hazardous events two to three times more often than those with normal olfactory functions.

This is not an exhaustive list of the negative effects of smell loss. As the catalogue of ailments continued to grow, I had to ask Caroline, "Can we reverse all of these risks and impairments by strengthening our sense of smell?" If I could grow my olfactory bulb through smell training, and a bigger olfactory bulb could offer some protection against COVID-19-related smell loss, it seemed logical to me that it could protect me from all of these frankly scary afflictions.

"Huh. It's a good question, it's interesting." She slows down to think through it. "Hm. We know that if you have olfactory dysfunction, then you have a higher mortality risk and so on . . ." She trails off, pauses, and repeats my question. "If you train your sense of smell and if you improve your sense of smell, does it change something for your brain health or, um, biological age? We don't know that. To my knowledge, there are no studies."

I take this as scientist speak for "maybe."

THE LARGEST SCIENTIFIC SAMPLING EVER CONDUCTED WAS A STUDY OF smell. In September 1986 *National Geographic Magazine* included a six-panel scratch-and-sniff test in the magazine sent to roughly eleven million subscribers. The scents were accompanied by a questionnaire asking for more information about each scent: "Did it evoke a vivid memory?" or "Would you eat something that smelled like this?" as well as information about the participant, like gender, age, and whether they smoked or had allergies. There was also a space for notes where readers could expand on their experiences with smell and memory. (Some readers used it as a chance to scold *National Geographic* for including a page so smelly they had to take it out of their home immediately. Maybe they were supersmellers—or maybe they were just grumpy.)

About 1.5 million subscribers followed the request and mailed in the questionnaires to the team researchers at the Monell Chemical Senses Center in Philadelphia (where Pamela Dalton is a member), making it one of the largest scientific studies ever conducted.

Readers were so jazzed by the opportunity to participate in a real research study that some made photocopies of the questionnaire to mail in, quite a feat considering copy machines were not widely accessible in the late 1980s.

Only 50 percent of respondents were able to smell all six odor panels—hey were rose, clove (eugenol), sweat (androsterone), banana (iso-amyl acetate), musk (Galaxolide), the sulphury smell added to natural gas (mercaptans). This means half of the respondents were affected by some kind of genetic blindness or specific anosmia.

Those who could smell odors couldn't necessarily identify them. Only 65 percent of respondents could smell androsterone and just 25 percent could call it sweat. For the rose scent 99 percent of people could smell it but still only 84 percent of respondents knew it was floral.

"Odors that were identified correctly were much more likely to evoke a memory, often a very specific one," says the results of the study, published in the October 1987 issue of the magazine. "Sample 6 [rose] on the survey was not merely 'floral' to a woman living in England; it was the perfume of the 'deep red rose called Dr. Charles De Bat,' last smelled 19 years ago in her father's mum garden in Africa."

Participants didn't always have a memory tied to one of the six scratch-and-sniff scents, but many were able to recount some odor-evoked recollection. Several readers said the smell of *National Geographic* reminded them of their childhood basement or other times perusing the magazine. There was also this touching story: "After my husband died, I would go into his closet and hug his suits, because they smelled of his own body odor, slight cigarette smell, and aftershave. I'd stand there, hugging his clothes, making believe, close my eyes, and cry."

So, having these odor-induced memories may be one method for keeping our olfactory abilities sharp and our minds nimble. The study in *National Geographic* found that the capacity to sense odors lasts well into our seventh decade, though the capability to identify the odors started to decline in participants' thirties. However it doesn't necessarily have to be this way. Especially by creating memories around scents, we can keep our noses sharp well into our later years.

When Dr. Bill Simpson was recruiting panelists to train for his sensory panel in Leatherhead, England, in 2018, he started with an open application. Around 450 people filled out a questionnaire asking about their sensory abilities and lifestyle, and from that group 140 were chosen for in-person sensory testing. From there the herd was narrowed to forty people. They were evaluated by industrial psychologists to eliminate people "who might disrupt a group." And the result was thirty-two capable panelists who were ready to be trained as sensory assessors and be part-time employees at AROXA. Bill's panelists undergo perpetual smell training to keep their sensory abilities sharp so they can better assess samples submitted by clients. There are some 165 compounds they are able to identify by odor alone; imagine the size of those olfactory bulbs!

"Once we had the thirty-two, I had them fill out a job application so I could get them in the system as registered employees," says Bill, "This is the first time I found out their ages. And one of the panelists was seventy."

She's now seventy-four, and Bill said she is one of the top performers on the panel. "The main thing is health. People who are healthy, and have good training," he said, "then age is not a factor."

And when our faculties do start to decline from natural aging or diseases like Alzheimer's, Parkinson's, or dementia, studies show that we hold on to these smell and taste memories the longest. You may notice that a loved one with Alzheimer's wants to constantly recount their first time tasting a milkshake or how the scents of the pine forests around their childhood home used to blow in through the windows at night.

THE PROFOUND STAYING POWER OF THESE SCENT MEMORIES IS EQUALLY fascinating to memory researchers and brands. "If companies are conscious of scent strategy," says Dawn Goldworm about her work crafting fragrances for businesses large and small, "what they want you to do is smell their scent somewhere else after having experienced it in their environment. All of a sudden, all you want to do is go on another cruise, buy another gown, buy another car. And it brings you back to not just buying any car or any cruise or any flight, but specifically that brand."

In her work with Nike she uses scents of sweat, and rubber, and dirt, and grass, and that "smell of a new basketball as it gets oily from your hand."

The "scent signature" of Nike doesn't smell like your personal sports memories; it is made up of the smells that trigger those personal emotions of victory, teamwork, loss, and triumph.

Lest you think it is only brands that can command our recollection by foisting specially designed fragrances upon us, we can control our own scent destiny. If you're looking to "start fresh" after a bad break up, or moving to a new city, or just because you want to, a fast track to resetting your mood is to replace all the scents in your life.

"You would need new hand soap, new dish soap, to change detergents, maybe some new candles or room scents," says Dawn, "but if you're going through a change and want to have some semblance of consistency, that's when you pay attention to these things. Bring the detergent you've always used. Make sure you have the same shampoo. You'll feel much more settled."

If you want to be able to forever transport back to a specific day, or moment in time, you can control that by introducing a new scent, too. The obvious example is wearing a new perfume on your wedding day, a scent that you like but smells totally out of the ordinary from what you'd normally wear. Or purchasing a scent on the last day of your big family vacation and having everyone wear it together.

I was leaving the Château de Sacy in France, doing my best to thank the concierge in my rudimentary French. After I said thank you and goodbye one more time, he responded with something I couldn't understand at all. "Mhmmm," I said with a smile and continued to back away, "Merci!"

Finally he blurted out in English, "No, wait, wait! Your gift box!"

I blushed when I realized he was placating my fumbling attempts to speak his language the whole time and accepted the bag he held out to me. Inside was a small bottle of champagne and a scented porcelain figure imprinted with an outline of the hotel sealed in plastic.

"Oh, what is this?" I held up the little white square.

"It carries the smell of all the rooms here. We have the scent in pockets all over the château." He told me it's the (fragrance of champagne) mixed with almond cookies and white flowers.

"If you quite like it, we have it as a candle, too." He motioned toward a wooden display. "Every time you light it you will think you're here in Sacy."

And so I left with both my gift bag and the candle. This wasn't my only opportunity to neatly pack a prefabricated scent memory in my suitcase to bring home. Every French hotel, and also a few restaurants, offered such a souvenir. Even the cramped quarters I booked in Paris that simply reeked of spilled brandy and old cigarettes had a branded candle in a locked display case. I don't think the aroma of that candle would bring back memories of the hotel unless it truly smelled of stale smoke and alcohol.

But it seems the European tourism industry is well aware of the connections we form between scents and emotions and memory. The smell of the porcelain is nearly gone now, but when I want to pretend I'm in the vineyards of Sacy, all I need to do is light my candle.

YOU ARE WHAT YOU TASTE

"YOU ARE WHAT YOU EAT." THERE'S A REASON WE'VE ALL HEARD THIS saying: It's true. What you eat literally builds and maintains the physical you. What about the metaphysical you, the you that is your personality and memories and experiences and heritage? In reference to that you, then I propose a new aphorism: "You are what you taste."

Eating is passive and as you've learned in these pages, tasting is anything but passive. The beginning of your personal taste history may have been influenced by others like the preferences you adopted from your family and your culture. And of course there is the impact your genes have on exactly what compounds you're capable of tasting. But the flavors you spend time with, the ones you actively notice and pay attention to, those are up to you. Every time we eat, we have a chance to taste. And now you're equipped with the tools to observe, talk about, and communicate a whole new world of flavor.

Before reading this book, you ate oysters. Now, you will taste

them. You'll notice that the merroir of Canadian waters makes especially briny oysters and that Pacific oysters from California have a subtle note of melon. It may register that they taste sweetest in September
and October. This curious fact sparked by taste may push you to go
learn that early fall is when oysters are holding onto nutrients to prepare for winter. Upon tasting the oysters on a vacation in France, the
surprise will create a new flavor memory for you. That is, if this is your
first taste of the potent coppery and sharply mineral species of Belon
oyster, native to Europe. All of the nuances and memories are things
you'd miss if you were to simply eat the oyster, rather than taste it.

In these pages you discovered your retronasal passageway for the
first time. You determined your personal supertaster status. You realized why all those ice cream shops are painted pink. And learned the
seven step tasting method. You picked up some exercises for recognizing flavors and filing them into your personal memory. You learned
the tricks our eyes play on our taste buds and how professional tasters
work around them. I introduced you to the four Cs of flavor interaction
and told you that there is no secret to food pairing. (Remember, if you
like it, it's a good pairing!) You found a new favorite flavor wheel and
you're now equipped with a template to describe flavors. You learned
how to plan your next trip with a balance of foods you're anticipating
and opportunities to taste something truly surprising.

Finally, you learned how to create sensory memories with real
staying power. Like the scent memory I made an effort to create on the
day I finished the last interview for this book. As I pulled away from
Tillamook Creamery, I rolled down my window and sharp citrusy pine
mixed with the decay of the swamp wafted in. *Now all I have to do is
finish writing it,* I thought and inhaled the aroma of damp earth and
sulfur. Six years ago, I would have called that whiff of sulfur an "off
flavor." Now, I know better. Until three years ago I wouldn't have been
able to tell you what this forest smelled like at all. Maybe I would have

said "trees." I give the air a few short sniffs and I think, *This is the smell of the forests of the West Coast after it rains. A rainy Oregon forest.* If I smell this again, hopefully I'll remember this moment. It smells nothing like the forests I drive through in Vermont; they're filled with the subtle spice of maple bark and mint wisps from yellow birch.

Underneath the swamp and pine trees there's the minerality of damp rocks, still wet after last night's storm. This took my mind to the pang of panic I felt on the too-narrow road of a New Zealand mountain pass and the hundreds of tiny waterfalls that trickled down the rock walls right beside my car. Right after we drove through those mountains, I tasted the flinty smoked note of a New Zealand chardonnay for the first time. It's the same chardonnay I paired with the kangaroo we grilled outside the tent later that week. The gamey flavor of the meat complemented the smoke in the wine.

That wasn't the first time I'd tasted kangaroo. The first time was at my college job at The Lonesome Dove in Fort Worth. The kangaroo was topped with avocado as part of an "elevated nacho." It was maybe the first flavor I'd ever purposely added to my mental flavor collection. I couldn't believe you could put a marsupial on a menu in Texas.

"In one mile, stay right." The GPS snapped me out of my daisy chain of flavor memories and I'm back in my rental car. I smiled a little in my quiet car. I was more sure in that moment than ever that focusing on taste is a good idea. I think that I will show people how caring about flavor will make life better. more vivid. more connected. I try to get another whiff of rainy Oregon forest to take me back to the memories of kangaroo nachos and New Zealand mountains. But the moment had passed, so I rolled up the window and switched on the music.

Now, it's time for you to start your tasting adventure and collect flavor memories like these. You're armed with the tools you need (especially the tasting method in Chapter 4, the flavor gathering exercises in Chapter 5, the four Cs of flavor pairing on pages 170-173, and the flavor description template on pages 198-201) to seek out, experience, and appreciate tastes of all kinds. Soon you'll have a robust library of your life experiences and emotions cataloged by taste. And, since we are all what we taste, it's time to get out there and get tasting.

PS- You don't have to start your tasting adventure alone. You can find me and a group of flavor obsessed tasters at howtotastebook.com.

ACKNOWLEDGMENTS

To my parents, Kris and Joe, who raised me in a curious, science-loving household and made sure I knew that if you ask enough questions you'll find the answer. To my incredible agent Stacey Glick who I immediately recognized as a fellow flavor fanatic. To my editor Denise Silvestro who took this book from tasty to truly indulgent with patience and insight. To my copy editor, Erica Ferguson, who helped me find the right words and my production editor, Rebecca Cremonese, who shepherded the book through the production process. To Kristine Mills for the cover that made this book a feast for the eyes. To Ann Pryor for publicity and marketing expertise. To Steven Zacharius, Adam Zacharius, Jackie Dinas, and Lynn Cully, and everyone at Kensington for believing in this book. To the dozens and dozens of people I interviewed who don't appear in print in these pages but very much do in spirit, especially Ken Selby, Olivia Haver, Jennie Ripps, Tom Shellhammer and Amy Dubin. Thank you.

To the teams at Tillamook, Oregon State University, and Bardstown that let me invade their spaces and their inboxes. To the people in these pages who shared their expertise and time in the name of great taste. To the librarians and staff at the New York Public Library who helped me track down magazines from the 80s, textbooks from the 90s, and journal articles from 2022 with creativity and enthusiasm. To the teams at Black Fox Coffee and McNally Jackson Seaport who let me write in the corner for hours and occasionally slipped me a treat. Thank you.

To my study buddy Shelly Smith, who talked beer and pairing with me weekly for nearly a year. To Kristen Tolman, who inspired me and made me believe this is possible. To my fellow tasters in the basement crew. To all the people who showed me that truly special ideas arise around food long before this book was even an idea, including Ariel Lauren Wilson, Dan Pashman, Cat Wolinski, and Claire Bullen. Thank you.

To my friends who let me disappear for months at a time, who watched Chewy when I had to take a trip, who told me this book was going to be even better than I hoped it would be. Thank you.

To all the people who have found me in corners of the internet and followed along as I learned what I was talking about, then realized I had no idea what I was talking about, and started learning again. Here's to the never-ending cycle that you make possible! Thank you.

To all of the servers and bartenders and baristas and craftspeople and chefs and bakers and artisans and bar owners who answered my questions and made me believe in flavor and humanity. Thank you for your time, your passion, and your tastes. To those who shared samples from the barrel of vinegar in the corner, sips of wine from the crazy bottles, book recommendations, and thoughtful if slightly hazy conversations, I wish I could list you all by name. Thank you.

To my husband, Wes, who believes in my dreams and cooks the white parts of the chicken that I like. Thank you.

And finally, to anyone who takes silly questions seriously. To anyone generous with their knowledge and expertise. To anyone who has cradled a single perfect petit four in their hands and realized the smallest things in life are worth appreciating. Thank you.

SELECTED REFERENCES

INTRODUCTION: TASTING IT ALL

"Consumer Expenditures-2021 A01 Results." U.S. Bureau of Labor Statistics. U.S. Bureau of Labor Statistics, September 8, 2022. https://www.bls.gov/news.release/cesan.nr0.htm.

Ustun, Beyza, Nadja Reissland, Judith Covey, Benoist Schaal, and Jacqueline Blissett. "Flavor Sensing in Utero and Emerging Discriminative Behaviors in the Human Fetus." *Psychological Science* 33, no. 10 (October 2022): 1651–63. https://doi.org/https://doi.org/10.1177/09567976221105460.

CHAPTER ONE: THIS IS YOUR BRAIN ON FLAVOR

Breslin, P. A. "Human Gustation and Flavour." *Flavour and Fragrance Journal* 16, no. 6 (2001): 439–56. https://doi.org/10.1002/ffj.1054.

Breslin, Paul A.S., and Alan C. Spector. "Mammalian Taste Perception." *Current Biology* 18, no. 4 (2008). https://doi.org/10.1016/j.cub.2007.12.017.

Martini, Frederic. *Anatomy and Physiology.* San Francisco, CA: Benjamin-Cummings Publishing Co., 2005.

Prescott, J., J.E. Hayes, and N.K. Byrnes. "Sensory Science." *Encyclopedia of Agriculture and Food Systems*, 2014, 80–101. https://doi.org/10.1016/b978-0-444-52512-3.00065-6.

Shepherd, Gordon M. *Neurogastronomy: How the Brain Creates Flavor and Why It Matters.* New York: Columbia University Press, 2013.

CHAPTER TWO: A MATTER OF INDIVIDUAL TASTE

Doyennette, Marion, Monica G. Aguayo-Mendoza, Ann-Marie Williamson, Sara I.F.S. Martins, and Markus Stieger. "Capturing the Impact of Oral Processing Behaviour on Consumption Time and Dynamic Sensory Perception of Ice Creams Differing in Hardness." *Food*

Quality and Preference 78 (2019): 103721. https://doi.org/10.1016/j. foodqual.2019.103721.

Essick, Greg K., Anita Chopra, Steve Guest, and Francis McGlone. "Lingual Tactile Acuity, Taste Perception, and the Density and Diameter of Fungiform Papillae in Female Subjects." *Physiology & Behavior* 80, no. 2-3 (2003): 289–302. https://doi.org/10.1016/j.physbeh.2003.08.007.

Hayes, John E., Linda M. Bartoshuk, Judith R. Kidd, and Valerie B. Duffy. "Supertasting and Prop Bitterness Depends on More than the TAS2R38 Gene." *Chemical Senses* 33, no. 3 (2008): 255–65. https://doi.org/10.1093/chemse/bjm084.

Iannilli, Emilia, Antti Knaapila, Maria Paola Cecchini, and Thomas Hummel. "Dataset of Verbal Evaluation of Umami Taste in Europe." *Data in Brief* 28 (2020): 105102. https://doi.org/10.1016/j.dib.2019.105102.

Jaeger, Sara R., Jeremy F. McRae, Christina M. Bava, Michelle K. Beresford, Denise Hunter, Yilin Jia, Sok Leang Chheang, et al. "A Mendelian Trait for Olfactory Sensitivity Affects Odor Experience and Food Selection." *Current Biology* 23, no. 16 (2013): 1601–5. https://doi.org/10.1016/j.cub.2013.07.030.

Keller, Andreas, and Leslie B Vosshall. "Better Smelling through Genetics: Mammalian Odor Perception." *Current Opinion in Neurobiology* 18, no. 4 (2008): 364–69. https://doi.org/10.1016/j.conb.2008.09.020.

Melis, Melania, Iole Tomassini Barbarossa, Thomas Hummel, Roberto Crnjar, and Giorgia Sollai. "Effect of the RS2890498 Polymorphism of the OBPIIA Gene on the Human Ability to Smell Single Molecules." *Behavioural Brain Research* 402 (January 2021): 113127. https://doi.org/10.1016/j.bbr.2021.113127.

Moskowitz, HW, V Kumaraiah, KN Sharma, HL Jacobs, and SD Sharma. "Cross-Cultural Differences in Simple Taste Preferences." *Science* 190, no. 4220 (1975): 1217–18. https://doi.org/10.1126/science.1198109.

Ruffner, Zoe. "This Vegan Japanese Dessert Is the Feel-Good Treat to Turn to This Holiday Season." Vogue. *Vogue*, November 8, 2019. https://www.vogue.com/article/yokan-japan-dessert-new-york-city.

Sollai, Giorgia, Melania Melis, Iole Tomassini Barbarossa, and Roberto Crnjar. "A Polymorphism in the Human Gene Encoding Obpiia Affects the Perceived Intensity of Smelled Odors." *Behavioural Brain Research* 427 (2022): 113860. https://doi.org/10.1016/j.bbr.2022.113860.

Spence, Charles, and Heston Blumenthal. *Gastrophysics: The New Science of Eating*. New York: Penguin Books, 2018.

CHAPTER THREE: THE FLAVOR OF A DINING ROOM

Buford, Bill. *Dirt: Adventures in Lyon as a Chef in Training, Father, and Sleuth Looking for the Secrets of French Cooking.* New York: Random House Large Print, 2020.

Dirler, Julia, Gertrud Winkler, and Dirk Lachenmeier. "What Temperature of Coffee Exceeds the Pain Threshold? Pilot Study of a Sensory Analysis Method as Basis for Cancer Risk Assessment." *Foods* 7, no. 6 (2018): 83. https://doi.org/10.3390/foods7060083.

Fiegel, Alexandra, Jean-François Meullenet, Robert J. Harrington, Rachel Humble, and Han-Seok Seo. "Background Music Genre Can Modulate Flavor Pleasantness and Overall Impression of Food Stimuli." *Appetite* 76 (2014): 144–52. https://doi.org/10.1016/j.appet.2014.01.079.

Hasenbeck, Aimee, Sungeun Cho, Jean-François Meullenet, Tonya Tokar, Famous Yang, Elizabeth A Huddleston, and Han-Seok Seo. "Color and Illuminance Level of Lighting Can Modulate Willingness to Eat Bell Peppers." *Journal of the Science of Food and Agriculture* 94, no. 10 (2014): 2049–56. https://doi.org/10.1002/jsfa.6523.

Spence, Charles, and Fabiana M. Carvalho. "The Coffee Drinking Experience: Product Extrinsic (Atmospheric) Influences on Taste and Choice." *Food Quality and Preference* 80 (2020): 103802. https://doi.org/10.1016/j.foodqual.2019.103802.

Talavera, Karel, Keiko Yasumatsu, Thomas Voets, Guy Droogmans, Noriatsu Shigemura, Yuzo Ninomiya, Robert F. Margolskee, and Bernd Nilius. "Heat Activation of TRPM5 Underlies Thermal Sensitivity of Sweet Taste." *Nature* 438, no. 7070 (2005): 1022–25. https://doi.org/10.1038/nature04248.

Zellner, Debra A., Christopher R. Loss, Jonathan Zearfoss, and Sergio Remolina. "It Tastes as Good as It Looks! the Effect of Food Presentation on Liking for the Flavor of Food." *Appetite* 77 (2014): 31–35. https://doi.org/10.1016/j.appet.2014.02.009.

CHAPTER FOUR: THE TASTING METHOD

Arakawa, Takahiro, Kenta Iitani, Xin Wang, Takumi Kajiro, Koji Toma, Kazuyoshi Yano, and Kohji Mitsubayashi. "A Sniffer-Camera for Imaging of Ethanol Vaporization from Wine: The Effect of Wine Glass Shape." *The Analyst* 140, no. 8 (2015): 2881–86. https://doi.org/10.1039/c4an02390k.

Dalton, P., N. Doolittle, H. Nagata, and P.A.S. Breslin. "The Merging of the Senses: Integration of Subthreshold Taste and Smell." *Nature News.* Nature Publishing Group, 2000. https://www.nature.com/articles/nn0500_431.

Diamond, J. "Flavor Processing: Perceptual and Cognitive Factors in Multi-Modal Integration." *Chemical Senses* 30, no. Supplement 1 (2005): i232–i233. https://doi.org/10.1093/chemse/bjh199.

Eng, Monica. "Most Produce Loses 30 Percent of Nutrients Three Days after Harvest." *Chicago Tribune,* November 3, 2021. https://www.chicagotribune.com/dining/ct-xpm-2013-07-10-chi-most-produce-loses-30-percent-of-nutrients-three-days-after-harvest-20130710-story.html.

Fabien, Beaumont, Cilindre Clara, Abdi Ellie, Maman Marjorie, and Polidori Guillaume. "The Role of Glass Shapes on the Release of Dissolved CO2 in Effervescent Wine." *Current Research in Nutrition and Food Science Journal,* April 25, 2019. https://dx.doi.org/10.12944/CRNFSJ.7.1.22.

Shirai, Tomohiro, Kentaro Kumihashi, Mitsuyoshi Sakasai, Hiroshi Kusuoku, Yusuke Shibuya, and Atsushi Ohuchi. "Identification of a Novel TRPM8 Agonist from Nutmeg: A Promising Cooling Compound." *ACS Medicinal Chemistry Letters* 8, no. 7 (2017): 715–19. https://doi.org/10.1021/acsmedchemlett.7b00104.

CHAPTER FIVE: COLLECTING FLAVORS, REFERENCES, AND REFLEXES

Herz, Rachel S, and Julia von Clef. "The Influence of Verbal Labeling on the Perception of Odors: Evidence for Olfactory Illusions?" *Perception* 30, no. 3 (2001): 381–91. https://doi.org/10.1068/p3179.

Reichl, Ruth. *Garlic and Sapphires.* London: Cornerstone Digital, 2013.

Santo, Kathy. "How to Teach Your Dog Scent Work at Home." American Kennel Club. American Kennel Club, May 27, 2020. https://www.akc.org/expert-advice/training/how-to-teach-your-dog-scent-work.

"Volatile Sulfur Compounds in Food." *ACS Symposium Series,* 2011. https://doi.org/10.1021/bk-2011-1068.

CHAPTER SIX: BLINDED BY THE SIGHT

Brochet, F. *Chemical object representation in the field of consciousness.* Application presented for the grand prix of the Académie Amorim following work carried out towards a doctorate from the Faculty of Oenology, General Oenology Laboratory, 351 Cours de la Libération, 33405 Talence Cedex. (2001)

Gottfried, Jay A, and Raymond J Dolan. "The Nose Smells What the Eye Sees." *Neuron* 39, no. 2 (2003): 375–86. https://doi.org/10.1016/s0896-6273(03)00392-1.

Morrot, Gil, Frédéric Brochet, and Denis Dubourdieu. "The Color of Odors." *Brain and Language* 79, no. 2 (2001): 309–20. https://doi.org/10.1006/brln.2001.2493.

Sage, Adam. "Cheeky Little Test Exposes Bad Taste of Wine 'Experts'." Independent.ie, November 24, 2012. https://www.independent.ie/world-news/europe/cheeky-little-test-exposes-bad-taste-of-wine-experts-26061451.html.

Schmidt, Liane, Vasilisa Skvortsova, Claus Kullen, Bernd Weber, and Hilke Plassmann. "How Context Alters Value: The Brain's Valuation and Affective Regulation System Link Price Cues to Experienced Taste Pleasantness." Scientific Reports 7, no. 1 (2017). https://doi.org/10.1038/s41598-017-08080-0.

CHAPTER SEVEN: CRITICS, JUDGES, AWARDS, AND GRADES

Gawel, R, and P.W. Godden. "Evaluation of the Consistency of Wine Quality Assessments from Expert . . . " Australian Journal of Grape and Wine Research, 2008. https://onlinelibrary.wiley.com/doi/10.1111/j.1755-0238.2008.00001.x.

Hodgson, Robert T. "An Analysis of the Concordance among 13 U.S. Wine Competitions." Journal of Wine Economics 4, no. 1 (2009): 1–9. https://doi.org/10.1017/s1931436100000638.

Hodgson, Robert T. "An Examination of Judge Reliability at a Major U.S. Wine Competition*: Journal of Wine Economics." Cambridge Core. Cambridge University Press, June 8, 2012. https://www.cambridge.org/core/services/aop-cambridge-core/content/view/S1931436100001152.

Steiman, Harvey. "Behind the B.S.. about Wine Tasting." Wine Spectator. Wine Spectator, July 3, 2013. https://www.winespectator.com/articles/behind-the-bs-about-wine-tasting-48608.

"What Is a Michelin Star?" MICHELIN Guide. Accessed September 17, 2021. https://guide.michelin.com/us/en/article/features/what-is-a-michelin-star.

CHAPTER EIGHT: ONE PLUS ONE MAKES SEVEN

Ahn, Yong-Yeol, Sebastian E. Ahnert, James P. Bagrow, and Albert-László Barabási. "Flavor Network and the Principles of Food Pairing." Scientific Reports 1, no. 1 (2011). https://doi.org/10.1038/srep00196.

Blumenthal, Heston. "Naivety in the Kitchen Can Lead to Great Inventions, but Too Much Can Take You to Some Strange Places." The Times. August 19, 2010.

Breslin, Paul A.S. "Interactions among Salty, Sour and Bitter Compounds." Trends in Food Science & Technology 7, no. 12 (1996): 390–99. https://doi.org/10.1016/s0924-2244(96)10039-x.

Holmes, Bob. Flavor: The Science of Our Most Neglected Sense. New York, NY: W.W. Norton, 2017.

Junge, Jonas Yde, Anne Sjoerup Bertelsen, Line Ahm Mielby, Yan Zeng, Yu-an-Xia Sun, Derek Victor Byrne, and Ulla Kidmose. "Taste Interactions between Sweetness of Sucrose and Sourness of Citric and Tartaric Acid among Chinese and Danish Consumers." *Foods* 9, no. 10 (2020): 1425. https://doi.org/10.3390/foods9101425.

Keast, Russell S.J, and Paul A.S Breslin. "An Overview of Binary Taste–Taste Interactions." *Food Quality and Preference* 14, no. 2 (2003): 111–24. https://doi.org/10.1016/s0950-3293(02)00110-6.

Rune, Christina J., Morten Münchow, Federico J.A. Perez-Cueto, and Davide Giacalone. "Pairing Coffee with Basic Tastes and Real Foods Changes Perceived Sensory Characteristics and Consumer Liking." *International Journal of Gastronomy and Food Science* 30 (2022): 100591. https://doi.org/10.1016/j.ijgfs.2022.100591.

Schmidt, Charlotte Vinther, Karsten Olsen, and Ole G. Mouritsen. "Umami Synergy as the Scientific Principle behind Taste-Pairing Champagne and Oysters." *Scientific Reports* 10, no. 1 (2020). https://doi.org/10.1038/s41598-020-77107-w.

Wang, Sijia, Maria Dermiki, Lisa Methven, Orla B. Kennedy, and Qiaofen Cheng. "Interactions of Umami with the Four Other Basic Tastes in Equi-Intense Aqueous Solutions." *Food Quality and Preference* 98 (2022): 104503. https://doi.org/10.1016/j.foodqual.2021.104503.

CHAPTER NINE: A POET OF THE PALATE

Alley, Lynn. "Wine Sensory Scientist Ann Noble Retires from UC Davis." Wine Spectator. Wine Spectator, August 21, 2002. https://www.wine-spectator.com/articles/wine-sensory-scientist-ann-noble-retires-from-uc-davis-21376.

Huxley, Aldous. *Time Must Have a Stop.* Normal, IL: Dalkey Archive Press, 1998.

Lee, Hazel. Taste With Colour, July 2017. https://tastewithcolour.com/pages/how-to-use.

Melcher, Joseph M., and Jonathan W. Schooler. "The Misremembrance of Wines Past: Verbal and Perceptual Expertise Differentially Mediate Verbal Overshadowing of Taste Memory." *Journal of Memory and Language* 35, no. 2 (1996): 231–45. https://doi.org/10.1006/jmla.1996.0013.

Mora, Pierre, and Florine Livat. "Does Storytelling Add Value to Fine Bordeaux Wines?" *Wine Economics and Policy* 2, no. 1 (2013): 3–10. https://doi.org/10.1016/j.wep.2013.01.001.

Rozin, Paul. "The Psychology behind a Memorable Meal | Paul Rozin." YouTube. MAD: MADSymposium YouTube, November 22, 2012. https://www.youtube.com/watch?v=5jv2WNrnS0c.

Wilson, Timothy D., and Jonathan W. Schooler. "Thinking Too Much: Intro-spection Can Reduce the Quality of Preferences and Decisions." *Journal of Personality and Social Psychology* 60, no. 2 (1991): 181–92. https://doi.org/10.1037/0022-3514.60.2.181.

CHAPTER TEN: TRAVEL LIKE A TASTER

Burdack-Freitag, Andrea, Dino Bullinger, Florian Mayer, and Klaus Breuer. "Odor and Taste Perception at Normal and Low Atmospheric Pressure in a Simulated Aircraft Cabin." *Journal für Verbraucherschutz und Lebens-mittelsicherheit* 6, no. 1 (2010): 95–109. https://doi.org/10.1007/s00003-010-0630-y.

Deutsche Welle. "Airline Food – DW – 10/15/2010." dw.com. Deutsche Welle, October 15, 2010. https://www.dw.com/en/lufthansa-investi-gates-the-science-of-airline-food/a-6114748.

Robinson, Eric. "Relationships between Expected, Online and Remembered Enjoyment for Food Products." *Appetite* 74 (2014): 55–60. https://doi.org/10.1016/j.appet.2013.11.012.

Rode, Elizabeth, Paul Rozin, and Paula Durlach. "Experienced and Remem-bered Pleasure for Meals: Duration Neglect but Minimal Peak, End (Re-cency) or Primacy Effects." *Appetite* 49, no. 1 (2007): 18–29. https://doi.org/10.1016/j.appet.2006.09.006.

Zhu, Jiang, Lan Jiang, Wenyu Dou, and Liang Liang. "Post, Eat, Change: The Effects of Posting Food Photos on Consumers' Dining Experiences and Brand Evaluation." *Journal of Interactive Marketing* 46 (2019): 101–12. https://doi.org/10.1016/j.intmar.2018.10.002.

CHAPTER ELEVEN: WHAT TASTERS KNOW

Rice, Michael A. "Merrior – The Good Flavors of Oysters." *Aquaculture Mag-azine*, 2019.

Turbes, Gregory, Tyler D. Linscott, Elizabeth Tomasino, Joy Waite-Cusic, Juyun Lim, and Lisbeth Meunier-Goddik. "Evidence of Terroir in Milk Sourcing and Its Influence on Cheddar Cheese." *Journal of Dairy Science* 99, no. 7 (2016): 5093–5103. https://doi.org/10.3168/jds.2015-10287.

CHAPTER TWELVE: TASTES TO LAST A LIFETIME

Damm, Michael, Louisa K. Pikart, Heike Reimann, Silke Burkert, Önder Göktas, Boris Haxel, and Thomas Hummel. "Olfactory Training Is Help-ful in Postinfectious Olfactory Loss: A Randomized, Controlled, Multi-center Study." *The Laryngoscope* 124, no. 4 (2013): 826–31. https://doi.org/10.1002/lary.24340.

Doty, Richard L. "Olfaction in Parkinson's Disease and Related Disorders." *Neurobiology of Disease* 46, no. 3 (2012): 527–52. https://doi.org/10.1016/j.nbd.2011.10.026.

Gilbert, Avery N, Charles Wysocki, Mark Seidler, and Allen Carroll. "The Smell Survey Results." *National Geographic*, 1987.

Glachet, Ophélie, and Mohamad El Haj. "Emotional and Phenomenological Properties of Odor-Evoked Autobiographical Memories in Alzheimer's Disease." *Brain Sciences* 9, no. 6 (2019): 135. https://doi.org/10.3390/brainsci9060135.

Huart, Caroline, Philippe Rombaux, and Thomas Hummel. "Plasticity of the Human Olfactory System: The Olfactory Bulb." *Molecules* 18, no. 9 (2013): 11586–600. https://doi.org/10.3390/molecules180911586.

Hummel, Thomas, Karo Rissom, Jens Reden, Aantje Hähner, Mark Weidenbecher, and Karl-Bernd Hüttenbrink. "Effects of Olfactory Training in Patients with Olfactory Loss." *The Laryngoscope* 119, no. 3 (2009): 496–99. https://doi.org/10.1002/lary.20101.

Proust, Marcel, Christopher Prendergast, and John Sturrock. *In Search of Lost Time*. London: Penguin Books, 2003.

Van Regemorter, Victoria, Thomas Hummel, Flora Rosenzweig, André Mouraux, Philippe Rombaux, and Caroline Huart. "Mechanisms Linking Olfactory Impairment and Risk of Mortality." *Frontiers in Neuroscience* 14 (2020). https://doi.org/10.3389/fnins.2020.00140.

Wysocki, Charles J., and Avery N. Gilbert. "National Geographic Smell Survey: Effects of Age Are Heterogenous." *Annals of the New York Academy of Sciences* 561, no. 1 Nutrition and (1989): 12–28. https://doi.org/10.1111/j.1749-6632.1989.tb20966.x.

INDEX